DIPLOMATIC
REALISM

William R. Castle, Jr., by Harris and Ewing, Washington, D.C.
(Photo courtesy of Donald Winslow.)

DIPLOMATIC REALISM

William R. Castle, Jr., and American Foreign Policy, 1919–1953

Alfred L. Castle

Samuel N. and Mary Castle Foundation
Honolulu

Library of Congress Cataloging-in-Publication Data

Castle, Alfred L.
Diplomatic realism : William R. Castle, Jr., and American
foreign policy, 1919–1953 / Alfred L. Castle.
p.   cm.
Includes bibliographical references and index.
ISBN 0–8248–2009–6 (alk. paper)
1. Castle, William R. (William Richards), Jr., 1878–1963.
2. Diplomats—United States—Biography.   3. United States—
Foreign relations—20th century.   I. Title.
E748.C29C37   1998
327.73′092—dc21   97-36550
                                                        CIP

University of Hawai'i Press books are printed on acid-free paper
and meet the guidelines for permanence and durability
of the Council on Library Resources.

Distributed by
University of Hawai'i Press
2840 Kolowalu Street
Honolulu, Hawai'i 96822

Designed by Jennifer Lum

For Donald, Lilia, and Masha Castle

Contents

Preface   ix

1   A Moral Endowment for Public Service   1

2   The Beginning of Public Service:
     The American Red Cross Bureau of Communications   12

3   The Corporate State in the 1920s   21

4   The London Naval Conference   37

5   The Hoover Moratorium   50

6   The Manchurian Incident:
     A Study in Applied Diplomatic Realism   67

7   The Presidential Election of 1936   92

8   Opposition to Intervention in Asia, 1939–1941   106

9   Opposition to World War II Foreign Policy   119

10   Diplomatic Realism and
     the Postwar Transformation of Japan   144

11   An Aged Realist Examines Cold War Assumptions   158

Appendix   Selected Radio Speeches to Japan   167

Notes   195

Bibliography   231

Index   245

Preface

The release of the William R. Castle, Jr., diaries by Harvard University in 1985 and the heavy use of the Castle Papers at Harvard, the National Archives, and the Herbert Hoover Presidential Library have added considerable light to our understanding of the State Department in the interwar years. In addition, we now have a better understanding of the Hoover presidency, the relationship of Hoover to leading State Department officials such as W. R. Castle, Jr., and Castle's continuing impact on foreign policy beyond his years of public service.

The only full-length treatment of W. R. Castle, Jr., is J. L. Hollingsworth's unpublished dissertation, "William R. Castle and Japanese-American Relations 1929–1933" (Texas Christian University, 1971). The work, though groundbreaking at the time, did not refer extensively to Castle's career before or after the Hoover administration. Moreover, Hollingsworth did not have access to the diaries, which cover the years 1918–1956. Had these diaries and other sources been available, the author might have given greater explication of Castle's sense of diplomatic realism and the continuing importance of Castle's policy influence in the 1930s, 1940s, and early 1950s.

Although W. R. Castle, Jr., has many admirers among diplomatic historians and is frequently referred to in standard works on the diplomacy of the interwar years, no work has focused exclusively on his often subtle role in foreign policy. Further, although he was one of Hawaii's most influential citizens on the national scene, he is largely forgotten in the state today. The following essays, some previously published in regional and national journals since 1985, are an attempt to partially rectify this. The essays are far from exhaustive, and future studies of the man and his era will continue to shed new light on his effectiveness or ineffectiveness as a diplomat and his influence on important decisions made by policy makers over a long period of time.

Born in the kingdom of Hawaii in 1878, Castle as a teenager observed the overthrow of the last Hawaiian monarch, Queen Liliuokalani, and carried a rifle in the abortive counter revolt of Robert Wilcox in 1895. Although an admirer of Hawaiian customs, history, and language, he nonetheless felt with his father, a past member of the kingdom's legislature and Hawaii's minister to the United States in 1895, that Euro-American political culture, art, philosophy, and values were superior to non-Western values. He was particularly proud of the contributions of the Protestant mission to Hawaii, which began in 1820 and did much to prepare the way for the U.S. annexation of the Hawaiian Republic in 1898. He never doubted that American democracy was better for Hawaiians than monarchy or that literacy, private property, civil liberties, and Euro-American civilization were superior to ancient Hawaiian culture. His ethnocentrism, common in American universities and government agencies of the day, would remain part of his cognitive map of the world for the rest of his life.

In 1896, Castle graduated from Punahou School, a prominent preparatory school that his grandfather had helped to found in 1841. Matriculating at Harvard, he graduated in the distinguished class of 1900. At Harvard, Castle made contacts with the sons of prominent New England families, many of whom were destined to have lucrative careers in business and finance. Others, like Castle, would use family wealth to take prestigious but low-paying positions in public service. Castle's devotion to Harvard would last for a lifetime and would result in his service as an overseer from 1935 to 1941 and as a substantial donor and volunteer fund-raiser for decades.

Marrying Margaret Farlow, the scion of an old and prominent Boston family, in 1902, Castle returned to Honolulu to work in the real estate business. The financial opportunities in the new U.S. territory were great indeed, but Castle soon grew bored with the provincial capital and deplored his inability to find real meaning in business. Moreover, Margaret missed her family and the cultural excitement of Boston. In 1903, he accepted an appointment as an instructor of English at Harvard. In 1908, he was promoted to assistant dean of students. In that position, he was put in charge of advising freshmen, a job he enjoyed greatly. In 1912, he took Margaret and his young daughter Rosamond on a two-year leave of absence to Algeria, where he devoted himself to writing. Returning to Harvard in 1914, he was appointed editor of the prestigious *Harvard Graduate's Magazine* and continued to teach courses in literature and writing.

In these years, Castle considered his future to be in writing rather than in traditional scholarship or teaching. Eschewing the laborious training for the Ph.D., a training that bored him, he chose to write for a popular audience. In 1912, Dodd, Mead and Company published the first edition of *Hawaii, Past & Present* (the enlarged second edition was published in 1926). This popular account of Hawaii's history, topography, and prospects became, for several decades, a standard account of the territory. To some extent a travel guide for an island group still exotic to most Americans, it was also an ethnocentric account of Hawaii's cultural and historical development. While admiring many of the qualities of the Hawaiians, Castle clearly felt that true civilization began with the coming of Western influence, most particularly the Protestant missionaries. As he saw it, American religious, economic, and cultural dominance had greatly improved life in Hawaii. U.S. annexation in 1898 and the acquisition of territorial status in 1900 were natural and beneficial outcomes of Hawaii's growing integration with the U.S. economy, which corporations such as Castle & Cooke (founded in 1851) had made possible. Liberal democracy, a bill of rights, capitalism, a vibrant not-for-profit sector, and Protestantism, as he saw it, were the keys to a better Hawaii and, indeed, a better world.

Castle's early experiences were partly shaped by the unique multiracial, multicultural, and multilingual society that Hawaii had become by the 1880s and 1890s. Unlike any other American diplomat of the interwar years, Castle had extensive experience with large numbers of non-European immigrants. Hawaii since the 1860s had increasingly sought inexpensive, cost-effective labor to serve the chief export crop, sugar. In the last fifty years of the nineteenth century, Hawaii's planter elite, in league with Hawaii's government, sought laborers from China and then, after the 1880s, increasingly from Japan. By 1900, Honolulu was a cosmopolitan territorial capital with a substantial majority of Chinese and Japanese immigrants. The importance of a free flow of labor from Asia made Hawaii's planter class, which dominated society, politics, and business, intimately aware of U.S. foreign policy in Asia as well as the politics of foreign policy in China and Japan. Moreover, the victory of Japan over China in 1894 impressed Hawaii's oligarchy with the need to respect Japan as a rising power in the East.

As a boy and young man growing up under the rule of King Kalakaua, Queen Liliuokalani, the Provisional Government of Sanford Dole, the Hawaiian Republic, and finally the first years of the territory of Hawaii, Castle came to admire Japanese culture, language, and history. In Eurocentric fashion, he adjudged Japan to be a more significant nation than China as it had emulated European technology, appeared to be developing the beginnings of Western forms of government, and looked to the West for some of its future direction. He also contrasted Japan's political order, capitalist development, and excellent educational facilities favorably to China's disorder, monarchy, and stubborn reluctance to adapt to Euro-American modernity. In the first two decades of the twentieth century, after U.S. labor laws went in effect, Castle nonetheless argued that Hawaii's plantations needed reliable Chinese labor. With the rise of Japanese-led labor unrest on the sugar plantations, he argued with most planters that Japanese were less likely to accept low wages and long hours of work. Further, Japanese laborers tended to be more "independent" due to the power and prestige of their mother country. U.S. law had excluded Chinese immigrants in 1884, and in 1900 the laws applied to the Hawaiian territory. This strengthened the potential bargaining power of Japanese workers as seen in the strikes of 1908 and 1920. Unless the United States made an exception for Hawaii, Japanese cultural and political influence would continue to grow in the Islands.[1] Hawaii's political leaders knew better than mainland congressmen what was possible in the territory, Castle believed. Asian laborers were, moreover, limited in their understanding of democracy and therefore were vulnerable to Bolshevik propaganda and "emotional" appeals to protest Hawaii's social and economic order and were a danger to Hawaiians, who were a diminishing minority in their own homeland.

Though Castle would, after the failed 1920 sugar strike, be an opponent of official discrimination by the U.S. government against Asian citizens in Hawaii, he always felt more comfortable with Japan's aristocratic government and economic elite. Castle became close friends with Japan's elite, most of whom were highly Westernized, and he was often described as a "special friend of the Japanese." This would make his work in Japan in 1930 and his continuing advocacy for some of Japan's interests in the 1930s and beyond a hallmark of his diplomatic career. A collector of Japanese literature and art, he truly admired much of Japan's history while distrusting those who underestimated Japan's resourcefulness and usefulness to U.S. interests in the Pacific. Philanthropically, he made personal gifts and gifts from his family foundation, the Samuel N. and Mary Castle Foundation, to selected Japanese colleges and universities as well as to projects to aid the Japanese after the 1923 earthquake.

Dodd, Mead and Company, pleased with the excellent reviews of *Hawaii Past & Present* and Castle's accessible prose, subsequently published his only two novels. *The Green Vase* (1912) and *The Pillar of Sand* (1913) drew mixed reviews but had a modestly successful sales record. Both novels explored themes related to the social complications that resulted from wrong ethical choices. Castle's two novels built plots that revolved around protagonists of "character, breeding and refinement" who, despite economic obstacles, prevailed in conflicts with unethical social climbers whose prosperity was only a surface one. Reflecting the years of economic and social displacement by an emerging corporate class of newly wealthy, felt by many of New England's oldest families, the novels struck a nerve in New England in the Progressive Era. The two novels seemed to accurately reflect, for many of Castle's readers, the stress of rapid economic change at the end of the nineteenth century.

In 1916, Dodd, Mead issued Castle's last published work before he entered the State Department. The short work, *Wake Up, America,* was full of invective toward those who would not support a call for universal military service in the midst of World War I. Feeling that the United States would eventually enter the war, Castle agreed with his hero Teddy Roosevelt that the country had become too soft and that too many lacked a sense of national responsibility. The reviews of the book were mixed and reflected the position of the reviewers on the issue of U.S. preparedness for war. The book, in retrospect, is valuable for describing Castle's passion for public service and his deep desire to "make a difference" in life.

Rejecting the life of a Harvard professor, a writer, or a businessman, he sought with great restlessness a meaningful public career. World War I, Woodrow Wilson's idealism, and a renewed sense of an engaged civil life led him to volunteer for military service shortly after America's entry into the war in April of 1917. Unable to qualify physically, he offered his service to Eliot Wadsworth, head of the American Red Cross. Moving with his wife and daughter to Washington, D.C., he could not have realized how his Red Cross service would revivify his life and lead to an influential diplomatic career.[2]

The following essays attempt to analyze Castle's influence on foreign policy during his years of State Department service (1919–1933) and his continuing activity into the early 1950s. Five of the essays have been previously published in somewhat different form: chapter 1 in *Christian Scholar's Review* (1991), chapter 4 in *Naval History* (1989), chapter 6 in *Mid-America* (1996), chapter 8 in *Pacific Historical Review* (1985), and chapter 10 in *Wisconsin Magazine of History* (1990–1991).

The research was made possible through grant support from the National Endowment for the Humanities, the Hoover Presidential Library Association, The Coolidge Fellowships program at Episcopal Divinity School (Cambridge, Massachusetts), and institutional support from New Mexico Military Institute, Hawaii Pacific University, and California State University at San Marcos. The work would not have been possible without the mentorship and critical reviews provided by my many colleagues and journal editors. Most of all, I owe a deep debt to Robert Ferrell, the distinguished diplomatic historian recently retired from Indiana University; Dwight Miller, chief archivist at the Herbert Hoover Presidential Library; and the former director of the Hoover Library, Robert S. Wood. I would also like to thank Michael E. Macmillan for the hours he spent editing the book. His expertise has helped pull together the somewhat disparate essays, published and unpublished, that make up this book.

The work, in fine, attempts to update our understanding of an influential diplomat while also encouraging further work on the man and his era.

DIPLOMATIC REALISM

1 A Moral Endowment for Public Service

Born into an old Boston family that had come from England in the 1650s and had gone to Honolulu as Congregational missionaries in 1837, William Richards Castle, Jr., was tutored in the values of public service, duty, honor, and philanthropy.[1] His grandfather was Samuel Northrup Castle (1808–1894), the stern and often rhadamanthine cofounder of Castle & Cooke, Inc. (1851). At the feet of his grandfather, the future diplomat, policy maker, and under secretary of state learned that the central fact of man's life was his fallenness and radical limitation. From his gentle and spiritual grandmother, Mary Tenney Castle (1819–1907), the notable abolitionist, educational reformer, Christian feminist, and philanthropist, he learned that man still retained the capacity for positive action through faith in God's grace.[2] These general orientations were reinforced by his father, W. R. Castle, Sr., attorney general under King Kalakaua, in the 1870s, and by his professor and mentor at Harvard, Barrett Wendell.

By his graduation from Harvard in 1900, W. R. Castle, Jr., had converted to Anglicanism while retaining his family's strong Christian realist values. These provided a general framework by which events could be interpreted and responses formulated.[3] Like the Christian realist theologian Reinhold Niebuhr, W. R. Castle, Jr., came to believe that the multiple ills of the world cannot be cured through human action. Since all individuals and groups are prevented from attaining perfection by their deep-rooted egotistic pride, he particularly distrusted those who responded to complex social movements in simple black and white terms.[4] Crusading fanatics, be they communists, capitalists, fascists, or nationalists, tend to oversimplify complex reality and seek a false, seductive clarity. Through their pride in the absolute rectitude of their position, they tend to create as many problems as they solve. With Niebuhr, he felt that the essence of original sin is to absolutize a partial perspective, which is all that man is capable of, and to rationalize selfish human interests by incorporating these interests in political, economic, and social structures.[5] Such structures, whose apparent permanency lends legitimacy to often evil and destructive actions, are difficult to deracinate once their self-interested and relative origins are disguised and forgotten.[6]

Postlapsarian man, according to Castle, must constantly be self-critical, cautious and humble in light of man's radical limitation and sin. We sin when in our self-centered existence we turn from God to self. Further, human anxiety, caused in part by our ontological contingency, leads to sin when we seek to control unpredictable aspects of ourselves and our social existence by human power, knowledge, and virtue. Totalitarianism, the primary political hamartia and innovation in the twentieth century, resulted from the effort to impose faulty solutions to multifarious and illusive problems. In response, Castle argued consistently for the relative virtues of democracy as a political response to man's need for organization. For him, as for Niebuhr, democracy was good not because men are wise and good, but because it is a safeguard against the human tendency toward injustice.

Mary Tenney Castle (1819–1907) was probably the most influential person in shaping the world view of William R. Castle, Jr. (Hawaiian Mission Children's Society photo.)

His grandmother, Mary Tenney Castle, was perhaps the most influential person in shaping his view of the world. From his grandmother, he absorbed the basic values of the American mission to Hawaii as well as a set of values that would help shape a lifetime of public service. A review of her ideas and activities, therefore, casts important light on the future diplomat's life.

Mary Tenney Castle's life is best understood if we study her society and beliefs. Born in Plainfield, New York, a little farming community in Otsego County, she was the daughter of Levy Tenney and his wife, Mary Kingsbury. Her father was a stern Puritan in religious belief and a respected farmer in prosperous west-central New York. Her mother was deeply intellectual and a devoted, active Christian.

Mary was the fourth of nine children. For a family that valued education and Bible reading as the basis of meaningful participation in democracy, the available village schools proved inadequate. Many of the children, therefore, continued their education in seminaries. After the marriage of Angeline Tenney to missionary Samuel Northrup Castle and their subsequent departure for the mission in Hawaii, young Mary left home and obtained her secondary education at Deerfield Academy in Massachusetts. Due to financial setbacks associated with the depression of 1837, Mary was forced to leave Deerfield and return to Plainfield, where she lived quietly with her parents and taught in the district schools. In the fall of 1841, she accompanied her invalid aunt, Miss Jeddiah Kingsbury, to Columbus, Georgia, where she witnessed slavery for the first time. Her strong opposition to it was expressed in letters to her parents and would likely have led to active engagement with the various antislavery societies of her day had she not accepted the widowed (Angeline had died in 1841) Samuel Castle's offer to serve as his "companion" to the mission in Hawaii.

Samuel Northrup Castle and Mary Tenney shared similar experiences and common theological guidelines for their lives. Both from their parents and from the intellectual and moral life of the Congregationalist mission, Samuel and Mary absorbed the central points associated with New Divinity theology and its leading adherent, Samuel Hopkins (1721–1803). The distinctive features of this thought centered on the radical corruption of humanity and the nature of regeneration. Following the lead of the eighteenth-century theologian, Jonathan Edwards, Hopkins taught that sin, though not transmitted to humanity via the imputation of Adam's disobedience and fall, is exhibited in selfishness and inordinate self-love. For Hopkins, the sincere unregenerate seeker-after-righteousness was ultimately motivated by wicked self-interest. This assumption led Hopkins, Joseph Bellamy, and other New Divinity theologians to declare the liabilities facing unregenerate persons who actively used the means of grace in their search for salvation.

Significantly, Samuel and Mary Castle held to Hopkins' more optimistic view of virtue. For them, the center of spiritual regeneration lay in a convert's new access to "disinterested benevolence." Thus, despite the assumption that this hyper-Calvinistic metaphysics would lead humanity away from righteous social action, for the Castles it had just the opposite effect. Seeing the heart of Christian virtue as a selflessness (i.e., disinterested charity for all of God's creatures), Hopkins' theology created a strong apologia for social reform.

Both Samuel Northrup Castle and Mary Tenney had experienced conversions to Christianity during the Second Great Awakening. Begun in Connecticut during the 1790s, this broad movement set ablaze one section of the nation after another during the first half of the nineteenth century. The important theological theme of the social and religious movement was the rejection of the Calvinist belief that humans had a natural and inevitable inclination to sin (the doctrine of human depravity). Rather, the leaders of the Awakening, such as Charles G. Finney, affirmed that sin was purely a voluntary act; no one was drawn irresistibly to sin and the consequent rejection of the Lord's will. Men and women could will themselves out of sin just as easily as they had chosen sin. Indeed, for both Castles, it was theoretically possible (if very unlikely) for men and women to will themselves free of sin, align one's will with God's, and live perfectly.[7]

An additional component of the Castles' moral universe was the teaching of postmillennialism. First formulated by Puritan theologians in the seventeenth century and developed by Jonathan Edwards in the eighteenth century, postmillennialism was the relatively optimistic belief that the return of Christ would take place after the millennium, which might be a literal period of peace and prosperity or a symbolic representation of the final triumph of the gospel. This new age would come through Christian teaching and preaching. Further,

Samuel Northrup Castle (1808–1894), grandfather of William R. Castle, Jr., arrived in Hawaii as a Congregational missionary in 1837 and later cofounded the highly successful firm of Castle & Cooke, Inc. (Hawaiian Mission Children's Society photo.)

the Holy Spirit would use such activity to shape a new world characterized by prosperity, peace, and righteousness. Evil might not be totally
eliminated, but it would be substantially reduced because the moral and
spiritual influence of the church would be greatly increased. During the
new age, Christians would solve many of humankind's most persistent
social and economic problems. The period would close with the second
coming of Christ, the resurrection of the dead, and the last judgment.
Such an eschatology sanctioned Christian "disinterested benevolence"
and world-enhancing altruism while retaining much of the original Puritan caution about human motivation and achievement. Postmillennialism, despite its realism about the fallibility and ambiguity of human effort was, for the Protestant missionaries, galvanizing.

For Mary Tenney, the process of conversion so central to Protestant
thinking in the early 1800s was particularly problematic. The experience of conversion was generally thought to be an overwhelming, all-
encompassing transformation in which a person's entire being was al-
tered. After conversion it was accepted that a sense of peace and spiritual
confidence would provide comfort and support for believers for the rest
of their lives. But for young Mary conversion at Deerfield and membership in the Presbyterian Church failed to bring a radical change from her
preconversion experiences. She could not feel that deep contrition and
conviction of sin that she believed was essential to the authentic conversion experience and consequent salvation. Despite joining the church,
she doubted she was among the saved or that she was of any special
worth. She feared that perhaps she had "grieved away the spirit" and salvation was not for her. In a letter written to S. N. Castle, who was asking for her hand in marriage and service to the Hawaiian mission, she
wrote of her trials:

Dear Brother Castle,

I received your letter of May 13, this morning somewhat
surprised at the so early arrival of yourself & little girl & far
more so at the proposal it contained, also regretting to hear of
the illness of both of you.

I thank you for the free & open manner with which you presented this subject & I find that it demands the same return—
When five years ago I for the first time indulged the hope that I
was made a partaker of the benefits of Christ's death my attention was immediately turned to the work of personal effort for
the salvation of souls & also to the Miss'y field. Those efforts
were characterized by an ardent but ill governed zeal resulting
from ignorance & moved in some degree by a sense of the dan-

gerous situation of sinners and from much spir. pride & self conciet [*sic*]. In looking back on that state I am not surprised that I fell—but you know the history. Since then I have been most of the time in a very careless state except slight alarms which have been more like mere specks—far—apart—Last August I began to feel the necessity of making vigouous [*sic*] efforts of taking a decided stand for God repenting & forsaking my sins & obeying him—which has been my general feeling & determination ever since, though my feelings have not been *deep*, my efforts feeble & my only evidence of sincere repentance *has been & is some* desire accompanied by feeble & compar'y unsuccessful efforts to forsake known sin & return to neglected duty—I united with the church here (on prof. of faith) because I felt it to be my duty, but greatly fearing that I was an object of God's obhorance [*sic*]. I had previously been consulting whether it was not duty to make a written dedication of myself to God on the plan pro by Doddridge, but I *could* not write it down. *I will henceforth obey thee at all hazards.* I thought it would be cold & insincere & then I was perplexed with reflections that if my *heart* was really engaged the work would be easy—but at the same time I thought I could say I trust thou, O Lord, knowest that it is my sincere wish & humble though feeble determination by thy grace to serve thee—In looking back to last Aug. I think I can see a steady but slow progress of rel. interest I have not regarded myself as having an established christian character but on trial to be developed by circumstances—At any time between Aug— & this if I have been asked what was my religious estate, looking upon another person as I could see myself I should have said at the best a superficial Christian—(I have not had the *presumption* to *indulge* the thought of a miss'y life).[8]

Mary's self-doubt and introspection, which her grandson, W. R. Castle, Jr., would share, slowed her approval by the American Board of Commissioners for Foreign Missions to become a missionary. The Prudential Committee, which approved all requests for mission work and passed on spiritual fitness, had doubts about her qualifications. They wanted as missionaries people who had no reservations, for whom all questions were settled; for Mary, incessant and reverent self-questioning was the sine qua non of true faith. The intensity of her spiritual faith made her suffer because she could not accept, without soul-searching, all the teachings of the Presbyterian Church. Specifically, she found the peace that followed the conversion elusive, while at the same time choosing to take an independent stand with regard to women's churchly role. Later, this streak of independence would earn the unhappiness of some of the Hawaiian missionaries when she quietly challenged the accepted and narrow public female roles dictating loyal, submissive mission wives. For example, her insistence that both sexes pray aloud at public gatherings was frowned upon in an age when women were not to usurp the dominance of men in church.[9] For Mary Tenney, neither the church nor the mission would ever provide sufficient opportunity for a woman to exercise her duty to better society.

For years after arriving in Hawaii with her new husband, the old questions about conversion, forgiveness of sin, worthiness, and her ability to love Christ in a full and disinterested way continued. Peace did not come easily, and she supplemented her reading of the *Oberlin Evangelist* by studying the writings of certain Christian mystics. Most compelling to her were the thoughts of François Fénelon (ca. 1651–1715) and Jeanne-Marie Guyon (1648–1717). Specifically, Mary, who was in need of a certain grant for faith, found the quietist doctrine of grace enticing. Quietists such as Guyon and Fenelon argued that the love of God moves eventually into a state in which God is loved for himself alone, without any admixture of hope for salvation or personal reward. One is now so filled with the desire to please God in all things that one would abandon all hope of eternity if such were indeed the will of God. Indeed, the soul is entirely passive in the hands of God, in a state of perfect quiet, unaware of itself or its acts. Moreover, the mystic doctrine of disinterested love, a basic feature of Christian spirituality during the Middle Ages, declared that even if there were no heaven and the soul were

William Richards Castle, Sr., set an example for his son through his participation in the political life of Hawaii, serving in the legislature, as attorney general under King Kalakaua, and later as the Hawaiian Republic's minister to the United States in 1895. (Hawaiian Mission Children's Society photo.)

consigned to deepest hell, the lover of God would be its own reward. As her son, and perhaps closest counsel, would later recall,

I did not know then what it was all about but years later it all came to me, partly in questions addressed to her, partly in remembering the books I used to see her reading, such as Upham's "Holiness," "Guyon and Fenelon," some works by Mr. Finney and others of the same type. It all meant an intense spiritual conflict. Mother felt and Mrs. Parker with her, I think, that a Christian was not really that, unless the perfection of Jesus Christ was really attained. She took literally the words, "Be ye therefore perfect even as your Father which is in Heaven is perfect." "Finally brethren be perfect." "I in them and they in me, that they may be made perfect in one." &c. She used often to repeat these and many similar passages and read the Bible diligently, looking for comfort and peace. In those days she believed that absolute faith was the only avenue to a pure and perfect life. I think she suffered a great deal during these years, for instead of looking placid and happy, she appeared more than serious, almost unhappy and anxious. Her reading and praying evidently did not bring at once the longed for sense of rest and peace which she would have had if she had been convinced that she had become "perfect even as Christ was perfect." I think Father did not sympathize with Mother's feelings and desires. He felt and lived up to the belief, that if the Christian lived up to his convictions, and in short obeyed the statement of requirements in Micah, which he often repeated, "what doth the Lord require of thee, but to do justly, and to love mercy, and to walk humbly with thy God," it was all that could be done and every thing else must be left with God. He certainly in those years got more satisfaction out of his religion than did Mother.[10]

As Mary sought reasons for needless suffering in the world and a rationale for unwavering belief, she found quietism and its doctrines of disinterested love helpful in leading her to a fuller acceptance of the Bible itself. She came, especially in her later years, to feel that the love of Jesus was sufficient grounds for belief. For her, by the 1880s and 1890s, it was enough to trust to Christ's love for her, despite her unworthiness to be loved so perfectly. She also felt energized by the concept that her Christian ideals, though impossible to realize in this world, were worth pursuing. Such qualified confidence in her worth, in her place as a community leader, would play a major role in her philanthropic activities in the 1880s and 1890s.[11] The limits of temporal institutions, no matter how structured, were another basic theme of Mary Castle. Her skepticism that earthly institutions could ever perfect life would shape her philanthropic thought and the thoughts of her children. Her Christian realism would, moreover, always view philanthropic support as an imperfect way of ameliorating imperfect social institutions.

Postlapsarian man, according to Christian realists, must constantly be self-critical, cautious, and humble in light of man's radical limitation and sin. We sin when in our self-centered existence we turn from God to self. Further, human anxiety, caused in part by our ontological contingency, leads to sin when we seek to control unpredictable aspects of ourselves and our social existence by human power, knowledge, and virtue. Totalitarianism, the primary political hamartia and innovation in the twentieth century, resulted from the effort to impose faulty solutions to multifarious and illusive problems. In response, Mary Castle argued consistently for the relative virtues of democracy as a political response to man's need for organization. For her, as for her grandson W. R. Castle, Jr., democracy was good not because men were wise and good, but because it was a safeguard against the human tendency toward injustice.

The implications of these theologically based values for W. R. Castle, Jr., were important and affected his entire public career. Throughout this

William R. Castle, Jr.'s introduction to public life included participation, along with his father, in Squad 3 of the Citizen's Guard of Honolulu. The Castles were absent when this photograph was taken in 1895. (Hawaii State Archives photo.)

public life, he equally opposed extremism on the right and the left of the ideological spectrum. Ideological fervor and clarity, he argued, often concealed selfish and partial economic, demographic, technological, and material interests.[12] As a pragmatist and advocate of *realpolitik,* he urged moderation, nonpartisan criticism, and "straight thinking." For the conservative Castle, change should be gradual and constantly checked by reason and caution. Domestic change, moreover, must never endanger the basic civil liberties that protect citizens from government interference. Most importantly, he consistently argued that war could be avoided if all nations acted in a self-interested rather than selfish way. Peace could best be retained through creating and maintaining the conditions that would make it the most economically rewarding condition for nations. Castle was, thus, a free-trade and open-door advocate.[13] He would even allow strong foreign nations the same right to an economic and regional sphere of influence that the United States had claimed for Latin America in the Monroe Doctrine. Further, the United States should balance its commitments overseas with the available resources it could marshal to effect change. For the United States to impose its version of society on foreign countries was dangerous and costly. Furthermore, permanent alliances with other self-interested countries were also to be avoided, as George Washington had suggested in his Farewell Address (1797). Because of the unavoidable centralization of government that accompanies it, war was to be avoided unless the country was being attacked. The loss of precious civil liberties and access to information was a threat to the viability of any democracy. Moreover, propaganda, often the effort of a centralizing state preparing for war, made it difficult for the citizen to exercise his duty to impartially evaluate and guide the nation's action.[14]

Finally, Castle's realist perspective continues to challenge those opposed to force as a means to resolving disputes. We still seek alternatives to increasingly devastating and internecine wars. His points, which have recently received a friendlier historiographical reception, were perhaps best summarized in his 1934 article written for the *Rotarian.* In his analysis of international comity, he concluded that obtaining a permanent and just peace could not

> be accomplished over night but it would be great to see the U.S. take the lead in a great campaign to bring it about. We do not want to develop in this country pacifists and weaklings but rather unselfish men and women who are strong for a righteous peace and will strive unceasingly for social justice and for inter-

national justice. Then peace will become inevitable. We want in this country men and women who always put their own nation first in their affections and in their intellects, but who realize that their own nation can be safe only as it plays a high and worthy part internationally. We want to do away with the kind of sentimentality which sees an easy national safety in a formula, whereas there is no such thing as safety without hard work just as surely as there is no such thing as prosperity without hard work. We want people who will . . . understand that there is no real safeguard aside from the right thinking and the right feeling of human beings.[15]

2 The Beginning of Public Service: The American Red Cross Bureau of Communications

Dissatisfied by the mixed response to his written work and feeling unchallenged by his part-time teaching at Harvard University, William R. Castle, Jr., found opportunities for public service during World War I a vital source of renewal. Indeed, Castle's energetic book, *Wake Up, America* (1916), argued for the redemptive efficacy of universal military service and national preparedness as U.S. interests were challenged by Germany. As he noted,

> Now the War has forced upon us the need of instantly so ordering our internal affairs that we may be able to meet all our external obligations efficiently and honorably. We need not mobilize our troops—if indeed we may have any to call to the colors—but we must mobilize our industrial forces to meet the shock of the world reconstruction period, to hold for ourselves, as our right, what we have gained by accident. We must also prepare to defend ourselves and our possessions, for when the war is over we shall probably not be greatly loved and we certainly shall be, comparatively, very rich. We have no great leader whose reasonableness, strength, sincerity, vision, will lure us all into the path of high, unselfish progress. Our great need may yet call forth such a man, but if not we must ourselves realize the crisis, break away from the fatal belief that the state exists to aid us individually and without recompense.

We must realize that it is time to drop all the alluring reforms that masquerade under the name of panaceas—suffrage, prohibition, government ownership, the single tax, socialism can wait to a more convenient season; the safeguarding of national life cannot wait. We must spontaneously mobilize for the defense of our industries, our democratic institutions, our national ideals.

We are free citizens of a great republic and each one, therefore, owes the best that is in him to the state. Each one of us is a trustee of the United States of America, bound to uphold his country with his vote, cast thoughtfully for the highest good, with a due proportion of his property, with a part of his time, if need be with his life.[1]

Failing the physical exam for military service, Castle approached a friend, Eliot Wadsworth, president of the American Red Cross. Castle suggested that he be allowed to serve in any post that would make a real difference in the war effort. In obtaining a top-level position with the Red Cross, Castle entered an organization that, since 1905, had been closely tied to the federal government. His two years of service would redirect his career to public service, confirm his organizational skills, provide numerous international and national contacts, and provide a sense of public purpose and identity that the cloistered halls of Harvard had not provided him.

Castle's entry into Red Cross service became better defined when, one month after the U.S. declaration of war against Germany, Wadsworth directed him to establish the Bureau of Communications. The chief responsibility of the office was to hurriedly prepare for casualty and prisoner-of-war reporting. This was a new activity of the American Red Cross, initiated in the midst of unprecedented U.S. military engagement in Europe. Organizationally, the existence of the

William R. Castle, Jr., with his daughter, Rosamond, in 1906. (Photo courtesy of Donald F. Winslow.)

new office was challenged by Secretary of War Newton D. Baker as a duplication of traditional War Department responsibility.[2] Castle's challenge was to organize an effective office, with minimum staff and budget in the face of unknown need and bureaucratic competition. The job required an ability to maneuver politically while also outperforming the larger War Department and its established bureaucracy. With little specific direction from Wadsworth, Castle began his office with only a file clerk, a stenographer, and a secretary and devised a plan of operation *ab ovo*.[3]

Examining the various international treaties governing the treatment of war prisoners, he realized that the work of prisoner relief and of getting information concerning prisoners was closely related to the work of tracing the missing in action. All foreign Red Cross chapters as well as the American Red Cross engaged in this work. Working closely with Ian Malcolm, former head of the Wounded and Missing Department of the British Red Cross, he developed an ambitious plan by mid-May of 1917. Castle then told the newly appointed War Council of the Red Cross that the new bureau could draw its authority and organizing principles from the traditional task of serving as a vehicle of communication between soldiers on duty and their families. In addition to prisoner relief, the new bureau would act as an agent for obtaining, on request, information for families on men reported as missing in action, killed, or wounded. This would be accomplished by assigning volunteers known as "searchers" to question friends of the missing. These efforts would be complemented by arrangements through the International Red Cross for prompt exchange of prisoner lists between the United States and Germany.[4]

William R. Castle, Jr., in Red Cross uniform in 1917. (Photo courtesy of Donald F. Winslow.)

A doubtful Baker immediately objected to the apparent replication of services already provided by the adjutant general. After a personal meeting with Castle, however, he was convinced to approve this private-sector initiative; perhaps mindful of the powerful friends of the American Red Cross inside the government and its bipartisan acceptance as a cost-effective alternative to undue government bureaucracy, he agreed to cooperate with Castle's plan. In no case, however, did he permit the Red Cross to make initial notifications, and it was restricted to issuing only reports that supplemented the War Department reports. Clearly Baker was unprepared in May of 1917 to foresee the War Department's inability to deal with the complexities of a world war or to predict the department's failure to report casualties in a timely fashion. Indeed, by 1918, he would welcome any help his department could get dealing with unprecedented requests for information.

In June 1917, Castle left for Europe to establish his bureau's operations. He spent considerable time with British and French Red Cross officials studying their modes of operation and asking their cooperation in shaping the bureau's own plans. Castle assigned volunteer "searchers" to occupy offices in American hospitals to collect information which would then be sent on to Washington, D.C., headquarters. An organization was established in Paris to process all inquiries from the United States. Trained volunteers, in addition to writing letters at the request of wounded soldiers and responding to inquiries passed through the Paris office, were assigned the more assertive task of sending unsolicited information to Washington. This action, to be reserved for "serious cases," as judged by the volunteer, would avoid the delays of information requests to be processed.

After a final consultation with the International Red Cross in Geneva, Castle returned to Washington to defend the position of the Bureau of Communication against the War Department. During the summer, the adjutant general had solidified plans for casualty reporting. The well-worded plan, however, concealed the reality that army lines of communication were already snarled. Growing complaints about slow mail and long delays in processing inquiries revealed defects in the government system. Seeing any opportunity to advance the Red Cross agenda, Castle steamed the bureau's activities by giving up the function of relief for future American captives. A Bureau of Prisoner Relief was created under the direction of Frank Abbott with Castle's Bureau of Communications focusing on reporting and communications responsibilities.[5]

To deal with the anticipated volume of work, Castle moved his bureau out of Red Cross headquarters and set up shop at 1818 H Street. A complex casualty card file was started along with a letter file for correspondence. In the winter of 1917–1918, the bureau expanded its services to domestic posts, camps, and stations within the United States. By January of 1918 Baker had, under public pressure and outcries of government incompetence, allowed Castle to inform families of the medical status of soldiers requiring hospitalization on domestic posts. A senate committee disclosed that the War Department had failed to notify families in these situations in a timely fashion. The Red Cross initiative was, therefore, key in remedying a need in the system. The value of this initiative proved particularly meritorious during the influenza epidemic in the autumn of 1918.

The growing popularity of Red Cross services led to new initiatives. In May of 1918 the State Department requested that the bureau begin a system that would allow American citizens to make inquiries into the welfare of relatives behind enemy lines. Prior to this, all such inquiries had been prohibited by law. Britain and France had allowed such inquiries from its citizens, and public outcries in the United States led the Wilson administration to relax censorship of such inquiries.[6] The procedure, which was a typical one for the bureau, was summarized by Castle in his final report written in 1919:

> Anyone in this country wishing to forward a message to Germany, etc., writes in duplicate in the Chapter office in his locality and files there a letter of recommendation from some accredited citizen. One copy of the message is then forwarded to Washington. It is there censored and paraphrased. The paraphrased version is sent to the International Red Cross in Switzerland, where it is translated and forwarded to the Red Cross, or some like organization in Germany, etc., for delivery to the addressee. The answer is returned to Washington through the same channels and is likewise censored and paraphrased and forwarded to the Chapter office from which it was received for delivery to the original inquirer.
>
> Messages and inquiries originated abroad are received in Washington from the International Red Cross, from the Bureau of Peace, from the Bureau Zuricois, and from the various Legations and Embassies of neutral countries. These messages are handled in a similar manner, the answer being filed at the local chapter offices.
>
> All messages leave this country in English and the answers are returned in English to the inquirers.[7]

By the end of 1918, this popular service handled ten thousand letters weekly. The heart of the bureau, however, lay in its obligations to report casualties promptly and accurately. Castle summarized this activity in his final report:

The aim of this department is to answer the inquiries about casualties and to secure the desired information from whatever source it is possible. In the case of a sick or wounded man, we try to secure a report on his condition and the nature of his wounds, the hospital in which he is located, and to transmit any special message which the family may wish to send—such as that they are writing regularly even though the soldier may not be hearing from them

In the case of a man who has been killed in action or died of wounds or disease, we attempt to secure a detailed report of his death and burial, the location of his grave, and, when requested, a photograph of the grave. We tell the family where to write for the soldiers personal effects and answer any questions, concerning back pay, the bringing home of the bodies, etc.

The mail is sub-divided into chapter and family mail for the reason that many letters going to chapters are answered by a form letter, whereas all letters to families are personal.

Both sub-sections again classify this mail into officially wounded, unofficially wounded, officially killed, and unofficially killed. In the case of wounded men, we notify the family that an inquiry is being sent abroad: that it will take at least six weeks to receive the report; and that we will notify them as soon as we have news. We assure them of the care the wounded and sick receive in our splendid hospitals, and add a personal touch to the letter. If a hospital report on the man comes in, in the meanwhile, it is forwarded direct to the family. In the case of Chapters, we write direct to them, asking them to notify the family of the action we have taken, and upon receipt of the news from abroad, we send it direct to the family, and a duplicate of the information to the Chapter.

Our object is to answer every question, even if we have to acknowledge that we know nothing about it. When it does not come under the jurisdiction of this Bureau, we try to advise them where to write to secure the information they want.

When the letters come to the correspondents, they have passed through the casualty files, and if there is an official report on the man, it is so noted on the letter. The former correspondence, if there is any, is also attached, and the letters are then distributed to be dictated on.

A great many letters are received asking about men who have been unofficially reported dead. We acknowledge these immediately, sending an inquiry abroad, and advise the family that we are making an investigation in the War Department to find out the truth of the unofficial report. In a few days we write them again to tell them the result of the investigation. If the report is confirmed, we write them; but, if it is not, and the source of their information appears to have been authentic, then we cable. Of course, the inquiry which went forward at the time of our first letter brings back the details of whatever the case turns out to be.

Whenever a man is said to be a member of the American Expeditionary Forces, and is not reported as being in another country, we take for granted he is in France.

The inquiries deal not only with men in the Expeditionary Forces, but also with those still in this country, and with the wounded and sick returned to this country. All these, however, are referred to the American Hospital Section.

The mail conditions in Russia have cleared up considerably and we are now able to secure details of the death and burial of men in that country, and even receive pictures of their graves. We have representatives in both Vladivostok and Archangel.

The correspondence are allowed to develop a style of their own and to express as much sympathy as they see fit.

The Casualty section, it will be seen, looks after all the preliminary correspondence concerning casualties. The final reports as they come in from abroad are sent on to families by the Foreign Mail Section of the Bureau.[8]

Clearly the quality of the casualty reporting service depended on a minimum of red tape, the ability of individual searchers, and their work load. Castle's summer trip to the battlefront in the summer of 1918 improved the training of the invaluable searchers while ensuring that every cooperation with the army was forthcoming. The results were, in the eyes of the public, impressive. When, for example, American soldiers arrived in Italy the Red Cross was already in place and functioning. Facilitating communication reassured soldiers and their families back home while improving morale in the army.[9] The Red Cross also preceded U.S. troops into Belgium, where high U.S. casualties taxed the efficiency of dedicated searchers.[10]

The Red Cross concentrated the greatest number of well-trained searchers in France. Operating with combat units, searchers kept up an exhausting pace compiling casualty reports from interviews with surviving soldiers, visits to aid stations, and even when possible through interviews with enemy prisoners.[11] The heavy U.S. casualties in the Argonne fighting would nearly overwhelm the bureau's capacities through the November 1918 armistice. Castle, betting on the rapid reduction of requests to the bureau with the coming of peace, mistakenly reassigned some of the searchers to social service tasks. This mistake led to an immediate backlog of cases that would take several months to clear.[12]

The final activity of the bureau was providing photographs of graves, so far as was possible, of all of the men who had died in the war. Cooperating closely with the Graves Registration Bureau of the army, the Red Cross had two or three prints of each photograph sent to families. By December of 1918, these were being supplied at the rate of seven thousand a month. The success of this unhappy concluding activity led to a reservoir of good feelings for the Red Cross and in particular for Castle's leadership.

When Castle resigned his directorship in February of 1919 the bureau was the dominant agency in the Red Cross and the most visible. During his wartime tenure, inquiries had increased from a few hundred letters a week to a high of 150,000 a week. The bureau had grown from the original staff of three to more than 350 people in the Washington office and more than 1,400 personnel in the field. Working around government regulations where he could while soothing bureaucratic opposition in the War Department was an accomplishment in itself. This successful international mission made Castle a popular figure in Washington as well as in Europe. Un-

A family gathering observed the golden wedding anniversary of Mr. and Mrs. William R. Castle, Sr., in 1925. Standing behind the Castles are, from left, Gwen Castle, Beatrice Castle, W. R. Castle, Jr., and Donald Castle. Behind them are Mr. and Mrs. Alfred L. Castle and Alfred L. Castle, Jr.
(Photo courtesy of Donald F. Winslow.)

der Secretary of State Frank Polk, who respected Castle's creativity, his ability to work with people of diverse backgrounds, his many international contacts, and his intimate knowledge of Europe, urged him to become a special assistant in the State Department's Division of Western European Affairs. The appointment, which Castle eagerly accepted, was applauded in influential government circles and would lead to a lifetime engagement with foreign affairs.[13] His basic philosophy of realism with respect to what was possible, given the ambiguity of human motivations and behavior, reinforced by his observation of men and nations at war, would serve as an organizing paradigm for understanding policy issues in the decades to come.[14]

3

The Corporate State in the 1920s

Although W. R. Castle's major influence in U.S. foreign policy would not come until after 1929, when he concentrated on Japanese-American affairs, the period of 1919 to 1929 was not without consequence. During his successful service for the Bureau of Communications, Under Secretary of State Frank Polk recognized Castle's ability to handle multiple tasks in an international environment and his ability to make and sustain European contacts. Polk, knowing of Castle's penchant for fulfillment through public service, urged him to become a special assistant in the State Department's Division of Western European Affairs. Accepting the post in February of 1919, he would slowly but steadily rise through the ranks, becoming chief of the Division of Western European Affairs in 1921 and assistant secretary of state in 1927. By the end of the decade, he had closely observed all levels of State Department activity and was widely respected for his knowledge of the "nuts and bolts" of implementing foreign policy, most often in a low-key manner.

After the failure of the U.S. Senate to ratify the Treaty of Versailles for the second time in March of 1920, the State Department entered a period of active cooperation with private business. Continuing the cooperative approach of Presidents Taft and Wilson, the Republican administrations of Harding, Coolidge, and Hoover believed that government should assist business to expand internationally while serving the greater good of the United States. This era, which up until the 1970s was thought to have been an "isolationist" and relatively inactive period in U.S. foreign policy, is now widely regarded by historians as an energetic era of foreign engagement though corporatism.

Corporatism refers to a system that is founded on officially reorganized functional groups, such as organized labor, business, and agriculture. In such a system, institutional regulating and coordinating mechanisms seek to integrate the groups into a whole; elites in the public and private sectors thus collaborate to ensure stability and harmony. This collaboration creates a pattern of interpretation and power sharing that blurs distinctions between sectors. Corporatism (or the associative system, as it is also called) is a "middle way" between laissez-faire capitalism and a state command economy. Class warfare would be avoided as prosperity would help all major groups in society. Group conflict would be contained, while organizational structures could harmonize differences. Historians such as Michael J. Hogan, Joan Hoff, Burton Kaufman, Charles S. Maier, Ellis Hawley, and Melvyn P. Leffler have seen 1920s Republican foreign policy as playing an active role in promoting initiatives and in organizing the private sector for overseas expansion. In the international arena, as on the home front, "realist" diplomats such as W. R. Castle argued that state trading, national autarky, and unregulated rivalries posed a threat to global peace and stability. Economic growth and armament reductions were ways to eliminate autarky and integrate national economies into a world capitalist order. The U.S. State Department, in league with the private sector, sought to further economic prosperity by unleashing private market initiatives through most-favored-nation treaties, convertible currencies, the reduction of armaments and international indebtedness, and the export of private capital and technical expertise.[1]

Although a somewhat minor figure in the State Department for much of the 1920s, Castle's sense that the anarchic proliferation of armaments could be halted through rational appeals to the self-interest of civilian leaders was a reflection both of his realism and his acceptance of the basic corporatist paradigm. For him, as for Secretary of Commerce Herbert Hoover and Secretary of State Charles Evans Hughes, international peace could best be secured through partial and mutual discouragement combined with mutually advantageous trade relations. If peace brought greater profits, leaders would be less likely to waste funds on war preparations, munitions, and war itself. Disarmament and economic promotion and expansion were, for Castle and most of the State Department, mutually supporting. Further, Castle shared the assumption of Hoover, Hughes, and Frank B. Kellogg that "scientific" settlements of war debts and tariff rates by nonpartisan experts and semiautonomous commissions was the best way to "depoliticize" differences between the United States and postwar Europe. Military involvement in international conflict should be minimized and identification with the League of Nations avoided.

Like the secretaries of state he worked for, Hughes and Kellogg, Castle assumed a mutuality of interests of the public and private spheres. Limited government could fulfill national interests by assisting business and other private groups to make money or gain influence internationally while also serving the public's good. The government's role was to share information, provide limited technical assistance, work to gain access to as many foreign markets as possible, reduce expensive armaments to secure most-favored-nation status from as many countries as possible, and seek economic connections with other countries that would bring reconciliation and peace. Private loans and investments would provide a basis for sustaining international prosperity and security. Conducting foreign policy through the private sector clearly had limitations and these limitations have been carefully documented. Nonetheless, the 1920s were among the most economically expansionist years in America's history. In this cooperative effort Castle would play a small part. His experiences, however, set the stage for his far more substantial role in shaping relations with Japan after 1929 and deserve some examination.[2]

Secretary of Commerce Herbert Hoover, left, and Secretary of State Charles Evans Hughes in 1924. (Library of Congress photo LC-USZ62-111374.)

Because of his numerous contacts in and out of European government, Castle's opinions on postwar Europe were solicited more than was common for a tyro in foreign affairs. Moreover, he would soon become accustomed to writing public position papers, often anonymously, as a vehicle for his views.

It was, for example, Castle's realist view that the key to a revived and stable Europe was a reformed, democratic Germany. A prosperous, democratic Germany would, in addition to purchasing American goods, serve as a barrier to possible future Soviet expansion into an influence over Central Europe.[3] However, Castle warned policy makers and the public not to assume that the defeat of the Kaiser generated a quick acceptance of a democratic culture. Drawing on his missionary heritage, he argued that converting autocratic Germany, like converting a sinner, would be a slow, even painful, process in which success was far from guaranteed. Indeed, he sounded the warning that some German political leaders were reviving the cry of "Drang nach Osten" to undermine the fledging states of Poland, Czechoslovakia, Rumania, and the Baltic countries. Castle cited evidence of German propaganda and overt threats in upper Selesia and covert aid to the communist governments in Russia and Hungary. Disorder in this strategically important area could lead to renewed war.[4]

In the spring of 1920, Castle kept in close touch with official and unofficial contacts in the recently formed moderate government of Friedrich Ebert. Squashing the extreme left, Ebert had called for a national election on January 19, 1919. The delegates to the new National Assembly were generally from the moderate left. The assembly met in Weimar to elect Ebert the first president of the republic and Philip Scheideman the first chancellor. Although suspicious of both the autocratic nationalists in the "hypocritical devious" socialists in the assembly, Castle urged the West to support the vulnerable Ebert regime by every legitimate means.[5] Later, he traveled to Germany in September of 1920 to report the prospects for Germany after the adoption of the July 1919 constitution. The provisions of the Weimar constitution included universal suffrage, proportional representation, a bill of rights, and separation of church, state, and school. Behind the liberal facade, however, much of prewar Germany persisted. The industrial cartels and monopolies were fundamentally unchanged, local leadership was largely the same, and the Junkers of East Prussia retained their landed estates. Castle reported his suspicions, which would prove to be accurate, that the Weimar Republic could depend on the loyalty of bureaucrats, army officers, and landed gentry only so far as relative prosperity was maintained.[6] The financial chaos of 1919 and 1920 was due to Germany's unwillingness to pay reparations to the victorious allies. Deploring French self-righteousness and arrogant demands on Germany, he could not sympathize with those who would destroy Germany while requiring it to pay the substantial indemnity. A fair reparation, combined with firmness in insisting on a reasonable timetable for payment, would permit justice to be done. France, he noted, had paid an onerous reparation to Germany as a result of the Franco-Prussian War of 1870–1871. So now could Germany.[7]

Castle's first two years in the State Department were influenced by the postwar Red Scare. The Scare was fueled by social and economic change after the war, a rising cost of living, a postwar recession, labor unrest, and the atmosphere of intolerance toward dissenting opinion fostered by wartime propaganda. Isolated cases of terrorism combined by a record number of strikes seemed to evidence the Comintern.

Like most of the State Department elite, Castle deplored the Soviet attempt to "poison" domestic and international affairs. He claimed to have unearthed confidential dispatches from the Soviet government to agents planted in most important European countries. In all cases, the dispatches called for the use of sabotage, assassination, obstruction, and deceit; most important, the agents were called on to take advantage of postwar confusion, dislocation, poverty, and hunger to advance the message of radical socialism. Castle noted that the Soviets had, in his opinion, little actual concern for the proletariat and used the language of social justice to mask the horror of their secret police, physical coercion, brutality, and mendacity. Castle, who would always deplore bloated and insincere rhetoric and excessive claims to virtue, warned that the Soviet rhetoric would be accepted at face value by "American parlor Bolsheviks and certain sentimental paper-radicals." He nonetheless wanted Americans in 1920 to avoid damaging traditional civil liberties and individual rights, while being diligent in protecting the country from subversion. The balance was delicate but essential to the health of the country.[8]

Although he did not fear communist influence in the economically stable and democratic United States, he did fear its impact in devastated countries in eastern and central Europe, which lacked democratic traditions. For example, in the communist regime of Béla Kun (March–July 1919), communist ideology had taken advantage of economic dislocation to kill many bourgeois reforms and self-rule. Educated people had fled the country fearing for their lives. Farmers, the backbone of the economy, had refused to plant crops that they could not own. Small manufacturers, also fearing that their property and profits were in danger, had cut production. To Castle's relief, the government of Béla Kun was short-lived. Herbert Hoover, Wilson's food administrator, brought extreme pressure on Béla Kun by manipulating food supplies, but Castle chose to see the reasons for the collapse in the defeat of the Red Army by the Rumanians. Communism in Hungary, he argued, had flowered briefly by claiming it could defend the fledgling country against the rapacity of its neighbors. When the threat ended, a more conservative regime was installed.[9]

The severe instability of the infant nations of the Danubian basin also concerned Castle. The sudden dismemberment of the venerable Austro-Hungarian Empire had produced a crisis through the multiplication of customs barriers and economic dislocation. The inability of these states to cooperate in establishing workable trade and lines of communication was, Castle reported to the State Department, producing negative consequences. For example, hunger and deprivation were worsened by the inability of trade to move across newly established boundaries. Thus surpluses of wheat in one country could coexist with hunger just a few miles away across international boundaries. Moreover, the new and fledgling state of Austria was already discussing the possibility of a union with Germany. Such a union could threaten future peace and independence in Central Europe while threatening the precarious "friendship" celebrated in the Treaty of Rapallo. He remained skeptical throughout the 1920s of this region's ability to withstand future German aggression.[10]

Before the official change in administration from Wilson to Harding in March of 1921, Castle publicly attacked the practice of rewarding party workers and contributors with appointments in the foreign service's overseas posts. Committed to the Progressive Era's ideals of disinterested and expert service for the government, and appalled at the unfairness of political rewards for the merely wealthy, he urged government reform of the diplomatic corps. The continued practice of the spoils system was no longer possible, he argued, given the enlarged role of the United States in foreign affairs. Voters should demand, he felt, the separation of the foreign service from politics in order to ensure that objective expertise was rewarded in the State Department.[11] To this end, Castle strongly endorsed and informally lobbied for the reform legislation sponsored by Congressman John Jacob Rogers of Massachusetts. This long-awaited reform passed Congress in May of 1924 and provided for the new professionalization career men Castle, Bill Phillips, Joseph C. Grew, J. P. Moffat, and Wilbur J. Carr had been advocating.

Specifically, the Rogers Act provided for the unification of the diplomatic and consular services and renamed the unified body the Foreign Service. The law further provided for a graded merit system for appointment and promotion. Salaries were, in many cases, increased, and a regular retirement system was put in place. To provide the instruction necessary to support the increased professionalization of service, the Foreign Service School was established. The term of instruction in the school was one year, which was considered a period of probation for new appointees. Castle would be an active instructor in the school, and it was there that many of his ideas about the importance of diplomatic realism were imparted to novice officers.

Castle was a frequent and popular lecturer for the Foreign Service School through the 1920s. A former lecturer and assistant dean at Harvard, he quickly gained a reputation for an ironic wit and a facility with words. More importantly, his lectures featured his developing and distinct sense of diplomatic realism.[12]

Significantly, he urged professional diplomats to look beneath the surface of nationalist, ethnic, racial, and religious claims to superiority. They were far from being the the key driving causes for international action. Castle argued that commercial economic, demographic, and material realities were, in the main, the primary causes for state action. Sentimental citizens, after World War I, for example, had applauded the creation of economically unviable states fashioned from the former Austro-Hungarian and Russian empires. Misled by their sentiments, many Americans had supported the nationalist and racial strivings in Europe. By doing so, the United States had contributed to the deconstruction of the viable economic unity of Central Europe. For Castle, the seeds of future economic collapse and racial horrors had thus been sown. He implored aspiring professional diplomats to remain aloof from pressures to back European nationalist aspirations and, by studying the realities of world economics, to render balanced judgments on territorial questions. Well-educated, impartial diplomats would find that economic, demographic, and material considerations "seem more vital and more lasting than any others. They are permanent while others, such as race, nationality and political form, fluctuate."[13]

William R. Castle, Jr., in 1923 when he was chief of the Division of Western European Affairs in the Department of State. With him in the photograph is his son-in-law, Alan F. Winslow, diplomatic secretary. (Photo courtesy of Donald F. Winslow.)

Furthermore, since the United

States had developed in a unique atmosphere of relative prosperity and national abundance while avoiding involvement in European rivalries, American diplomats could better judge the competing claims of European rivals than could the Europeans themselves. The suffering of World War I and historical rivalries made most European politicians blind to the limitations of self-determination. Blind ambition mixed with ethnocentrism and racial and religious differences had produced an economic tragedy when the Hapsburg Empire had disintegrated to satisfy "the selfish" aspirations of Czech, Polish, Slovak, and Magyar nationalists.[14]

Like most State Department leaders, Castle taught aspiring diplomats that international law, though limited in its impact, made international commercial conflict predictable. The principles of international law regulated but could not end competition among states. Properly constructed, all nations accepted the role of law in containing costly international anarchy. Because of this, the governments that put themselves outside the pale of international law, most specifically the Soviet Union, should be isolated. Application of international law made the world more stable and predictable, thus facilitating U.S. trade interests.[15]

No international arrangement could, for example, address the dominating social, economic, and political realities that rendered post–World War I Germany a threat to permanent peace. Castle warned throughout the 1920s that democracy in Germany had emerged "artificially," not through any fundamental social or political change. Moreover, the Kaiser had provided Germany with a "center of gravity" that it lacked in the Weimar Republic.[16] The multiparty system of Weimar Germany guaranteed instability; should a severe economic downturn occur, a strong man would likely emerge to subvert the vulnerable democracy.

Finally, Castle consistently argued in his instructions that America's interests were best served by professional diplomats who really knew how nations worked. Trained diplomats would check popular passions for idealistic crusades to change world politics. If the public could be made to understand the value of disinterested, cautious, careful expertise, the jobs of foreign service officers would be secure. He further urged novice officers to learn, in close association with seasoned veterans from similar educational, social, and economic backgrounds, the intuitive skills needed to supplement the necessary technical skills of the diplomat. For Castle, the best diplomats required a rigorous liberal arts education and were able to analyze and synthesize information about a country. Such diplomats, moreover, understood the psychology of a country and of human nature. Professional diplomats could teach Americans the hard realities of international affairs while diminishing strife between nations through careful, cautious negotiations which advanced national interests. Such diplomatic professionalism would garner the respect of the diplomatic guild throughout the world.

Castle's view of the appropriate range of philosophy and activity for the foreign service was reinforced by the appointment of Charles Evans Hughes as secretary of state under Warren G. Harding. Perhaps Harding's best appointee, Hughes named Castle chief of the Western European Division in 1921. Hughes was a fellow foreign-policy realist, and the two men developed a warm personal relationship. His goals were necessarily limited by public opinion and a Congress opposed to any actions that would limit American independence or freedom of action. No bold innovative moves were expected by Harding, who promised the electorate a return to "normalcy" in foreign policy. Hughes' real ability to operate within these limitations while still retaining boldness and originality made him one of the best secretaries of state in the twentieth century.

One of Castle's earliest responsibilities was to assist in the separate peace with Germany necessitated by the defeat of the Treaty of Versailles in the Senate. Shortly after Harding's inauguration, the Senate passed a resolution declaring the wars with Germany and Austria-Hungary over. It also reserved for the United States all rights, reparations, and other advantages to which the United States had been entitled under the armistice agreement and failed Versailles Treaty. To obtain German agreement with this unilateral declaration, the State Department prepared a treaty incorporating the language of the July 2nd declaration ending the war officially with a series of selected references to the Versailles Treaty which listed various rights and advantages to the United States. An exhausted German government, satisfied that it had gotten what it could from a noninternationalist United States, signed the Treaty of Berlin on August 25, 1921. Austria and Hungary followed with similar treaties almost immediately.

After assisting in the drafting of the successful language of the Berlin Treaty, Castle next worked to reduce lingering problems between the two countries. A year after the treaty, Senator Oscar W. Underwood proposed that American claims arising out of Germany's wartime activities be resolved through an all-American commission. Castle and Hughes agreed that such an arrangement would not be acceptable to Germany and obtained an executive agreement from Harding creating a German-American Claims Commission. Such an agreement, they argued, possessed international precedence and could speed normalized trade relations.[17] Moreover, Castle continued to worry that German prisoners convicted of espionage were being released all too slowly. Fritz W. Bischoff was the last to be released. Delays in the Department of Justice had infuriated German opinion and led Castle to ask Hughes to intervene in 1924.[18] Although the matter was settled quickly, much of the Castle's time during his period as chief of Western European Affairs was consumed with repairing friction between American and German citizens.

A particularly bothersome matter was German offense taken at films inspired by World War I. American opinion of German political and military leaders had been shared by organized propaganda during the war. Germans were, in government, viewed as the opposite of the liberty-loving, pragmatic, liberal American. The German embassy, for example, protested at a scene in the film *Mare Nostrum* that depicted the crew of a German U-boat laughing at the drowning victims of their torpedoes.[19] Castle's response to the embassy was to explain that the State Department could not contend an expression of any kind or account for the taste of moviegoers. Still, Castle used his friendship with Will H. Hays, president of the Motion Picture Producers and Distributors of America, to urge filmmakers to tone down overt anti-German bias. He made his case by telling Hays and others that the films would sell better in Europe if simple stereotypes of Germany were left out. On other occasions, Castle arranged for private showings of films that might ignite opinion in the German embassy.[20] Castle even urged Consul General William Coffin in Berlin to quietly survey German films for examples of anti-American themes. Due to a higher tolerance of censorship, Coffin could not find comparable examples.[21] The endless protests so irritated Castle that his famous dry, sardonic humor was evoked. Once, a German diplomatic official complained about the American *The Four Horsemen of the Apocalypse* even though the producers had cut out several objectionable scenes. When the official belabored the offensiveness of the scene, which featured a German general eating an apple while civilians were being machine gunned, Castle was tempted to ask him if substituting a banana for the apple would satisfy the German government.[22]

Secretary of State Hughes would also rely on Castle for analysis and recommendations on the European debt question. During October of 1922 Castle was part of a U.S. delegation that gathered in Berlin under the leadership of Under Secretary of State Joseph C. Grew. The goal of Grew and his commission was to study the European economic situation and to recommend actions on assessing and collecting war debts. Particular attention was given to Germany's ongoing economic crisis.[23] U.S. Ambassador to Germany Alanson Houghton proposed that the United States cancel the war debts in return for guarantees of partial disarmament and guarantees of avoiding war for fifty years.[24] Castle cautiously agreed with the ambassador that debt cancellation could secure peace and prosperity in Europe but argued that the State Department would first have to sell the idea to the American people.[25] Writing Hughes, he proposed that the secretary call for an international conference similar to the Washington Naval Conference, held a few months earlier, to create a greater acceptance for negotiating debt cancellation.[26] Hughes, believing that Congress would never accept such an arrangement, rejected the idea and proposed instead negotiations on the payment schedule. After that, Castle, a loyal assistant, never publicly referred to the Houghton proposal again.

The reparations question quickly became a crisis in December of 1922 when Germany failed to meet its scheduled payment.[27] In January, after the French occupied the Ruhr, Castle's division advised Hughes that opinion in France, England, and Switzerland was that, according to French Premier Raymond Poincaré, the ruin of Germany was preferred to timely reparation payments. The Ruhr occupation, Castle argued, would be counterproductive for France because anti-French feeling there was violent. Moreover, the French lacked the necessary organization to last in the Ruhr; a long-term occupation would be a minimal condition for the occupation to be cost-effective.[28] Shortly after the January occupation, Castle recommended that the State Department treat the occupation as a fait accompli without promises to Germany or to France that would constrain future U.S. action. On the other hand, the State Department should insist that American businesses in the Ruhr be free from any discrimination. Should the French not guarantee this, economic sanctions could be used as a measure of last resort.[29]

When Frank B. Kellogg became secretary of state in 1924, Castle found him cantankerous and occasionally inattentive but nevertheless achieved a closer relationship than did many of the secretary's other subordinates. (Library of Congress photo LC-USZ62-92303.)

To Castle's great sorrow, his mentor, Secretary of State Charles Evans Hughes, left the office shortly after election of Calvin Coolidge in November of 1924. Under the new secretary, Frank B. Kellogg, Castle would, like Under Secretary Joseph Grew, find communication with the cantankerous new cabinet member difficult. Although Castle was closer to Kellogg than most of the secretaries' subordinates, lived in the same neighborhood, and often walked to work with him, Castle quietly doubted whether he was given the whole story on certain questions. When Kellogg chose, Castle could tone down the secretary's harsh first response to foreign matters.[30]

Because of Castle's relative closeness to the quarrelsome and occasionally inattentive secretary, he was frequently approached by foreign diplomats to serve as a sounding board. (Castle's interpersonal skills and ability to keep confidences made him an attractive sounding board for a large range of diplomats throughout his life.)

Even with his promotion to assistant secretary of state in 1927, a natural promotion for someone of his experience and length of service, Castle's duties were much as they had been under Hughes. Questions regarding the funding of international debts, the processing of claims, questions about exceptions to immigration quotas, and efforts to promote international arms reduction occupied most of his time. In addition, Castle's division was active in soothing friction with Canada and other countries which from time to time objected to the enforcement of America's prohibition laws. Much of the rest of his time was spent with routine administration of the division and helping Americans with problems overseas. (Castle continued to benefit from his contacts in the U.S. Senate to support the foreign-policy initiatives of Kellogg. The powerful Republican senator from Pennsylvania, David A. Reed, often reported legislation helpful to the State Department while also pressuring the Tariff Board and other government agencies to cooperate.)[31]

Much of Castle's time as assistant secretary of state was devoted to advice and comment on the Kellogg-Briand Pact, a multiparty peace agreement that came to symbolize the wishful thinking of Republican Party foreign policy in the 1920s. The pact, which outlawed war and was signed in Paris in 1928 by virtually every nation in the world, appeared at the time to be a naive alternative to giving the League of Nations real teeth. As futile as the treaty would prove to be in preventing war, it was far from an example of a temporary lapse in the realism that dominated State Department thought in the 1920s.

In April of 1927 the clever French foreign minister, Aristide Briand, offered to Secretary Kellogg a bilateral pact between France and the

United States pledging both countries to perpetual peace. The seemingly benign offer was actually an attempt to commit France to the security system of Europe, most specifically the series of pacts that France had signed with many countries in a desperate effort to discourage future German aggression. The bilateral pact, if signed, was a negative military alliance that would have tied the hands of the United States in future relations with France and, indeed, all of Europe. The proposal was quickly supported by many civilian pacifist organizations in the United States, including those led by Jane Addams and Carrie Chapman Catt. Political pressure mounted for Kellogg to do "something" for peace.

As Robert Ferrell, the distinguished historian of U.S. foreign policy discovered in conversations with W. R. Castle in the early 1950s, Kellogg had turned to his advisors to find a politically acceptable way to change the terms of the pact, while appeasing the substantial support for it in the country. Castle, who always feared the meddling of nonprofessionals in the complex, often ambiguous world of diplomacy, was a primary architect of Kellogg's counterproposal in December of 1927. Arguing that the more signatories to an agreement the less binding in practice it becomes, Castle urged Kellogg to propose a multinational agreement renouncing war. If the language of the revised pact contained enough guarantees that the that signatories would not give up the right to conduct defensive warfare, no country could object. The counter offer, once made, proved to be very popular in Europe and the United States. The trick turned, Briand attempted to delay his decision by proposing that a committee of

President Hoover, standing center, meets in the East Room of the White House on July 24, 1929, with representatives of the governments that had ratified the Kellogg-Briand Pact. (Library of Congress photo LC-USZ62-1117222.)

impartial jurists examine Kellogg's proposal. The tide of public opinion, however, pressured Briand into acceptance of a pact that had no more than symbolic authority.[32]

Castle spent the winter of 1927–1928 selling the idea of a multilateral pact to doubters. Admitting that the language of the proposed pact was stuff for "Pacifists and Earnest Christians," he nonetheless argued internally for the trick to be accepted. Castle recorded the confidential discussions in his diary:

> The last three or four days of the year were so busy, while I was in the office, that I wrote nothing. I took two or three afternoons off because it is a long time since I have loafed and it seemed hardly worth while to go away anywhere for only two or three days. On the 28th the Secretary sent a note to Claudel [Paul Claudel, the French ambassador to the United States] enclosing a copy of an arbitration treaty which we should be willing to sign with France—a treaty which is far stronger that the Root Treaty—and another note that, although we could not sign a bilateral treaty with France on the subject, we should be willing to sign a multilateral treaty to be subscribed to by the principal nations of the world renouncing the resort to war as a national policy. Claudel immediately came in to see me about it. He said that Briand was not yet ready to accept the idea of a multilateral treaty. He asked me why a bilateral treaty would not be acceptable. I told him that public opinion would not stand for it for one thing, that such a treaty would inevitably have more the appearance of a treaty of alliance than a treaty to advance the cause of world peace. I said that we were not particularly interested in the question of peace between France and the United States which, after all, was academic, but that we were enormously interested in advancing world peace. I said that a bilateral treaty might have just the opposite effect. He asked why and I countered by asking him what effect he thought a treaty between the United States and Germany outlawing war would have in France. He admitted that it would have a very exciting effect, that people would say that Germany was purchasing security from attack by the United States so that she could more readily attack her neighbors. I asked him whether he did not think a French-American treaty would have the same effect on German opinion and possibly on English opinion and he admitted it would. He asked if I would be willing to instruct Whitehouse [Sheldon Whitehouse, counselor of

the U.S. embassy in Paris] to say similar things to Briand and I promised to do it, did it as soon as he had left. This showed very clearly that Briand was dissatisfied with the way Claudel has been carrying on the negotiations but I nevertheless want to do everything possible to keep all negotiations right here. We cannot trust them to Herrick [Myron T. Herrick, the U.S. ambassador to France], who supposedly returns on the 14th, and in any case Claudel is a keen, sane man. It is not his fault that we have gone Briand one better. He has always understood that we cannot make a treaty with one country which we are not willing to make with others and has, I have no doubt, transmitted that fact to Briand. It is more and more evident to me that Briand made his first suggestion for political reasons solely and that he has now got a bad case of cold feet. They will be positively frozen when we drive him into the open and make him do something, or refuse to do something, which on paper at least is a step toward prevention of war.[33]

While advising Kellogg on the way to sidestep the bilateral offer of Briand, Castle was dismayed at the inability of Britain, Japan, and the United States to advance disarmament at Geneva. The Geneva Naval Conference was being called by President Coolidge in an effort to extend the category of ships that would be subject to restrictions (smaller warships, such as cruisers). France and Italy refused to attend. Great Britain, fearful of further declines and desperately trying to protect its empire, refused to reach an agreement with the State Department. Japan, no more interested in an expansion of the Washington naval disarmament arrangements, nonetheless convinced Castle that it might be amenable to future conferences that were more sensitive to Japan's increased influence in Asia.[34] This encouragement from Japan favorably disposed Castle toward Japan's "reasonableness." Japan's moderate civilian government was convinced that Castle would, for his own realist position, treat Japan fairly. This would make Castle a good choice for U.S. ambassador to Japan during the 1930 London Naval Disarmament Conference.

Castle spent much of 1928, helping Herbert Hoover achieve the Republican nomination and to be elected in November 1928. Castle and Hoover had known each other since World War I but had never been close. Indeed, Castle's diary indicates slight irritation with Hoover in the early 1920s when the State Department occasionally resented Hoover's Department of Commerce for "interfering" in foreign matters. Still, by 1926, Castle and Hoover had developed a friendly social relationship while also discovering that they fundamentally agreed on most points of domestic and foreign policy. Castle, who realized the substantial intellectual and political limitations of Harding and Coolidge, found Hoover to be the best hope for the Republican Party in the 1928 presidential election. Both believed strongly in the promise of the cooperative state, the rule of expert administrators and diplomats, the importance of disarmament and diplomatic realism, and the importance of Japan to America's economic and diplomatic future.

After the election of 1928, President Hoover and W. R. Castle, Jr., would grow even closer. Knowing of Castle's desire to serve in a more significant position than assistant secretary of state, Hoover appointed him to serve as special ambassador to Japan in the fall of 1929 to assist in the negotiations in the 1930 London Naval Disarmament Conference. In 1931, Castle would be promoted to under secretary of state. Much of Castle's significance after 1928 was due to his special friendship with Hoover. This friendship would continue beyond Hoover's departure in March of 1933 and, indeed, would help Castle achieve a continuing significance in diplomatic affairs into the early 1950s.

4 The London Naval Conference

A turning point in Japanese-American relations may well have come in 1930, when William R. Castle, Jr., served for four months as ambassador to Tokyo during the time of the London Naval Conference." President Herbert Hoover sent Castle to interpret the U.S. position to the government of Premier Yuko Hamaguchi and to facilitate acceptance of what proved to be a complicated naval treaty. Castle hoped that a stable, democratic Japan could have a legitimate interest in China while serving as a bulwark against Russian expansion. He was prepared to recognize Japan's aspirations for trade in China, while working to obtain concessions in naval armaments.

Before the talks began in London, President Hoover had taken measures to protect the American diplomatic position, appointing as ambassadors in the major capitals individuals who had sufficient distinction to lend prestige to his policy. He believed that the Japanese post would be particularly sensitive and consulted his minister to Switzerland, Hugh Wilson, who responded that Castle was the best man for Japan. Before the invitation was made, Castle let the president know that he would accept on the condition that the assignment cover only the period of the naval conference. With his developing close relationship to Hoover, Castle knew that his ability to get things done depended on being close to the White House.

The Hoover administration was delighted to have a man who was in touch with American policy. Henry Cabot Lodge, Jr., then a journalist, wrote in the *New York Herald Tribune* of Castle's special ability to sense the movements of public opinion.[1] The Japanese likewise looked forward to the mission. Because of the new envoy's closeness to the president, they felt that America was taking into account their increasing international prestige.[2]

Although Castle's instructions included no detail about negotiation with Tokyo, he did receive latitude to interpret American opinion and State Department positions. He was responsible for communicating Japanese opinion, and his instructions stressed that he should communicate directly to the American delegation to the London conference, led by Secretary of State Henry L. Stimson.

The ambassador's plan of action, which he did not substantially alter during his stay in Japan, was to concentrate on Japan's foreign minister, Baron Kijuro Shidehara. Castle hoped to identify four or five other individuals who stood between the foreign minister and the emperor and, hence, could prove helpful. The ambassador also hoped to get to know "as many kinds of people as possible."[3] He quickly discovered, however, that what seemed a common sense approach would hardly suffice against the extraordinary complexities of the naval conference. He found out that the Japanese navy, and in reality the entire Japanese government, was not about to accept the ratio for British, American, and Japanese ships that Secretary Stimson was offering in London.[4]

Members of the Japanese delegation arrive for the Washington Conference on October 24 1921. Pictured are, from left, Robert Woods Bliss, third assistant secretary of state; Baron Kijuro Shidehara, the Japanese ambassador to the United States; Admiral Robert E. Coontz chief of naval operations; Vice Admiral Kanji Kato, naval technical adviser; Major General Kunishige Tanaka, military adviser; and Brigadier General Andrew W. Brewster, chief of th War Department liaison mission with foreign military officers attending the conference. (Library of Congress photo LC-USZ62-92164.)

The crucial problem at the London Conference was the so-called 10:10:6 ratio. Invented by a newspaperman present at the Washington Naval Conference of 1921–1922—in the reduced form of 5:5:3—the ratio amounted, so Japanese critics had said at the time of the Washington Conference, to Rolls Royce : Rolls Royce : Ford. After the conference, the numbers 5:5:3 were scrawled across buildings in the cities of Japan as evidence of how Westerners had failed to appreciate a nation the late President Theodore Roosevelt once had described as the Anglo-Saxons of the Orient. Indeed, Japanese opinion was highly incensed by the ratio proposed by Washington.

The ratio agreed to in the early 1920s applied only to battleships and aircraft carriers. For battleships it was roughly comparable to hundreds of thousands of tons of displacement—500,000:500,000:300,000. The problem at London in 1930 was to extend the ratio to lesser categories of warships, that is, heavy and light cruisers, destroyers, and submarines. Opinion in Japan—and government policy—was strongly against extension and desired not 10:10:6 but 10:10:7, and ideally equality.[5]

The special sticking point at London turned out to be what was known in the interwar years as the heavy cruiser, a large ship that had become technically desirable because of the limitation of battleship tonnage at the Washington Conference. To prevent evasion of the battleship limitation, the diplomats had placed a limit on smaller vessels, stipulat-

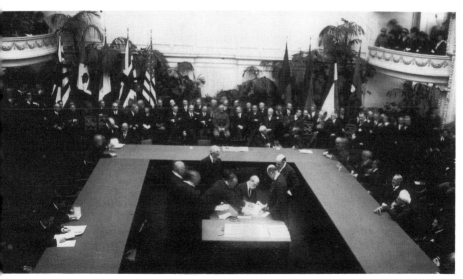

Secretary of State Charles Evans Hughes signs the treaties resulting from the Washington onference on the Limitation of Armament on February 5, 1922. Surrounding him are other members of the American delegation. (Library of Congress photo LC-USZ6-1755.)

ing that any ship over 10,000 tons displacement and with guns of more than eight inches would automatically be certifiable as a battleship. This sensible arrangement then became a sort of ideal definition for a heavy cruiser—the next largest ship to a battleship. In 1922 no cruiser had been built with a displacement of 10,000 tons and guns of eight inches. Immediately, the U.S. Navy undertook to build such ships, which became known as "treaty cruisers." It is fairly clear that they chose the size because it was the largest possible. The British and Japanese navies followed suit, and by the mid-1920s, a veritable race in heavy cruisers was developing. The London Naval Conference met in an attempt to halt that race.

The Japanese believed that construction of such large cruisers by the United States threatened Japan's control of the Western Pacific. Such, indeed, was the purpose of the U.S. Navy, although in retrospect it is clear that a dozen or so heavy cruisers would hardly have controlled that enormous reach of ocean that stretched from Hawaii westward to the Japanese Islands. In any event, the thought became reality, both in Washington and Tokyo. This, then, became the problem of Ambassador Castle.

Secretary of State Stimson seems never to have understood the nature of this treaty-cruiser problem. In addition, Castle soon discovered that his superior, negotiating in London, thought a 10:10:6 ratio in treaty cruisers—heavy cruisers—was easily possible. Castle's presumed task in Tokyo was to relate the obvious (Stimson's interpretation) to the Japanese and, perhaps as easily as Stimson had decided the issue, gain Japanese acceptance.

Stimson had little patience for the theoretical nature of the treaty cruiser's architecture. A complicating factor was that the 10,000 tons displacement was not enough of a platform for eight-inch guns. Moreover, an eight-inch gun had to be machine-loaded, meaning only three shells in the air a minute, as opposed to a six-inch gun that could be hand loaded. This would result in ten to fifteen shells in the air per minute. Further, the weight of the shells was 250 pounds compared with 100 pounds. Hence, if a light cruiser, the standard cruiser of the 1920s, could close the supposedly awful gap where it did not have the range, it could destroy a heavy cruiser by sheer numbers of shells in the air.[6]

Even before going to Japan, Castle had seen how awkward the treaty-cruiser issue was becoming and how dangerous it was for American-Japanese relations. In a letter to Hugh Wilson dated January 29, 1930, he wrote:

> One thing we certainly missed at home was the very widespread demand for the 10:7 ratio. There is no use in saying

that we should not consider ratios because the Japanese instantly point out that our entire policy is based on equal ratio with Great Britain. The Japanese government is certainly not going to capitulate right away on the matter, particularly at a time when capitulation would mean almost certainly defeat in the election of February 20.[7]

The Hamaguchi government's insistence on a 10:7 ratio with the United States in the heavy cruisers had originated in a October 10, 1929, meeting at the residence of the naval minister. The entire cabinet, leaders of the opposition party, and members of the Privy Council expressed unity in seeking the 10:7 ratio. To all important political and naval groups, this ratio was crucial to the security of the empire. The Japanese demand, going into the conference, was founded specifically upon the avowed defensive strategy of Japan's navy.

The U.S. Navy had assumed that the 10:6 ratio established for battleships and aircraft carriers at the Washington Conference could extend to all categories of ships. Throughout the London Conference, the Japanese insisted that the 10:6 ratio applied only to capital warships, and any comprehensive armament control over other categories of warships would have to be settled at the 10:7 ratio. Hence, as the American delegation took ship to London in January of 1930, no preliminary agreement had been achieved. Secretary Stimson's confidence that Japan would not insist on the 10:7 ratio because it needed relief from the ex-

Secretary of State Henry L. Stimson led the American delegation at the London Naval Conference though he had a poor understanding of the crucial issue of the status of cruisers under earlier disarmament treaties. (Library of Congress photo LC-USZ62-93488.)

pense of replacing old battleships accounted for his failure to arrive at a preconference arrangement.

As Castle's suspicions of Japanese intransigence on the 10:7 ratio were confirmed by early reports from London, he began to discover division in the Japanese position. His analysis of inner circles of the Tokyo government revealed that Hamaguchi still hoped to produce a successful conference while enhancing Japan's prestige. Before dissolution of the Diet in early 1930, the opposition party, the Seiyukai, made a loud but unsuccessful attempt to force the government to state that the 10:7 ratio was essential. "Big navy" supporters in Japan, prominent among the naval command, continued to insist that lessons of the battles of Tsushima in 1905 and Jutland in 1916 required the higher ratio.[8]

Castle also discovered that the chief Japanese concern was conflict with the Americans over China. By attempting to diminish Japan's fear that America would challenge its interests in China, the United States could make agreement at London more likely and also establish a basis for long-range cooperation. Although Japan was "a powerful and faithful ally in the Far East," he wrote to Hoover on January 27, 1930, "at present, it is a suspicious friend."[9]

Castle shared Hoover's long-standing belief that Japan was a possible check to Russian expansion in the Far East. Japanese desire for trade with China, he felt, was a reasonable demand, given their vulnerable economy. Indeed, Japan's legitimate economic interests in China could be acceptable to America. "From every point of view," he told the Japan Society of Boston on December 9, 1930, "the two nations need each other, and I think these people are not far wrong who assert that our continued friendship more than any other single thing depends on the peace of the world."[10]

Castle also believed that neither pacifistic ideals nor agreements could guarantee peace. Rather, enlightened self-interest among major powers and the peaceful flow of world trade were the keys. In 1930, and from the perspective of both the United States and Japan, a unified, prosperous, independent China was in the best interest of each.

In a private letter written on January 27, 1930, to his old friend, Senator David Reed, the top U. S. representative at the London Conference, Castle expressed his dismay over the ingrained American fear of Japan:

> It is a fantastic fear since I cannot imagine Congress declaring war on Japan because of anything Japan might do in China. . . . It is perfectly silly for us to pretend that Japan has not had special interests in Manchuria, and although the Japanese posses-

sion of the South Manchuria Railway may be irritating to the Chinese government, it is certainly not irritating to the Chinese people. Otherwise, they would not emigrate to Manchuria at the rate of 700,000 a year in order to live in safety and peace under the Japanese.[11]

In his initial conversation with Shidehara, Castle stressed the above points as well as belief that the 10:7 ratio for Japan was unnecessary as America would not possibly build beyond a 10:6 ratio. He stressed that armaments were an incitement to war. As was typical of State Department officials in the 1920s, Castle believed that military buildups had been one of the causes of World War I. Indeed, international tension did not so much cause armament races as races caused tension. Weapons tempted a country to try them.[12] Further, in a period when economic depression was worsening, he stressed the expense of military weapons. To the argument that arms gave jobs, his philosophy was that the money would have had benefit if it were used for constructive social purposes.[13]

As negotiation intensified in London, Castle focused on these themes both in public statements and in conversation. Despite a warning from Acting Secretary of State Joseph P. Cotton that he should be careful in his "phraseology" in explaining American-Japanese relations, Castle pressed the two countries' compatibility of interests.[14] His first speech was to an audience of press representatives, and he called the countries' aims identical and said that long-term self-interest would be predicated on a peaceful, sovereign China. The reception was positive. The influential *Nichi-Nichi* agreed that China was the crux of suspicion and hoped that Castle's understanding of China's importance to Japan was representative of future U. S. positions. Everywhere the ambassador went, he pointed to Japanese-American cooperation in education, economy, medicine, and in rebuilding Tokyo after the destructive earthquake of 1923. Speaking to audiences at universities, hospitals, businessmen's associations, and especially the press, he emphasized goodwill and the advantages of cooperation.

The American press took immediate interest in this active ambassador. In his call for reduced armaments and respect, he seemed to echo the thoughts of many Americans who felt he had identified the residual source of international tension.[15] Members of Congress quoted from Castle's speeches to bolster their argument that the Japanese "bugaboo" was being used to keep the arms race going. Senator Hiram Johnson of California, however, wondered publicly whether the ambassador had gone too far by implying that Japan would be the chief guarantor of peace in the Pacific, much as the United States was in the Western Hemisphere.[16]

The period of preparatory discussion in London ended by February 4, 1930, when the American delegation rejected Japan's claim for the 10:7 ratio. The head of the Japanese delegation, Reijiro Wakatsuki, protested that such a ratio was essential to Japanese security. Despite the offer of the U.S. delegation to accept eighteen heavy cruisers, Wakatsuki repeated that a 10:6 ratio was a harbinger of U. S. aggression in the Pacific.

As Castle and much of the London Conference delegation anticipated, the Japanese response remained rigidly negative until February 20, when the elections were held in Japan. Castle again pointed out that the 70 percent ratio was "a political doctrine" and the sine qua non of the Japanese program.[17]

Ambassador Castle's continued description of Japanese intransigence and his sensitivity to the policies of the Hamaguchi government irritated Stimson. Stimson feared that the popular ambassador might, in his effort to win Japanese approval, lead the Japanese to anticipate changes in American naval policy. On February 28, Stimson ordered the acting secretary, Cotton, not to repeat to Tokyo any details regarding the London negotiations unless he ordered it. Stimson, understandably, wanted one voice to represent U.S. policy. Castle, however, never could

Japanese Prime Minister Reijiro Wakatsuki photographed during an address before the League of Women in Tokyo in 1926. (Library of Congress photo LC-USZ62-110935.)

rid himself of the feeling that Stimson's action was in part caused by his embarrassment in being wrong about Japanese willingness to reduce their demands. In his extensive but unpublished memoirs of State Department affairs from 1914 to 1937, Castle later wrote:

> Agreement with Great Britain was certainly of prime importance, but the urge to secure that agreement somewhat obscured the importance of reaching understandings before the conference should meet with the other nations as well, especially Japan. Both Washington and London brushed aside as of little importance the Japanese request for a 10:10:7 ratio at least, and as a result, this question very nearly wrecked the conference. There was no conception—and there should have been—of the tremendous popular feeling on this subject in Japan.[18]

Castle then cabled the American delegation that the elections had resulted in a decisive victory for Hamaguchi. Defeat of the opposition meant that the government had an unassailable position and could prosecute its policies in a decisive manner. More importantly, he reported:

> I was told confidentially by Admiral Kichisaburo Nomura [commander, Japanese Third Fleet] that when the position of the Japanese government in the Diet is uncertain, it is apt to take a strong attitude in foreign questions, and when it is firmly entrenched in the Diet, it is apt to take a conciliatory attitude. . . . It was not meant by him at all that the government would not capitulate on the ratio which had been repeatedly pointed out by me as much more than a government demand, but that the government would be in a position to make compromises which before the public could be defended.[19]

The Japanese delegation again presented its proposal for a 10:7 ratio and then proposed a compromise. Japan would accept eighteen cruisers for the United States, if the American government would defer construction of the last three cruisers until 1935. Such a compromise might satisfy the American desire for the 10:6 ratio while assuring Japan's wish for a 10:7 ratio until 1936. In 1936, Japan would reopen discussion with the United States.

The proposal at first received a cool reception, but Stimson's attitude changed when President Hoover noted on March 5 that even if given a slowdown in American construction, the Japanese Navy would be greatly inferior. Additional pressure to consider the Japanese offer came from Senators William E. Borah and Claude Swanson, who agreed with Castle that Japan need not be an inevitable opponent.[20]

Stimson now notified Castle that he had authorized Senator Reed to accept the compromise, with one important variation. If Japan would sanction eighteen cruisers for the United States, the latter would defer construction of the last three cruisers respectively until 1934, 1935, and 1936. Ambassador Tsuneo Matsudaira, who came to London from Paris and took the lead in negotiation for a compromise, offered to accept this condition if Japan were allowed 20,000 tons in other categories of warships. To ensure that the Japanese did not get this last concession, Stimson called a meeting of the heads of the three delegations at the Ritz Hotel. There he summarily informed Watasuki that Reed's offer of March 8 was the final American offer. Further, if the Japanese were unable to accept, Britain and the United States were prepared to exclude Japan from their negotiation. Such an exclusion, he implied, would be disadvantageous to Japan's naval position.[21]

The so-called Reed-Matsudaira Compromise was arranged on March 13. Under the arrangement, the United States could construct fourteen heavy cruisers between 1930 and 1936. The delay in U.S. construction of its final three cruisers would give Japan a de facto 10:7 ratio until 1936.

Japanese Ambassador Tsuneo Matsudaira took the lead in negotiating a compromise on the issue of warship ratios at the London Naval Conference. (Library of Congress photo LC-USZ62-93487.)

Ambassador Castle at once became involved in obtaining approval for this agreement. Through informal meetings, he tried to convince Shidehara that American concessions were fair and that the Japanese had not been asked to make dramatic sacrifices. Castle had also received directions from Stimson to emphasize the impossibility of American compromise. The ambassador chose, however, to stress the fairness of the U.S. proposal rather than that Japan had virtually no real choice in accepting the final offer. He pointed out that even if concessions were possible, the British would not likely agree. Reluctantly, the Japanese envoys accepted a compromise rather than assume responsibility for failure of the conference.[22]

Even before the compromise, proponents of a large navy for Japan had been conducting a campaign to persuade their countrymen that America was a potential enemy and that any alterations in Japanese demands would be suicidal. The chief opponent of compromise was chief of the Japanese naval staff, Admiral Kanji Kato. Referring to the compromise as the American Proposal, he particularly objected to the low ratio in heavy cruisers and prohibition of new submarine construction before 1936. Most Tokyo newspapers echoed his objections.[23] Castle's strategy was to ignore the press complaints and to concentrate on key officials and Japanese public support.

Castle disagreed with Stimson's coercive approach. He observed that any sign of U.S. pressure would reduce chances that the proud foreign minister or the premier would support the compromise. Castle decried the earlier threats of an Anglo-American treaty made without regard for Japan's defense concerns.[24] Thus, in realizing that bold threats would weaken the ability to work with civil officials in the Hamaguchi cabinet and realizing that coercion would needlessly test Shidehara's statesmanship, he facilitated Japanese acceptance of the Reed-Matsudaira Compromise.

Castle was able to report on March 3 that the Hamaguchi cabinet had accepted the compromise and that instructions were to be sent to the delegation in London.[25] He believed the key to acceptance had been Shidehara's political courage and the influential Count Nobuaki Makino's representations to the emperor.

Although Stimson in London could report that the Japanese delegation had presented a reply that "amounted to a substantially complete acceptance of the compromise," Castle worried that acceptance by the Privy Council would not be automatic. He told Hoover:

> All this looks hopeful enough, but it does not take into account the Army and Navy, which are immensely powerful. At the time of the Russo-Japanese war the chiefs of the general staffs were given Cabinet rank so that they might approach the Emperor directly. This rank they have retained, and it makes them less responsible to the Ministers of War and Marine who are technically their chiefs.[26]

Indeed, before formal Japanese ratification in October 1930, the naval command challenged both acceptance of the treaty and civil control over military affairs. Shortly after acceptance and the treaty's return for ratification, Castle proved right. Led by Admiral Kato, the naval chief of staff, the opposition party and other nationalist groups argued the following:

- The London Treaty would adversely affect the empire's security.
- The proposal came within the "right of supreme command" defined by Article II of the constitution.
- Kato, as a head of the Naval General Staff, bore personal responsibility for exercising this right of supreme command.
- Through direct access to the emperor, he could prevent acceptance of this unsatisfactory treaty.[27]

The leading form of opposition other than appeal to the "right of supreme command" was to delay consideration by the Privy Council by insisting that the Diet debate the treaty.

Ambassador Castle knew better than to involve himself directly in Japanese politics and could only report the slow progress toward ratification. Noting the lack of enthusiasm for the treaty, he guessed correctly that the quicker the ratification the better. In private talks with Shidehara and Hamaguchi, he urged dispatch and claimed that although the treaty represented an imperfect compromise for all three powers represented at London, Japan's security would be assured for the duration of the treaty. He avoided the threat of an Anglo-American treaty and stressed the importance of goodwill, cooperation, and the compatibility of Japanese and American interests in China. To give weight to the American position, he urged Senator Reed and Secretary Stimson to set out publicly in the Senate hearings the concessions the United States had made.[28]

The conflict over ratification in Japan was, as Castle described, bitter because it was a conflict between the military and civil branches of government. After many weeks of opposition between Premier Hamaguchi's government, which fully supported the treaty, and Kato's forces, which denied the civil government's right to determine the size of the fleet, the Privy Council formally approved the treaty on October 1. At least temporarily, civil control of foreign policy had been asserted, and Hamaguchi could announce with Castle that the treaty marked a move forward.

In retrospect, the London Naval Conference proved less successful than Castle and the Hoover administration thought. That the forces of fanaticism were only beginning to show their strength was made painfully evident when Hamaguchi was assassinated in November 1930.[29] The appearance of democracy, which had so impressed Castle, proved illusory. Too, increasing Japanese investment in China seemed to require a big navy. Unrestricted access to China, viewed as the basis of future economic security, drove Japanese expansion. Even as ratification occurred in Japan, the Seiyukai was preparing to maintain Japan's position in Manchuria along with a foreign policy that denied the need for ongoing cooperation with Britain and the United States.[30] A treaty intended to increase the chances for peace produced political unrest and even galvanized the forces for war.

5　The Hoover Moratorium

The Hoover Moratorium of 1931 was one of those diplomatic accomplishments—and there have been many—that took an enormous amount of time and attention and seemed, when completed, to resolve a critical problem. It would fall far short, however, of providing a lasting solution to the financial chaos brought on by the Great Depression. Its very name is hardly known today, and even when known requires explanation. Yet at the time it preoccupied the governments of the United States, Germany, France, and England.

The need for a moratorium on intergovernmental debts was indisputable. A virtual crisis began on May 6 when both the German ambassador in Washington and the American ambassador in Germany, Frederick Sackett, told President Herbert Hoover that the principal bank in Austria, the Kreditanstalt, had failed and that its collapse was bringing down all the major Austrian and German financial institutions. The ambassadors drew the possible result—financial ruin to the Continent—in stark proportions. Sackett was appalled by what might happen and urged the Hoover State Department to take action.

Moreover, Germany was racked by political turmoil. Sackett saw the rise of Adolf Hitler as similar to that of Lenin prior to the November Revolution, and in fact felt there was a connection between the Nazi and Communist threats. The inevitable failure of the Nazis, the ambassador advised, would push such radicals as Josef Goebbels and Gregor Strasser to join with Communist leaders and plunge the country into Bolshevism. Only the continuation in power of Chancellor Heinrich Brüning, and an economically stable Germany, could prevent such a result.

What was Hoover to do? Despite the need to adjust Germany's reparations payments, provided for by the Young Plan of 1929 (which had reduced reparations to $8 billion, to be paid over fifty-eight years), the American president had to take action because of the continuing financial disorder in Germany and elsewhere. The Berlin stock market nearly collapsed on May 26. Admittedly Hoover believed the financial problem "primarily a European crisis in which responsibility of the Continent should be further developed."[1] Moreover, he feared a debt moratorium might involve America with postwar reparations, from which the United States had traditionally distanced itself. Hoover's decision to move slowly and investigate the issue first also stemmed from his fears of Democratic Party opposition in the 1932 presidential election; Americans, generally speaking, regarded payment of the debts as a matter of principle as well as a symbol of U.S. economic influence in the world. He also worried that U.S. relations with France, the country with the most to lose from a debt moratorium, would worsen.[2]

In deciding for a moratorium, Hoover seems to have been influenced by powerful Wall Street bankers and his close friend, Under Secretary of the Treasury Ogden Mills. On June 5 the senior partners of J. P. Morgan and Company, joined by the prominent financier Thomas Lamont, urged the president to provide "a life-saver for the world." Estimating that U.S. financial institutions held about 50 percent of the $2 billion worth of short-term credits in Germany, Lamont argued that small banks in the United States would become alarmed and call in their credits if Germany failed to pay reparations on schedule. Such an outcome would cause a "terrifying crisis" and endanger banking stability in the depression-weary

President Herbert C. Hoover photographed by Bachrach in 1929. (Herbert Hoover Library.)

United States.[3] Many American banks, he predicted, would find their assets frozen in Germany. To head off such an international crisis, the Morgan partners advised, the government should invite the country's debtors to avail themselves of the postponement clauses in the debt settlements.[4]

Turning to his advisors from the cabinet, Hoover found Secretary of State Henry L. Stimson adamant that he move toward a moratorium at once.[5] Irritated with Hoover's reluctance to act, Stimson urged Mills, who was closer to the president, to make a strong case for a moratorium. Mills reported to Hoover that Secretary of the Treasury Andrew W. Mellon, who was in London, had urged the necessity of committing to a moratorium.[6] Further, Mills argued that his European contacts indicated Germany would suspend payments as provided for by the Young Plan, and France would reciprocate by ending their scheduled war debt payments. Moreover, the United States could not in any case remain aloof from Europe; if the Hoover administration did not move first and declare a moratorium, America would nonetheless find itself involved with the economic problems, but on terms set by Germany and France. Worse, the United States could be asked to assume the major responsibility for guaranteeing the stability of European finances. Calling for a two-year U.S.-led moratorium, Mills advised the president to seek the bipartisan support of congressional leaders as well as the concurrence of France.[7] Somewhat reluctantly agreeing to the urging of Mills and Mellon, Hoover sought approval for his plan from Congress.[8] Such support was far from certain, as Under Secretary of State William R. Castle, Jr., confided to his diary. Congress might well find a two-year moratorium dangerous for the same reasons he did:

> (1) . . . people will rightly ask why, when we have a deficit of a billion, we should give up four hundred million more. (2) Economically dangerous: is there any reason to think that England and France and Italy will save the situation, which is in their hands, by remitting an equal amount to Germany, which is the nation that needs saving. (3) Dangerous for the cause of disarmament since in the present state of the European mind there is no reason to believe that France and Italy at least might not use all this extra cash to build up their military machines. If we are to cut down on the debt payments we should at least have the assurance that our doing so will assist our foreign sales. If the money we remit is used to purchase from Russia at cheap rates it will further depress business conditions here and, therefore, in the whole world.[9]

To Hoover's surprise, however, congressional leaders gave generally favorable responses. Indeed, many of them had anticipated such an invitation after Castle's press conference on June 14.[10] Noting his close relationship to Hoover, most of the press and many banking officials felt Castle's remarks suggested a healthy flexibility and possible departure from the intransigence of Hoover's predecessor, President Calvin Coolidge, on the war-debt issue.[11] While the press warmed to hints of an upcoming major announcement, the Reichsbank reported a loss of ninety million marks on June 19. Castle, Mellon, and Mills failed to convince the president to obtain approval of the proposal from France.[12] Abruptly notifying the French ambassador to the United States, Paul Claudel, Hoover did not wait for an official reply before announcing his unilateral plan to postpone the collection of war-debt payments for one year if other governments deferred the scheduled war debts and reparations due them.[13]

The moratorium announcement, which was positively received by the press, the public, Wall Street, and Congress, was a gamble to strengthen the existing financial order while retaining U.S. independence of action. Hoover argued that the moratorium was "entirely consistent" with U.S. policy since the Paris Peace Conference.[14] He also stressed the exigencies leading to his decision and continued to demand that European nations assume their share of the financial burdens and further reduce armaments.[15] At the last minute, however, Castle urged Hoover to create the illusion of German support for his one-year moratorium plan. To that end, Stimson and Sackett secretly arranged for President Paul von Hindenburg of Germany to cable an urgent request that the United States issue such a debt suspension.[16] Not emphasized in the June 20 announcement, however, was the fact that this proposal undermined the sanctity of contractual obligations, emphasized the hitherto controversial idea of the interdependence of war debts and reparation payments, and circumvented the Young Plan's provision for emergency debt suspension. Moreover, several of Hoover's advisors privately agreed with the president that the Young Plan itself needed substantial revision.[17] The theory of the unrelatedness of war-debt payments and reparations, a fundamental assumption of Republican foreign policy, had been dealt a severe blow in the face of German economic collapse.[18]

The enthusiastic reception of the announcement both domestically and internationally was quickly dashed by the furious indignation of the French government. As the other great creditor nation, France deplored Hoover's unilateral action. Since France had benefited from the Versailles order, French officials feared that circumventing the Young Plan would weaken France's financial grip on its traditional enemy, Germany. Furthermore, the French protested that the financial effect of the moratorium helped the United States more than France. Indeed, in strict financial terms, the French were being asked to give up more in lost reparations than they gained from postponed war-debt obligations.[19] As Ambassador Walter Edge in Paris noted:

> They believed that American and British finance had conspired to cheat France out of the fruits of the military victory. They would not accept the explanation that all we and the British wanted was to accelerate the reconstruction of Europe. In fact, they pointedly remarked that Europe in the eyes of Anglo-American financiers had come to mean the German Reich. They were also somewhat resentful of the sudden development of New York after the war as a financial center superseding Paris, and the fact that the way from New York to the Continent of Europe seemed to lead by financial as well as political channels through London. The French were to some extent to blame for this, for in their business relations they were difficult, indulging in pinpricks which may have given satisfaction to some of the more short-sighted of their leaders but which resulted in isolating France even more from the "Anglo-Saxons."[20]

The negative reaction of the French under Pierre Laval was, therefore, more political than economic. Laval feared suspension of the unconditional annuity would encourage Germany to seek permanent changes in the Versailles Treaty. Furthermore, he felt the German government would lack the political will to tax its people to resume payments after the year's suspension was over.[21]

Most important, the French suspected that the United States was imposing the major financial and political burden for effecting stability on their vulnerable and insecure shoulders.[22] For Laval and French Finance Minister Etienne Flandin, France's interests, particularly its need to shape events in Germany through the collection of debts, could only be maintained by driving a hard bargain with Hoover and his representatives.[23]

One of these key representatives was Acting Secretary of State William R. Castle, Jr. Secretary Stimson departed for a long-awaited vacation on June 26 despite the critical pending negotiations with France.[24] With Secretary of the Treasury Mellon on his way to France from England, Hoover turned to Acting Secretary of State Castle as his chief advisor and negotiator. For Castle, whose strained relationships with Stimson often excluded him from information and a key role in State Department matters, the chance to work closely with the president was a long-awaited opportunity.[25] Castle's active role in obtaining French agreement to the moratorium would ensure that his view of European relations would be a force for the rest of the Hoover administration.[26]

For the most part, Castle's views on foreign policy coincided with Hoover's, and the two men remained close personal friends until Castle's death in 1963. The relationship had begun when Castle committed himself in the fall of 1927 to Hoover's 1928 presidential campaign. Indeed, in the 1928 election Hoover relied heavily on Castle for advice on foreign policy, asked him to edit selective foreign-policy speeches, and requested his assistance in writing the speech accepting the Republican Party's nomination.[27] Their close relationship, which was a key to much of Castle's subsequent importance in foreign policy, was strengthened by a genuine personal bond, agreement that communism represented a chief threat to American core values, opposition to recognition of the Soviet Union, agreement on the basic parameters of foreign policy, and a shared understanding of Europe's debt structure.[28]

Hoover and Castle projected a limited role for U.S. intervention in foreign affairs. Castle saw the world as properly divided into three regional blocs. In the first, Latin America, U.S. interests were paramount; America would dominate through open trade, access to markets and raw products, and cooperative political arrangements. Europe comprised the second bloc. Here, Castle limited U.S. action to using economic leverage through the flow of private and government loans to provide for free-market stability, access to European markets, integrated economies, a stable Western and Central Europe serving as a bulwark against

Following negotiation of a moratorium on war debt in July 1931, Acting Secretary of State W. R. Castle, Jr., joined President and Mrs. Hoover at a baseball game between the Washington Senators and the Philadelphia Athletics. (Herbert Hoover Library.)

Soviet expansion, and disarmament. To this end, he advocated reform of the punitive postwar reparations intended to strip Germany of power through the Charles Dawes Plan (1924), limiting that country's debt to $250 million annually, and the Owen Young Plan (1929), which reduced Germany's reparations to $8 billion (from the nearly $33 billion set in 1921) payable over fifty-eight years. For Castle, a prosperous Weimar Republic was a sine qua non of the European balance of power, the continuation of America's economic influence and prosperity, and general peace and stability. He, like Hoover, had little patience for continuing cries from the French for security through a weakened Germany.[29] The final of the three blocs, East Asia, became increasingly interesting to Castle after 1930. Here he sought to safeguard U.S. trade interests by protecting the open door without risking war. To do this, he would increasingly turn to cooperation with Japan as a bulwark against Soviet expansion and constant instability in China.[30]

Both Hoover and Castle were "independent internationalists" in favor of keeping foreign policy as free as possible to build a world order in which Americans would prosper, individual freedom would be protected, military armaments would be reduced, and wars (devastating to trade, prosperity, and civil liberties) would be avoided.[31] Moreover, both men thought foreign policy should be guided by enlightened self-interest. The United States would, as they saw it, be well served by avoiding entangling alliances, economic boycotts, and military action. Both believed also that the Soviet Union was a dangerous outcast in a world dominated by the U.S. dollar and the Washington treaty system of 1921–1922, which had sought to guarantee the open door principle internationally, limit naval armaments, make Japan dependent on U.S. capital, and build a base for joint U.S.-Japanese efforts to develop China and other parts of Asia. Ultimately, Castle and Hoover agreed that a world in which Britain, France, and Germany were dependent on U.S. finance; in which the Soviet Union was isolated and its expansion contained; and in which a partially dependent Japan was a defender of the status quo in Asia was a world in which orderly democratic capitalism was most likely to prosper.[32] With these profound areas of agreement, Hoover found easy to entrust his acting secretary of state with an important, if today overlooked, role in the difficult negotiations with France over the moratorium.[33]

The immediate negative reaction of the French to Hoover's suspended debt payment plan gave testimony to how much Hoover's and Castle's goals for postwar Europe differed from those of France. For

Hoover and Castle, and Republican officials generally, European stability was primarily an economic matter which the United States could subserve without political or military obligations. The offer of a moratorium, therefore, was in line with U.S. expectations that financial adjustments to debt questions could ensure order, stability, and peace. For Prime Minister Laval, French public opinion and political pressure required him to put France's political and military interests above either rapprochement with Germany or financial adjustments to war debts and reparations.[34] Most significantly, Laval and the Quai d'Orsay strongly believed that future French security depended on a Germany weakened and partially controlled by reparation payments guaranteed by the Treaty of Versailles. To the United States, stability and peace depended on a prosperous and republican Germany. In the 1920s, the strong U.S. economy and steady flow of financial credits had guaranteed that the French would comply with America's version of how peace could be maintained and accept without too much protest the unwillingness of the United States to make a defensive treaty with France.[35] By 1931, however, the Depression had substantially weakened the U.S. economy and devastated the German economy, but had left the relatively stronger and diversified French economy with enough leverage to resist automatic agreement with a U.S. version of economic settlement.[36] The challenge of the crucial and heated negotiations with France, therefore, was the need to obtain French cooperation while avoiding any significant military or political guarantees on the part of the United States.

Laval wanted to reassure the French public that the proposed moratorium would not alter the Versailles Treaty's arrangements for unconditional reparation payments from Germany. Thus, he demanded that the unconditional annuities be paid, then relent through the Bank of International Settlement (BIS) to any economically needy country (including Germany) in Central Europe. Any loans made to Germany, moreover, were to be made to the railroads rather than directly to the German government, which might expend the funds on armaments. France further insisted that Germany's deferred reparation payments be made immediately after the termination of the moratorium in 1932 and that certain payments-in-kind be continued during the year. As a final concession, France sought guarantees that Germany would discontinue work on a number of battleships, abandon the Austro-German customs union project, and cease challenging French spheres of influence in central Europe and the Balkans.[37]

With the departure of Stimson on June 26, Castle conferred with

Hoover and Mills. French resistance to the debt suspension and the apparent intransigence of their counterproposal infuriated Hoover. To the president, the French position, given the circumstances of international financial collapse, was intolerable. Finding Laval's difficulty with French public opinion unconvincing, he felt the French reservations were "technical and fictitious." Moreover, Hoover had his own problems with Congress; Senator William E. Borah of Idaho, for one, had loudly warned that concessions to the French might force him to cancel his support of the moratorium.[38]

With Mellon and Edge in Paris to facilitate direct communications with Laval, and Stimson on his way to Italy to lay the groundwork for a 1932 disarmament conference, Acting Secretary of State Castle became a chief negotiator for Hoover.[39] Knowing Hoover's bargaining position would be strengthened if they could get the Germans to make at least symbolic political concessions to the sensitive French leaders, Castle asked Ambassador Sackett to pressure German officials. "It would be unfortunate," Castle told Sackett, "if the impression that the Germans are giving nothing and taking everything became general." While Germany could not be expected to make any financial sacrifices, acceptance of the plan would be facilitated if Germany made a spontaneous contribution toward the restoration of confidence. Castle urged Sackett to get the Germans to drop the proposed customs union with Austria and reduce or eliminate expenditures on a second battleship.[40] Castle found backing for his position vis-à-vis Germany from British Foreign Secretary Arthur Henderson. Agreeing that political conditions should not be attached to the Hoover offer, Henderson advised Sir Ronald Lindsay, British ambassador to the United States, that voluntary German concessions would make it easier for Europe as a whole to accept the Hoover plan. Lindsay was encouraged to openly support Castle and this position in the press.[41]

While working to obtain German concessions, Castle warned Edge that quick French acceptance was critical to the success of the plan and the restoration of faith in the international finance markets. After consulting with Hoover and Ambassador Claudel, Castle cabled Edge two plans on which to base his arguments for acceptance.[42] The French had, in fact, agreed in principle to the debt suspension, but they claimed that under the Young Plan they could not give up the nonpostponable annuities. They agreed, however, that this sum should be paid into the Bank of International Settlement and immediately be relent to Germany and other European countries needing it. This meant the money would have to be repaid a year later, which Hoover felt would not give Germany the needed relief. In urging Edge and Mellon to change the minds of the

French, Castle suggested that the nonpostponable annuities might be paid by Germany to the BIS. Since this would be done in reichsmarks, it would not upset the exchange and in any case the funds would be relent to Germany. Castle further proposed that this should be funded for thirty-five years (the life of the agreement), to be repaid annually. Edge and Mellon presented the offer to Laval but were told that the amount might be funded for payment in the next five years, but no longer.

Hoover flatly rejected this offer, since U.S. debts would have to be treated the same as reparations to have any hope of congressional approval. Indeed, the president refused to pass along the French offer to Germany or other U.S. debtors and directed Castle, in consultation with his State Department staff, to cable a counteroffer. Hoover subsequently agreed to Castle's suggestion to lower the repayment schedule from the originally proposed thirty-five years to twenty-five years but insisted (against Castle's advice) on telling Edge and Mellon that there would be no more U.S. concessions.[43]

In telephone conversations with Mellon and Edge on June 29, Castle learned that Flandin doubted Laval would accept the counterproposal because of domestic political pressure. Further, they defended Laval's position that the counterproposal seemed to ignore France's legitimate concerns that the moratorium would strengthen Germany to France's harm.[44] To increase the chances of France's acceptance, they suggested that the payments of the unconditional annuities be deposited in the BIS, that it be repaid in five years, and that a guarantee fund be created to ensure regular payments to France if Germany should declare its own suspension of debt payments. Castle fulminated to the U.S. representatives that these French conditions for acceptance were silly. After all,

> If Germany has to make some such declaration she will not suddenly be able to put up 800,000,000 reichsmarks. The French also insist that part of this unconditional annuity be loaned to Central European powers who are in need. This wording because the idea is to help Germany and the others, not to make Germany help the others.[45]

Throughout the hectic seventeen days of negotiations, Castle never relented in his pressure on Sackett to obtain concessions from the German government. Though warned by Hoover not to push too hard for fear of making the Brüning government intransigent, Castle knew of Sackett's close relationship with the chancellor and his liberty to speak freely to him.[46] Sackett's confidence in his ability to deal with Brüning and his solid record of achievement in Germany encouraged Castle to press Germany for concessions more than he might have. Castle's faith in Sackett's persuasive abilities was augmented by his knowledge that Britain would coordinate with the United States to obtain concessions from Germany. Specifically, Castle instructed Sackett to ask for suspension of the German naval cruiser while Britain would request that the customs union proposal be dropped. This dual strategy would avoid the United States having to take the brunt of German criticism alone.[47] Negotiations with the French were stalled, and fearful that the Germans would declare a unilateral moratorium before the July 15 Young Plan payment was due, Castle told Sackett the French would likely abandon the construction of a cruiser if Germany would reciprocate.[48] Sackett conveyed this offer to Brüning but met with obfuscation and delay. It was clear that Germany would not give up the cruiser or the customs union unless France accepted Hoover's moratorium offer in its entirety.[49]

Hoover despaired of an early acceptance of the moratorium and confided to Castle that he might offer an alternative plan, granting a moratorium to each debtor nation separately and with different conditions. Although Castle advised Sackett to confidentially "sound out" the reaction of the German government to this possible proposal, the ambassador ignored the request, thinking Hoover's consideration of punitive multiple moratoriums would undermine his patient efforts to obtain German concessions to France. Brüning's reluctance to make these concessions stemmed from his fear that a show of weakness on his part would alienate the Reichstag and Hindenburg, who had made the battleship project a favorite of his.[50] As Sackett further observed, "the present moderate Government is so essentially a government by a very small minority, as Embassy reports have emphasized, that it is not able to take a firm stand against the extremists in the Nationalist camp, no matter how blind their opposition may basically be."[51]

Much to Sackett's chagrin, news of Hoover's alternative plan was leaked to the press by Ogden Mills, apparently with Hoover's approval, in order to expedite discussions with the French.[52] Castle tried to issue a formal denial, but the damage had been done.[53] Brüning now knew that Germany could expect a moratorium in spite of French objections; a German concession would be gratuitous. Castle rushed a cable to Sackett giving him greater latitude to resume, as best he could, his negotiations with the Germans.

> In order to induce the Germans to give it an approval of this
> sort, act according to your own judgment. In the past week we
> have been considerably exercised over the failure of the Ger-
> man Government to respond to the different suggestions which
> have been made by us in our attempt to reach a general agree-

ment and gain the principal object in view. From the telegram being repeated to you from Paris, you will note that several points still remain to be settled and the attitude of Germany will the principal factor determining the spirit in which these points can be taken up with other countries involved.[54]

Knowing he had little to lose at this late date, Sackett quickly made his first push, encouraged by a midnight telegram from Castle. In it, Castle argued that even a weak statement from Brüning indicating his willingness to curtail expenditures on armaments would be a welcome boost to the discussions of Edge and Mellon with Laval and Flandin in Paris. Specifically, Castle suggested that the Germans guarantee a moratorium on new naval construction while retaining the right to recommence building after the year's respite.[55] Armed with this imprimatur, Sackett received the following statement from Brüning's cabinet: that Germany would use the savings from the moratorium only to stabilize the financial situation. Sackett further informed Castle the statement should not be made public but transmitted to Laval as inconspicuously as possible.[56] With this long-awaited gesture toward France's security jitters, the responsibility for acceptance was now clearly in Paris.

With President Hoover increasingly irritated about the nonproductive French negotiations, Castle was eager to use the Brüning statement to break the deadlock in Paris. He cabled Sackett asking him to convince Brüning to publish the German statement so that world opinion would pressure the French to agree to the debt suspension.[57] Moreover, Sackett was urged to obtain from the German foreign minister a guarantee that new naval construction would not be undertaken during the year the moratorium was in effect. Because the minister was reluctant, Sackett went beyond Castle's instructions by promising that the Hoover administration would provide continued economic support for Germany. This offer of exceptional U.S. support in the midst of a severe depression was a gamble—one rewarded at last with German compliance.[58]

Castle and Hoover's impatience with France stemmed from their conviction that the moratorium, as announced on June 20, left intact the whole complicated system of reparations and interallied debts, ready to operate again when the world eventually shook off the Depression. The moratorium was intended to save the debtor, not cancel the debt. By early July, with the stalled talks eroding the international confidence generated by the June 20 announcement:

> . . . France has lost the opportunity of years to put herself forward in the eyes of the world as a nation ready to play her part and take the leadership in Europe. Her silly quibbling over un-

essential points has done infinite harm to the good effect of the President's proposal and has deeply offended all of Europe. France is not the knight in shining armor but is the pettifogging attorney. She quarrels while the house is on fire and it is the quarreling which will be remembered, not the final agreement—if the agreement is reached.[59]

By July 3, with Germany about to make the concessions described above, the French agreed to give up any question of the guarantee fund if it did not have to deposit the entire amount as soon as Germany declared a moratorium but could make payments to the different participating nations only as payments fell due. The French were willing to drop the issue of loans to Central European countries so far as unconditional payments, if the central banks would agree to give help when and where it was needed. The French would agree to call this unconditional payment the amount turned over to the BIS by the German Railway Company. They would also permit the payment to be relent to the railway, which could in turn lend it to Germany.[60] Castle and Mills authorized Mellon to obtain a final agreement containing these provisions and ask the French to accept a period of at least twelve years for funding of the amounts not paid during the year of the moratorium.[61]

At Hoover's insistence, Castle spoke by telephone with Henderson, Sackett, Mellon, and Edge to garner support for the pending agreement with France. To Castle's and Hoover's dismay, the Foreign Office developed a case of nerves and was demanding guarantees from the United States and France that discussions with Paris would not lead to "further sacrifices unless other parties to Mr. Hoover's proposal are prepared to cooperate in making sacrifices."[62] The Foreign Office felt this precautionary statement was necessary to reassure a doubtful House of Commons that the United States would not make concessions to the French at the expense of the English. To compound the setback, Mellon reported on July 3 that the French disagreed on the period of refunding and insisted they would consent only if the United States agreed to their continuing to receive, during the year of suspension, reparations in kind. Castle knew Hoover would never accept this condition, as it would destroy the intent of the moratorium to give the European economy a chance to recover.[63]

Castle privately told Hoover that in his opinion Mellon was part of the problem in Paris. According to Castle, Mellon made the negotiations more difficult than they needed to be because he did not understand the implications of the question of deliveries in kind.[64] Moreover, Mellon suggested that perhaps Hoover should authorize some compromise on this matter in return for a French agreement on the question of time. Laval suggested that the United States be neutral on the entire subject of in-kind deliveries and allow the matter to be decided by a committee of experts. This, however, was not in the spirit of Hoover's plan, and in no circumstance would the president agree to it. Castle directed Edge and Mellon to break off discussions with the French if they would not budge from their position,[65] reminding them that the British would clearly not go along with any exceptions made for the sole benefit of the French. "The way to deal with the problem now," Castle said, "is to have the French Government accept the President's proposal outright, and leave the question of existing contracts covering deliveries in kind for settlement by experts of the interested powers, whose conclusions would be acceptable to us if they accord with the spirit of the President's proposal."[66]

The French, anxious not to be isolated at a moment of worsening financial conditions in Germany, quickly moved to keep the negotiations alive. Edge and Mellon, delighted at the continuing dialogue, cabled that they would agree to the twelve-year repayment period if an agreement could be reached with Germany on the matter of in-kind deliveries for the year 1931–1932.[67]

The cable was unsatisfactory to Castle, who had learned from American bankers that the German government could furnish no exchange to meet the scheduled July 15 payment. He called Claudel to his office and told him Hoover was intransigent about the matter of payments in kind. Castle further argued that the spirit of Hoover's moratorium would be fulfilled if Germany relent to the Reichsbank the amounts that came to it through the payments in kind, this being no out-payments by France and no strain on Germany. After Claudel cabled this information to Laval, Edge telephoned Castle to complain that this contact with Claudel had interfered with the negotiations in Paris. Castle, knowing that he alone spoke for Hoover in this situation, ignored the request to end such initiatives.[68] He also concurred with the president that, with German concessions guaranteed and now publicly stated, the United States should at least hint that if France remained intransigent, European nations might have to handle the financial crisis by themselves.[69]

Mellon telephoned Hoover, Castle, and Mills on July 6 to say that he had represented the U.S. position to Flandin, whose cabinet once again rejected the U.S. requirements.[70] A disappointed Hoover directed Castle to prepare a statement for the press explaining why the negotiations broke down while holding the offer of a moratorium open. At the same time, Hoover, Castle, and Mills proposed to Mellon in a telephone conversation early that afternoon that a last-minute effort be made to have the French take the outline of the U.S. position and make reservations to the points they disagreed with. The transcript of that conversation reveals the extent to which Hoover had come to distrust French intentions. The president told Mellon:

> It is very bad for us to have them write the document. They always put tricks in them. If we get them to interline our document, suggesting the changes that should be made in the document, using our document as the basis, it is rather important because we want to get out definitely what the things are. If they rephrase it through a few tricks which are difficult to examine—take our document and see what changes they would make in it. What we are anxious to do is to find out what changes they would make in the note which you have got before you. The easy way for them to make it is by way of reservations. No other way would do for them to suggest changes in the text but to hold on to our document as the basis of the discussion—not let them put forward another trick document like they did yesterday.[71]

To the surprise and delight of Hoover and his negotiating team, Mellon obtained a clear agreement from the French at 2:50 P.M. on July 6 and called Washington immediately. In exchange for Germany paying its unconditional annuity to the BIS so long as the annuity was relent to Germany, and for France's allies in Central Europe receiving financial aid through private banking channels, France accepted the one-year moratorium and Hoover's demand that the entire unconditional annuity be used for the relief of Germany. Both sides further compromised on the issue of repayments. Suspended payments were to be repaid over a ten-year period. Technical questions about in-kind deliveries and French payments into a guarantee fund, as provided for in the 1929 Young Plan, were referred to later adjustment among financial experts from Germany, France, and the United States.[72]

After a brief celebration, Castle called Sackett to make sure the time of repayment of German debts would be acceptable to Germany. Sackett confirmed that Brüning had found such a time period acceptable. Castle assured Sackett that although the compromise was subject to the agreement of Britain and other interested parties, any minor changes would not be to the detriment of Germany. Mindful of Hoover's need for positive publicity at home and in Europe for the success of the negotiations, he urged Sackett to coordinate a strong German statement praising

Hoover and the United States for its efforts on behalf of German financial stability.[73]

On July 7, Castle paused to savor the very favorable national and international press response to the compromise. While most of the press reports praised his personal work in seeing the compromise through, he privately reflected that Hoover and he had made some mistakes that delayed acceptance:

> In looking back on it all, I wonder what should have been done differently. As I may have noted before, it was probably unwise to make the concession as to the sacredness of the unconditional annuity, even though it was only a paper transaction. The President said that Stimson insisted on this. Stimson thought that, if we admitted the principle, the French would give way on details. The President was probably right that with the French one concession would probably lead to the request for others and drag negotiations on interminably. That concession, it seems to me, was a serious deviation from the spirit of the proposal. All that was done before Stimson left. I think we were also wrong in permitting ourselves to be dragged into the discussion of technical details with which we really had no concern. We were all to blame here, but not one of us could see the woods for the trees until H.H. went to the Rapidan and could get the perspective which we had lost.[74]

Among the many cables congratulating Castle for his patient efforts to reconcile Germany and France to Hoover's offer of a debt suspension was one from his superior, Secretary of State Stimson. Privately, Castle somewhat gleefully noted of his nemesis that "The poor man probably thinks that his cables of instructions from the CONTE GRANDE really put the thing through. If he knew that people really did not stop to read those cables he might be a bit surprised."[75]

Despite Castle's efforts, the delayed Franco-American Moratorium Accord provided only palliative and short-lived relief from the slide from prosperity and stability, in which had been Hoover's and the Republican Party's hope for a Pax Americana.[76] Indeed, the prolonged negotiations with France created additional uncertainty as well as lingering ill will between Hoover and French leaders.[77] Despite the reprieve from the German crisis, Hoover would fail to offer the massive U.S. economic resources needed to battle the deteriorating financial conditions in Europe.[78] When American bankers resisted additional credits to Germany, Hoover, through Castle, announced that the United States could not assume responsibility for maintaining German credit. Responsibility for stability in Europe would fall on Germany and other European governments.[79]

The moratorium and its aftermath marked the unraveling of an order established on the basis of U.S. economic strength. The recalcitrance of the French during the negotiation marked the beginning of a decade in which the United States lost the power to shape events in Europe. This weakness stemmed in part from the Republican Party's efforts to reduce the cost of defense expenditures and the retrenchment of the country's commitments and strategy abroad. This resulted in a foreign policy that

> lacked the military power to enforce the terms of the peace treaty. It could not forgive the war debts that Allied countries owed the American treasury, which in turn made it difficult for these countries to reduce the value of Germany's preparations. Nor could the American government play a financial role in reconstructing the European economy. Instead, the Republicans designed a foreign policy that relied on economic rather than military strategies to guarantee the peace and on private rather than public funds to rebuild Europe.[80]

The moratorium's failure saw an increase of isolationism. But Castle's part in the negotiations prepared the way for his substantial role in the Manchurian crisis, which occurred later that same year. It was another negotiation that took place within the new limits of American economic power. His work with Hoover for the Franco-American accord thus ensured his position as Hoover's closest diplomatic advisor.[81]

6 The Manchurian Incident: A Study in Applied Diplomatic Realism

The diplomacy of realism, understood theologically, is the diplomacy of original sin. Postlapsarian man, unable to expect more than proximate solutions to problems of international anarchy, injustice, violence, and aggression, must live with the strain of ambiguity. Diplomatic realism, a dominant thread in the life of William R. Castle, Jr., is a key to understanding his influential role in the pivotal Manchurian Incident of 1931–1932, which set the stage for Japanese-American relations for the rest of the pre–World War II decade.[1] An examination of Castle's philosophical presumptions, his friendship with President Hoover, and his uneasy relationship with Secretary of State Henry L. Stimson illuminate the strengths and weaknesses of this venerable strain in diplomatic praxis.

Castle entered the State Department in 1919 with a set of assumptions that he kept throughout his public career. Educated at Harvard, he had absorbed the diplomatic "realism" of his mentor, Archibald Cary Coolidge.[2] From "Archie" Coolidge and the writings of Paul S. Reinsch and Lewis D. Einstein, he understood the self-interest that moved human beings and nations, often behind a mask of idealism.[3] Skeptical of people's ability to understand national self-interest, Castle saw the United States as a flawed nation in a dangerously competitive state system, but with the ability to be a balance wheel in the world. Moreover, commercial strength required an open-door policy for access to foreign markets and resources and made U.S. "selfishness" compatible with world peace. A diplomatic corps able to read the cultural expressions of national self-interest could regulate differences and prevent international strife.[4]

Diplomatic realism defined Castle's general approach to policy during the Manchurian Incident and thus deserves some examination. As Castle used the term, realism demands that diplomats deal with a flawed world the way it is. Although nations have come and gone, mankind has consistently evinced the capacity both to compete for resources and to cooperate with others having similar self-interests. Nations have mirrored this dual tendency in their rapacious imperialist/nationalist moments and in their capacity for alliances, cooperative arrangements, and peace pacts. For Castle, the wise statesman was the one who could manage and constructively channel both tendencies. The genius of the founding fathers of the United States was their recognition of man's dual nature and their ability to forge a political system with checks and balances while directing self-interest and moral virtue toward practicable social goods.

Castle also felt that misdirected and self-righteous moral fervor could be destabilizing to the delicate international order. Idealists pursuing abstractions such as human equality usually ignored the historical fact that moral choices must be made in the context of political action, with all of the usual trade-offs. For the diplomatic realist, hard choices are a blend of moral considerations and political necessity (with moral and diplomatic imperatives often in conflict). Whereas the moralist often demands that a position be held without exception, the diplomatic realist must note exceptions and consider the political consequences of any action. Idealists could unsettle imperfect, fragile domestic and international arrangements by trying to rise above the rules of the political order. Moralists claiming access to a "Higher Law" would be less likely to accept provisional and gradual solutions to complex social problems. The simplicity of purist moral positions made them popular with a public weary of patient compromise, checks and balances, and concern for diversity of opinions. Moreover, nations claiming special access to moral truths were profoundly unsettling to the balance of power and interests which maintained the uncertain peace. Castle, a Christian realist, believed only God had complete certainty in the realm of morality. For flawed humans and the nations they made, morals were partial, contingent, and embedded in a nation's values, history, and culture. No nation, not even the United States, could claim its views were the same as God's universally binding moral purposes. In fact, national self-righteousness prevented dialogue, compromise, and patient negotiation with antagonistic nations.[5]

According to Castle, the circumspect diplomat must, therefore, recognize the virtue in other nations' positions, objectively seeing himself, the antagonist, and how the antagonist sees him. He must distinguish between America's interests and his personal moral sympathies and seek primarily to advance the nation's interests. Any private individual had the right to take inflexible, even sacrificial, positions in defense of moral principle, but international political action required prudence, moderation, and patience.[6] The diplomat must be able to tolerate considerable ambiguity in applying a nation's morals, which are usually tied to its self-interest and specific historical, economic, and social context.

Protecting and advancing national interest was the overarching goal of diplomatic realists such as Castle. All nations possessed a hierarchy of interests. Core interests included such basics as national sovereignty, territorial integrity, preservation of a nation's political order, its culture, history, and so forth. Peripheral interests (such as beneficial trade treaties) reflected shifting public opinion, variable sectional alliances, personal ties of political leaders, and the like. Generally, diplomats in the realist tradition advocated negotiation on peripheral interests and less or no negotiation on core interests. As outgoing Japanese ambassador, Castle explained in a speech to the Japan-America Society during the London Naval Conference,

> There was no sentimental internationalism in the Conference. No patriotic delegate was willing to sacrifice the interests of his own country in the name of humanity. On the contrary, all the delegates worked earnestly for the good of the nation they represented, but with no ill-will to the other nation. They were wise men who know that love of one's own nation, which we call patriotism, is the very basis of world progress. They neither gave up their own ideas not tried to impose them on others, and therefore each learned more highly to respect the others.
>
> There is a type of individual who runs about preaching love of our fellow men but goes at it from the wrong angle. He seems to think. . . . that one cannot aid humanity without neglecting one's own country. But the world cannot really progress unless we all go out to make our own nations the best possible. . . . This need not be at the expense of other nations but in such a manner that the good we do for ourselves will react on others. I believe the London Conference to be a living proof that this is the way of progress.[7]

Nations sought to achieve their interests and maximize their security through controlling or substantially influencing the actions of other nations. Diplomatic realists, however, rejected the needless use of martial force to advance interest, believing war reduced security, distorted a nation's economy and normal political process, and destabilized the international order. Except to protect core interests, realists would avoid war, stressing instead compromise, concession, patient negotiating, and adjustment of differences by knowledgeable diplomatic experts who could rise above popular emotions of the moment.

Distrustful of popular rhetoric and political meddling in the affairs of diplomatic specialists, Castle valued dealing with the world as it "really was." For him, there was no evidence of unilinear human progress, no chance of a changed human nature transmogrified by new political arrangements, no truly novel institutions, and no evidence that the United States had a special claim to being morally exceptional. These basic realist presumptions help to explain Castle's controversial role in the epochal events in Manchuria during 1931–1932.

By the early 1930s, China had suffered more than a decade of turmoil, fueled by anti-Western nationalism and Sun Yat-sen's successful fight against local warlords. After Sun's death in 1925, Chiang Kai-shek broke with his Soviet advisors and pursued a disruptive purge of Communists and their leftist allies in China. Led by Mao Tse-tung, renegade Communists escaped to the mountainous interior of South China and held out against Kuomintang forces. Although Chiang completed the unification of China by 1928, with substantial economic and diplomatic progress, his authoritarian one-party government neglected badly needed land reform, prevented the growth of democracy, and failed to secure the loyalty of land-hungry peasants, impoverished city workers, and disaffected students and intellectuals. China's instability, combined with the perception that Chiang and his Kuomintang movement were revolutionary and antiforeign, led the United States to look elsewhere for a guarantor of stability, predictability, and anticommunism in the Far East.[8]

In the midst of antiforeign violence associated with Chinese nationalism and the possibility of Soviet hegemony in Manchuria, British Ambassador Sir Ronald Lindsay invited then Assistant Secretary of State Castle to collaborate in boosting military forces to protect British and American lives. After discussing the proposal with President Hoover, Castle informed Lindsay that the United States did not want to increase its naval presence in Shanghai and that any international effort would have to be led by the British alone. Moreover, he stated, Japan had tentative plans to intervene in the disorders and would coordinate its efforts with Chiang's government. The United States would look favorably upon joint Japanese, British, and Nationalist Chinese efforts to restore order but would be a spectator only.[9] During the more significant events in Manchuria in 1931–1932, Castle retained his faith in Japan's right to maintain order in an area as crucial to that country as Latin America was to the United States. He saw Japan as the only country capable of making a credible show of force during a period of economic depression in both the United States and Britain. Although Japan's independence in its military maneuvers was a potential problem for the future, Castle saw this as a legitimate defense of national interest. Japan's considerable investments in China represented 81.9 percent of its total foreign investment. Much of this was in Manchuria, an area key to Japan's long-term economic health. The United States, despite its hopes for expanded trade with China, had only 1.3 percent of its total foreign investment there.[10] As long as liberal, pro-Western cabinets prevailed in Tokyo, there seemed every reason to look sympathetically upon Japan's motives.[11] Moreover, U.S. and Japanese interests were, in his view and in the long run, consonant. Normal trade "flounders only in times of peace and. . . . the most effective trade promotion is the promotion of all methods for the peaceful settlements of international disputes." The Japanese would, if a rational assessment of their self-interest prevailed, come to realize that peace with China, respect for the open door, and the basic Washington Conference peace structure held the best chance for Japan's economic penetration of new markets in Asia and the United States.[12]

Castle's promotion to under secretary of state in the spring of 1931 greatly enhanced his ability to influence foreign policy. Primarily occupied with the intricate negotiations for the Hoover Moratorium on war-debt payments during the summer of 1931, he could only look with concern at the mounting signs of a major Sino-Japanese clash in Manchuria. Rumors circulated freely that Chiang had united China chiefly to wage war on Japan. There were dozens of "incidents" including anti-Japanese boycotts, rioting, and attacks on "Japanese" (actually Korean) farmers around the village of Wampaoshan. These, plus Chiang's economic and political control of northeastern provinces, increased Chinese immigration into the area, and Chinese railroad construction was a part of this policy.[13] The ingredients for a major confrontation over Manchuria were clearly evident.

On September 18, 1931, Japanese troops (apparently acting independently of Foreign Minister Shidehara) set off an explosion on the South Manchurian Railroad, which Japan had controlled since 1905. Edwin L. Neville, consul of the U.S. embassy in Tokyo, downplayed the seriousness of the incident, describing it as a legitimate reaction to Chinese provocations. Moreover, although Japanese officers had acted independently, civilian control would soon be restored.[14] U.S. Ambassador Cameron Forbes, more concerned with the tardy reconstruction of the embassy in Tokyo, agreed,[15] but Castle feared that a chain of events had been initiated that would be difficult to reverse.[16]

Meeting with Secretary of State Stimson a few days later, Castle advised caution and restraint in dealing with Japan. He and Stimson hoped Japan's civilian government would regain control of its army in Manchuria and make amends for the aggression. Conflicting accounts of events and the Depression in the United States made it unlikely that Hoover would permit bold unilateral action. In addition, a U.S. challenge to the Wakatsuki-Shidehara government could damage its standing with the Japanese public. Neither Castle nor Stimson wanted to force this friendly government into a corner and drive it to defend the actions of its recalcitrant military. In their opinion, the League of Nations ought to take action to resolve the problem, with the United States (which continued to avoid membership in the League) being a nonparticipating observer at the council table.[17]

As Japan's Kwantung Army continued to advance in Manchuria, the foreign offices of England and France indicated reluctant acceptance of Japan's aggression and a hope that Japan had the best chance to impose order on this turbulent area of China.[18] Given the conflicting claims of Japan, Russia, and China to the area, a stable Manchuria controlled by democratic, capitalist, and essentially pro-Western Japan might be the lesser evil. This sentiment was succinctly summarized by the U.S. ambassador to London, Charles G. Dawes. Dawes advised a Japanese diplomat that "the Chinese are altogether too cocky. What you people need to do is to give them a thoroughly good licking to teach them their place and then they will be willing to talk sense."[19]

Castle's sense that the troubles in Manchuria stemmed from Chinese instability and irresponsible policy was reinforced by reports from the U.S. legation at Peking that a long series of "Chinese initiations" had forced the hand of the Kwantung Army on September 18. The Chinese government's unwillingness to recognize Japan's right to control its railway zone was partially responsible for the precipitate and unwise Japanese aggression. A legation official privately reported to Castle, "if you could take an x-ray picture of the brains of the Chinese in Manchuria, you would find an overwhelming sentiment in favor of Japanese control of the region and that, even outside of Manchuria, there would be large numbers of thinking Chinese who would agree that it was fortunate for China to have at least one province where somebody kept order."[20]

Notwithstanding heated rhetoric on both sides, the conflict was rooted in ascendant nationalism in Japan and China. Legally part of China, Manchuria was ruled by a local warlord and possessed informal independence. Moreover, as a result of agreements with Russia in 1905 and China in 1915, Japan had acquired substantial political and economic concessions in the province; Japan could station troops along the 690-mile South Manchurian Railroad while Chinese troops could operate in the rest of Manchuria. In addition, Japan's presence there had ostensibly been sanctioned by the Root-Takahira Agreement (1908) and the Lansing-Ishii Agreement of 1917.[21] Pledging to maintain commercial equality and the territorial integrity of China, and calling for mutual consultation should insular possessions be threatened, the signatories of the Four Power and Nine Power treaties nonetheless made no commitment to use armed force to redress grievances. The reliance on moral suasion to maintain the status quo in China was furthered by the Kellogg-Briand Pact (1928), in which sixty-two nations agreed to renounce war as an instrument of national policy. The real hope to contain Japan came from America's economic dominance in the 1920s and Japan's reliance on the West for supplies of capital and trade.

This delicate economic and political balance collapsed quickly with the onset of the Great Depression in 1929. With less demand in the United States for Japanese silk and other items, the volume of Japan's exports fell by 40 percent between 1929 and 1930. Exports from Japan to the United States were also hurt by the Smoot-Hawley Tariff of 1930. With loans from U.S. banks rapidly drying up, Japan grew more dependent on its spheres of influence, especially Manchuria. By 1931, Japan was dependent on Manchurian lumber, coal, iron, steel, and grain. Moreover, the Soviet Union under Stalin was rapidly industrializing, and leaders of Japan's Kwantung Army argued that Manchuria would be a strategic base against future Soviet expansion. The restless leadership also feared U.S. naval expansion, military budget cuts in Tokyo, civilian leadership which spoke of compromise, and Japan's economic dependence on the West.[22] Castle realized that the balance of power in Asia was changing, and U.S. policy was limited in what it could now do to force Japan's hand in Manchuria.[23]

As the United States and the League of Nations sought unsuccessfully to restrain Japan in the fall of 1932, Castle's brand of diplomatic realism was further refined. Castle was more pragmatic and generally calmer than Stimson. His time as special ambassador to Japan had convinced him that Japan would predominate in East Asia and be a stabilizing force there.[24] Moreover, he agreed with the U.S. minister to China, Nelson T. Johnson, that Sino-Japanese disputes were primarily the affair of two countries with strong nationalistic political forces; both countries would need to work out their destinies without U.S. entanglements.[25] While Japan had clearly violated the structure of peace established by the Washington Conference, Castle recommended that the United States avoid inflexibly enforcing the letter of treaties outdated by Japan's actual dominance in East Asia. Japan, as he saw it, had interests that coincided with America's and was the "one useful friend in the Orient" on which the United States could depend:

> What America must learn, and can far more easily learn in this era of post-conference trust and goodwill, is that just because Japan's interests here are vital, that just because Japan's trade with China is of paramount importance, Japan must be and will be the guardian of peace in the Pacific. I believe that Japanese commerce with Central and South America is likely vastly to increase. Japanese traders know that they can go about their business in that part of the world in security because the whole purpose of the United States is to maintain peace in the Western Hemisphere and to hold open the door of honest opportunity to all. America must learn to appreciate just as clearly the fact that Japan, the greatest progressive and peaceful power of the Orient, will be an equally faithful guardian of the rights and opportunities of all on this side of the earth.[26]

Moreover, the United States should support Japan's civilian leader, Baron Shidehara, and avoid sponsoring a humiliating commission of enquiry in Manchuria.[27] This also meant limited cooperation with the League of Nations, which, knowing little about the changing realities in Asia, would be likely to set an arbitrary deadline for Japan to withdraw from its recent seizures in Manchuria.[28]

At this early stage of uncertain events, Castle and Secretary of State Stimson agreed that the U.S. government should avoid precipitous action, while privately urging Japan's civilian government to control its army and arrange for gradual withdrawal.[29] (Indeed, Castle reassured the press that Japan's tardy withdrawal of troops was due to fear of reprisals against Japanese nationals in Manchuria.)[30] The United States, they felt, should avoid taking sides. In practice, this meant that the League should invoke the Kellogg-Briand Pact rather than the United States doing so and appearing hostile to Japan. In addition, the State Department should avoid recognizing that an act of war in Manchuria existed; to do so would open the delicate question of sanctions, which Hoover, Castle, and Stimson opposed at this early stage.[31] If necessary to prove goodwill, the United States could withdraw as a nonvoting observer in the League's proceedings and even recall the U.S. Asiatic Fleet on maneuvers near Manchuria.[32]

When Japan failed to heed the League's call to evacuate all conquered areas by November 16, 1931, Chinchow was bombed. As Japan continued its conquest of Manchuria, Stimson began to consider more serious U.S. responses. Some kind of U.S. sanction might be needed if League attempts to resolve the worsening conditions in Manchuria failed. Castle, however, strongly opposed even withdrawing Ambassador Forbes from Tokyo:

> It would have no effect except to throw Japan into the hands
> of the militarists and give them the feeling that, since the damn
> foreigners are out of the way they can do what they please.
> What would seem to me a wiser and more effective plan would
> be to announce, together with the rest of the world, that we
> shall not recognize treaties negotiated under present conditions
> as being negotiated under duress. But I pointed out to the Sec-
> retary that even then we must be very careful because, if the re-
> sultant treaties should be eminently fair and we then refused
> to recognize their validity either Japan or China could violate
> them later on with the idea that the rest of the world could not
> kick since in any case they were not valid.[33]

Hoover also felt that if the League failed to restrain Japan, the United States should not recognize treaties Japan might obtain from China under military pressure.[34] Castle supported Hoover's idea to please both China and Japan by replacing Manchuria warlord Chang Hsueh-liang with a viceroy appointed by Chiang Kai-shek.[35] He felt that time was working against Japan; its dependence on trade with China would mean economic destitution at home and growing domestic pressure on Tokyo to sue for peace in Manchuria.[36] Others in the State Department, such as China expert Stanley K. Hornbeck and former U.S. minister to Peking John MacMurray, also felt China was "reaping what it had sown."[37] The venerable secretary of state from 1905 to 1909, Elihu Root (long a hero to Castle), argued that Japan had every right to dominate an area as economically and militarily strategic for it as Cuba was for the United States.[38] Advising Hoover that Japan would not likely go along with or recognize any viceroy appointed from Nanking, he contended that U.S. sanctions in the form of economic boycotts would be futile while likely causing a war the United States could not easily win. In fact, Castle believed that "the world might be better off if Japan really and completely controlled Manchuria."[39] Castle also told Stimson that

> If the League invokes Article 15 it necessarily admits a state of war. Under these circumstances Japan would block Chinese ports and there would be very serious danger of involving the United States. A boycott of Japan would necessarily mean practical cessation of trade with China also. At this time of economic trouble the world cannot stand any further dislocation. If there is anything left of the stock market that little would disappear. Europe would be plunged more deeply into disaster. Our principal export to Japan is cotton. Certainly the South would not willingly see the sick man murdered in his bed. If an embargo were imposed by the League there are enough violent anti-Leaguers in Congress who would fight against it on general principles. The world is not inclined to take another material kick in the face to maintain the sanctity of treaties which it is not convinced have been violated.[40]

On December 10, the League, with the reluctant approval of China and Japan, ordered a temporary cease-fire while a neutral investigation committee was formed to examine the merits of the competing claims to Manchuria. Castle was alarmed when Tokyo's acceptance of the committee's investigation led to the fall of the Wakatsuki-Shidehara cabinet. A more militant party assumed power and Castle's limited influence in Tokyo was now further diminished. Skeptical that an impartial investigation could solve the real demands of conflicting ascendant countries, Castle looked gloomily upon the prospects for peace in 1932.[41]

To the surprise and dismay of the U.S. State Department, Japanese forces marched into Chinchow. It was not clear that Japan intended to seize all of Manchuria. A few days before the aggression, Chinese officials had fled the provisional capital. The invasion took place in spite of Stimson's pronouncements that continued aggression would endanger Japan-U.S. relations, confirming the limits of relying on world opinion to contain Japan.[42]

Ignoring the League of Nations and vowing to take unilateral action, a furious Stimson issued a nonrecognition note on January 7th. This note, which became the centerpiece of U.S. policy in the Far East, invoked the Kellogg-Briand Pact and the Nine Power Treaty and refused to admit the legality of any changes brought about in violation of the Kellogg Pact. Frustrated by lack of cooperation from leading European powers and the League, and angered by Japan's betrayal, Stimson reaffirmed, without specific mention of Chinchow or Manchuria, America's interest in protecting the sovereignty, independence, and territorial integrity of China.[43] The note was also motivated by an awareness that America's long-range economic interest lay in its growing trade with Asia. Japan's voiced intention to restrict foreign trade and business in Manchuria might foretoken greater trade restrictions in China and perhaps other areas of the Far East.[44] In the absence of any consensus for economic sanctions, it was the boldest yet safest action that could be undertaken, in Stimson's view.

In the perfervid days of the new year, Under Secretary of State Castle played a quiet but important moderating role in the preparation and delivery of the note. More immediate was a potentially explosive event in Manchuria: American Vice-Consul Culver B. Chamberlain was beaten by Japanese soldiers. Amidst howls of protest from the American press, Castle worked to minimize the jingoistic outcries and maintain calm, self-interested diplomacy. In a speech before the School of Politics of the Women's National Republican Club, he described the beating as an unauthorized act of a few renegades in the Japanese army. Japan, he insisted, was a responsible government and would swiftly discipline the soldiers and apologize.[45] Stimson, however, loudly insisted that amends be made and that no apology would be enough.[46] Ambassador Katsuji Debuchi quickly apologized on behalf of Japan. When it appeared that Stimson would refuse the apology without additional guarantees, Debuchi felt Stimson had insulted Japan. To soothe Ambassador Debuchi, Castle persuaded him that Stimson was only seeking more information about what had actually happened in Mukden before accepting the apology. Debuchi accepted this and quietly guaranteed to Stimson that the culprits would be dealt with.[47]

Castle also moderated Stimson's initial nonrecognition note, telling

Ambassador Katsuji Debuchi represented Japanese interests in Washington during the Manchurian Incident of 1931–1932. (Library of Congress photo LC-USZ62-93486.)

Stimson his appeal to the Nine Power Treaty appeared to guarantee the territorial and administrative integrity of China. Supported by Stanley Hornbeck, Castle persuaded Stimson to change the draft so that the territorial and administrative integrity of China were not so guaranteed. The phraseology agreed only to protect American rights insofar as the destruction of the integrity of China would affect those rights.[48] Stimson was also persuaded to encourage all Nine Power Treaty signatories to send similar notes of nonrecognition.[49] Playing a typically quiet behind-the-scenes role, Castle soothed the nerves of Ambassador Giacomo de Martino from Italy, who felt that Italian views had been ignored. Somewhat disingenuously, Castle explained to the fiery Martino that the only reason Stimson had talked to the French and British was that they had brought the matter up; that Stimson had not shown them the note; and that Martino was really the first who had seen it. "It is awfully difficult in all this work," wrote Castle, "to have to consider steadily the *amour propre* of a nation, but one has to think of that first and foremost when it comes to dealings with Italy."[50] Thus, although the Stimson Doctrine of Nonrecognition (as shaped by Castle and Hornbeck) did not dissuade Japan's military, the opportunity for further dialogue as an avenue for peace was maintained. As long as talks continued and economic or military sanctions were avoided, Castle hoped that his civilian friends in Tokyo would reestablish order and seek to normalize relations with its major trading partner, the United States.

Castle's faith was challenged severely by the events of late January 1932. Citing the murder of a Japanese monk on January 18th, Chinese attacks on Japanese civilians, and the continuing Chinese boycott of Japanese goods, Japan's Imperial Navy attacked the Chinese sections of Shanghai. Unlike the early victories near Mukden in September of 1931, the destruction of the suburb of Chapei and threats to the European-controlled International Settlement did not bring the Japanese a quick victory. World opinion quickly condemned Japan's aggression and called for immediate withdrawal.

In the face of Stimson's fury at such developments, Castle disguised his own anger with Tokyo and once again played the role of moderate conciliator. Believing it was in the U.S. interest to avoid war with Japan, America's substantial trading partner, buffer against the Soviet Union, and force for stability in a tumultuous China, he sought to check Stimson's inclination to use economic or military sanctions to bolster the moral sanctions called for in the Stimson Doctrine of Nonrecognition.[51] Publicly, Castle blamed the events in Shanghai and Mukden on a military driven to justify its self-importance in Japan, arguing that the United

States could still trust and work with Japan's civilian, democratic government. He warned Americans against stereotypical judgments about "the Japanese mind" and its warlike proclivities, urging them instead to see Japanese citizens as among the finest in the world.[52] Throughout the Shanghai crisis, Castle made himself available to Ambassador Debuchi and a host of unofficial representatives from Japan such as Count Katayama. Behind the scenes, he softened anti-Japanese pronouncements made by the secretary. In the midst of the heated exchanges between the United States and Japan over the invasion of Shanghai, Castle explained the U.S. position as essentially favorable to the count:

> This afternoon I had a sad talk with poor old Count Katayama. He did not know about the Nanking business, which almost made him cry. He said that he thought the three great men of Japan, Count Makino, Prince Saionji and Admiral Yamamoto, would feel about everything that happened exactly as I feel about it. He said they felt safe to have me here and I said that this was good to hear, but that Japan's present actions, or rather the actions of some of the Japanese military made it hard, if not impossible, to do anything. I know how the right thinking people are suffering, but the fact remains that Japan must and will be judged by the world in accord with the actions of its troops. I told Katayama that it was very hard for a friend of Japan to defend Japan when these things were happening. He said he knew this, that it was simple enough to answer the criticisms of the adversaries of Japan, but that it was impossible to argue against the distress of its friends.[53]

Castle's familiarity with influential Japanese business and government leaders led to frequent visits from Debuchi. Castle took advantage of this trust to urge moderation upon Japan. For example, Japan firmly objected to Stimson's call for withdrawal of Japanese troops from Shanghai and quick settlement of all outstanding controversies with China in the spirit of the Pact of Paris and the December 9th resolution of the League of Nations. Castle, however, urged Debuchi to have Japan cease all military operations in Shanghai and promise to consider future discussions on the issues. Discussions held well after fighting had ended would likely be acceptable to the United States and would obviate the hardening of its position. Debuchi agreed to this approach and so advised his government—unfortunately, with no result. Furthermore, as Castle noted in his diary:

> The Ambassador brought up a report that certain Japanese land forces had already been despatched to Shanghai. He said

that, although he could not deny this officially, he felt it was premature, that it would have been impossible for Japan to ask for good offices and then immediately despatch an expeditionary force. I told him I hoped he was correct. He said that undoubtedly the sending of a regiment from Manila would make the Japanese feel that, to protect their 25,000 nationals in Shanghai, they also should send land forces. I told him that the only reason we sent land forces was that they were the only ones immediately available and that obviously more assistance was needed in the Settlement. He said he understood this perfectly himself and was trying to make it clear to his Government.[54]

Japan soon decided not to reinforce its forces in Shanghai with the large numbers initially planned, but it also refused to accept negotiations of all outstanding issues in China.[55]

The U.S. response was announced in Stimson's letter (drafted by Hornbeck) to Senator William E. Borah, chairman of the Senate Foreign Relations Committee. Stimson first reviewed America's historic commitment to equality of commercial opportunity in China and the preservation of its territorial and administrative integrity. The letter went on to say that the provisions of the Washington Disarmament Conference, in which the United States had surrendered its commanding lead in battleship construction and its right to further fortify Guam and the Philippines, had been predicated on the signatories of the Nine Power Treaty guaranteeing equal access to China's trade and providing mutual support for its sovereignty. Japan could force an armed America, Stimson wrote, if it continued to violate the Nine Power Treaty. This unilateral pronouncement, issued with Hoover's blessing, was a demarche born of frustration with British and French inaction and Japanese intransigence.[56] Though Stimson's letter would later be criticized for substituting words for action, when first released it was a popular document in the United States.[57]

Anxiety over Shanghai was reduced when Japan and China agreed to a cease-fire on March 3rd. Within three weeks Japan began to withdraw its troops and shortly thereafter negotiated a permanent end to the conflict. By July 17th, all Japanese troops had vacated the city.

When Castle's only child, Rosamond, died suddenly on February 26th, he withdrew from further engagement with the affairs in China until his return to the State Department in late March. Concerned with the intricacies of the complicated European debt question, Castle became acting secretary of state in April. Stimson left for Geneva to serve as chairman of the American delegation to the World Disarmament Conference, and the difference between Hoover's interpretation of the non-recognition doctrine and Stimson's came to a head while he was away.[58]

Although the United States had six more battleships than the Japanese navy, it had failed to maintain a credible naval deterrent in the Far East. Japan had more light cruisers, one more aircraft carrier, and many more heavy cruisers than the United States. Moreover, the U.S. Navy faced budget cuts as a result of the continuing economic depression. More important, Japan's supply lines to Manchuria were very short compared to the existing U.S. supply lines. To Hoover and Castle, the numerical differences were another reason for caution. Navy Secretary Charles Adams agreed that the United States could expect to fight Japan from four to six years if Britain failed to cooperate. Even with a British military alliance, they estimated that a war could last two years, with devastating consequences to U.S. trade with Japan and China.[59]

Stimson, on the other hand, had clearly despaired of the efficacy of nonrecognition alone and urged Hoover to build naval strength in the Pacific.[60] Most importantly, Stimson believed that the United States must conceal its weakness and use the possibility of economic and even military sanctions to force Japan to settle the Manchurian affair according to the interests of the United States.[61]

Castle and Hoover discussed their concern over Stimson's position when they met privately on May 2 to discuss an upcoming Castle speech on nonrecognition and its relationship to the use of force. Specifically, Castle was to say that the United States would continue to employ moral opposition to Japanese aggression but would not use economic embargoes or military sanctions against Japan. Economic embargoes, he would argue, were rarely successful and in fact tended to harden positions, making peaceful negotiations less likely. The speech held out hope that Japan's government would negotiate an end

William R. Castle, Jr., posed for this photograph with his father, daughter Rosamond Castle Winslow, and Alan F. Winslow, Jr., about 1926. (Photo courtesy of Donald F. Winslow.)

to its occupation of Manchuria and reenter the universe of peace-loving nations more interested in mutually beneficial trade than in war.[62] Castle's speech was designed, in part, to disrupt any plans Stimson might have of proposing or threatening an economic embargo or military sanctions. Hoover told Castle that "he liked it and thought it well expressed but said also said that we must be prepared for a real row with the Secretary, who still yearns for the boycott. The President said he felt the time had come to speak out and that he was ready for the fray as I was."[63] Wanting the president to receive full credit for a generally popular foreign-policy principle during a difficult election year, Castle changed the name "Stimson Doctrine" to "Hoover Doctrine" and emphasized the exclusion of economic and military sanctions.

Castle's speech was received positively, and a delighted Hoover asked him to write the foreign-affairs plank in the Republican platform as he had in 1928.[64] Stimson, as expected, was furious that an important speech had been given undermining any future use of a bluff with regard to economic or military sanctions.[65] The Hoover-Castle understanding of nonrecognition would dominate in future negotiations with Japan and virtually assure that the United States would not engage in unilateral steps to undo Japan's advances in China.[66]

Without the threat of economic or military sanctions, options in dealing with Japan in Manchuria were limited. The depression worsened in the United States, the political future of President Hoover appeared bleak, and the State Department's role in Manchurian affairs was reduced to that of a bystander. By July 17, 1932, Japan had withdrawn its troops from Shanghai, but its presence in Manchuria was solidified. Prime Minister Admiral Makoto Saito, Foreign Minister Yasuya Uchida, and Minister of War Sadao Araki made it clear to the world that Japan would not surrender its interests in Manchuria. In June, the artificial state of Manchukuo seized the customs collected by the Chinese Maritime Service at its ports, particularly Dairen. When China protested this action, Japan threatened to send military support to Manchukuo. Ignoring warnings from the Western powers, Japan offered official recognition to Manchukuo on September 15.[67] Castle and Hoover continued to hope that Japan and China would work out a compromise that would "include the recognition of Manchuria as an integral part of China, the appointment by Nanking of a governor general acceptable to the Japanese, a large measure of autonomy, clear recognition by China of Japanese rights and paramount interests in Manchuria."[68]

Throughout the difficult summer and fall of 1932, Hoover and Castle consistently resisted Hornbeck's and Stimson's arguments for a stronger stance against Japanese support of Manchukuo. Their differences were in method and action rather than principle. Though all four deplored Japan's actions, Castle asserted that "we must not nag, we must not act independently of others, and we must not risk war." [69] Unwilling to drive the Japanese to seek an ally in Stalinist Russia, fearful of disrupting international trade with Japan in the midst of America's worst depression, mindful of the unlikelihood that Britain or France would support a hard-line position against Japan, and still hopeful that Japan's government would come to its senses and negotiate a compromise solution with China, Castle and Hoover isolated the secretary. Meeting privately at Rapidan (Hoover's retreat outside of Washington, D.C.) on August 20, the two friends talked about Manchuria:

> That is always a little difficult because we want to be loyal to the Secretary and yet cannot be dishonest. Yesterday there was no trouble because the President was not, as H.L.S. told me he was, feeling more violent against Japan than the Secretary himself. He said he was always afraid Stimson would get us into real trouble through his earnest and entirely laudable desire to support the various peace treaties. He said he was thankful he had forced Stimson to omit the last three pages of his speech on the Kellogg Pact because in those pages he went the whole limit, expressed our willingness to join in sanctions, etc., the kind of thing Japan would never in this world have forgiven. I told him that I thought the Secretary's ideas on the situation were absolutely correct, but that he did not see quite as clearly as I the necessity of not taking the lead, both because the matter is in the hands of the League and because anything we say will cause more irritation in Japan than anything the League says. Japan will always be there and we need her as a friend in that part of the world—not as a supine friend who follows her bidding, of course, but that nevertheless we should not give the impression that we are egging people on against her. I told him that the only danger I foresaw was at the time the League Commission Report is handed in, that I felt then that we should state to the press that our own information corresponded with that of the Commission and let it go at that, that the Department has a long report on what happened, based on our own sources and that Stimson would probably want to publish this also. The President agreed that we must stand by the League Commission and go no further. He thinks that the nations of Europe will have a pretty hard time in taking any action on the

League report, but that whatever happens we have already made our own position clear and must simply stand on that. He feels that the Tories in England and the French in general are really sympathetic with Japan so far as Manchuria is concerned and that they will not want to come out clearly in condemnation. The President thinks that Japan may still come to her senses and talk with China in a reasonable way, that there is still a possibility that Japan might admit Chinese overlordship on condition that China appointed a viceroy friendly to Japan. This probably depends almost entirely on whether the radical military control is weakening. At least the President agrees with the diplomatic corps in Tokyo that silence is best just now and that time inevitably works in our favor.[70]

In this atmosphere of caution, born of an assessment of the country's self-interest, Castle found little to disagree with in the release of the League of Nations' Lytton Commission report on October 2nd. The result of an extensive and impartial investigation of a five-member multinational committee in the winter and spring of 1932, the document condemned Japan for its actions in Manchuria. It also found Manchukuo to be an artificially created state with little support for the area's large Chinese population. As such, no official recognition of Manchukuo would be consistent with recognized international obligations. Finding both the Chinese and Japanese to blame for the crisis, the report called for a new administration in Manchukuo, one that would contain substantial foreign influence while protecting the legitimate right of Japanese residents.[71] Hoover, Stimson, and Castle agreed that the report was fair and thought its recommendation would, in time, be followed by Japan. Rising expenses in controlling the restive Chinese population, possible diplomatic isolation, and endangering trade with the West would be too high a price for even fervent Japanese patriots to abide for very long. It seemed that the worst of the crisis was over.[72] Even Hornbeck, as skeptical of Japan's intentions as anyone in the State Department, felt Japan would eventually comply with the report.[73]

While League members debated ratifying the findings of the Lytton Commission (which they finally did on February 24, 1933), Castle tried to stem the growing mutual distrust between Japan and the United States. Though no longer certain that Japanese civilian moderates like Count Makino and Baron Shidehara would restore friendly relations with the United States, he continued to hope Japan would compromise with China and avoid costly prolonged military engagements. In a November meeting, Prime Minister Saito told Castle that tension between the two countries was being fueled by Hoover's retention of a large naval fleet at Pearl Harbor.[74] Assuring Saito that the U.S. fleet presence was not unusual and in no way threatened Japan, Castle privately felt Saito was partly correct:

Why do we keep our fleet in the Pacific where it obviously irritates Japan and is considered by the Japanese as a threat?" I always answered that it was a question of money, etc., but that never satisfies anyone. And it is not easy to answer because that is a point on which the Secretary and I have never seen eye to eye. When the Secretary was in Europe and Admiral Pratt came to me as Acting Secretary to ask whether he might not bring to the Atlantic at least part of the fleet, it was my impulse to say "yes" and when I discussed the matter with the President he felt the same way. I pointed out, however, that the matter was close to the Secretary's heart and that it would be wise to postpone any action until the Secretary got back. To this he willingly agreed and I so informed Pratt. It has been hard from me to see ever since what advantage there was in having the fleet in the Pacific to compensate for the disadvantage of keeping the Japanese stirred up. In case of war it could get back quickly and in case of war we should not risk a general fleet engagement in any event. What I want to think of always is the prevention of war, the avoidance of anything which might cause an incident that would rouse warlike feelings and if the presence of our fleet in the Pacific intensifies to any degree anti-American feeling in Japan, the fleet should not be there. I wish we knew what the Embassy thinks about it. One thing is certain and that is that, ex-

Count Nobuaki Makino was one of the civilian moderates to whom W. R. Castle, Jr., looked for aid in maintaining friendly relations between Japan and the United States. (Library of Congress photo LC-USZ62-112106.)

cept for the pacifists, nobody in America wants war with Japan whatever the Japanese may do in Manchuria.[75]

In the same meeting, Castle reassured Saito that the United States would not pressure the League, which was considering ratification of the Lytton Report.[76] Privately, however, he harbored the same reservations about League action and its efficacy that his close friend, French Ambassador Paul Claudel, did. Claudel feared that the League, under the domination of numerous but impotent small nations, would censure Japan, refuse to offer realistic alternatives, and leave the major powers with the responsibility of providing possible military opposition to Tokyo. Castle wrote:

> With all that Japan has done, which M. Claudel disapproves as much as any of us, he feels that Japan still remains the only link the western nations have with the Orient and that it would be a world disaster to have Japan made impotent, perhaps develop into a communistic state and thus open the road for propaganda; he says he is honestly attached to all the good there is in Japan and does not want to see the rest of the world assist in the destruction of that good, although he admits that he has himself no constructive suggestion to make. He thinks that the only course is to refuse to have any dealings with Manchukuo and then wait patiently to see how the matter will work out.[77]

The brutal truth, as Castle and Claudel saw it, was that a chaotic China was not much worse off in 1932 than it had been in 1930. Rhetoric to the contrary, militants on both sides were recklessly sacrificing the long-term national interests of their respective countries. In doing so, the normal give and take associated with the diplomacy of realism had been lost and the seeds for a future war sown.

In the closing weeks of the lame-duck Hoover administration, Castle watched with dismay as the Chinese, embittered by lack of Western support and dilatory League action on the Lytton Report, resumed diplomatic relations with the Soviet Union. The Soviets, worried about a Japanese move against vulnerable Siberia, were all too ready for such a relationship. Moreover, by March 4th, Japan had captured the province of Jehol, which consolidated its hold on Manchuria and put it within striking distance of Peking and Tientsin.[78] Stimson, in his self-proclaimed role as "acting secretary of state" for incoming President Franklin Delano Roosevelt, was reassured that Hoover's policies in Manchuria met with approval by the new administration.[79] (Indeed, no new initiatives against Japan would be taken by the new secretary of state, Cordell

Hull.) On May 31, 1933, Japan signed a truce with Chinese representatives establishing the borders of Manchukuo at the Great Wall, allowing the Kwantung Army to control Shanhaikuan Pass, and establishing a demilitarized zone east and north of the Peking-Tientsin district.[80]

The lugubrious events of 1931–1932 had permanently alienated Stimson from Hoover and Castle. But for Castle, the reliance Hoover had shown on his positions would ensure a fruitful collaboration between them for the next twenty years. As Castle saw it, Hoover had been an "enormously stabilizing influence" in steering the United States through the temptation to do nothing in Manchuria, or to do too much. Hoover confessed to Castle, "I think that you and I can congratulate ourselves in having kept this country out of war with Japan, which would have been inevitable if Stimson had gone along unchecked." Castle recorded this in his diary, adding:

> I told him that I thought the speech I made about our resorting to sanctions had been useful even though it had made Stimson dislike me more than ever. The President remarked that he thought the speech had been an essential step in our policy and that I ought to feel that its value nationally more than compensated for any disagreeable consequences to me personally. He said that in the Far East we have been up against an almost impossible situation, that we could not sit back and see the treaties violated, but that on the other hand any move on our part

The under secretaries and assistant secretaries of the retiring Hoover cabinet called on the president on March 3, 1933, to say their farewells. Under Secretary of State W. R. Castle, Jr., is standing at Hoover's left near the center of the picture. (Herbert Hoover Library.)

made the danger of war very great, granted the inflamed state of Japanese public opinion and the total unreliability of the military forces in control of the Japanese government.[81]

For his part, Castle confessed to Hoover that:

> If he had been re-elected I could not have stayed on another four years under Stimson and [Hoover] said the situation was really impossible, that he could not possibly have kept Stimson. He said the Secretary was really a pathological case, that he thought clearly for a couple of hours and then crashed mentally because not enough blood went to his brain. He said that he had insisted on appointing me as Under Secretary because he thought it would strengthen the Department and that I could take two thirds of the work off Stimson's shoulders.[82]

As Castle prepared to leave office, refusing to pursue a vague appeal of Hull that he remain in the State Department in some responsible position, he promised Hoover to record the history of Hoover's foreign policy in a full-length book. More significantly, he concluded that even he could be of considerable use to Hoover's noninterventionist values as a member of the loyal opposition.

In retrospect, the inability of the West, the League of Nations, or the United States to mount a vigorous challenge to Japanese aggression in Manchuria left the way clear for Japan's expansion throughout Asia. Perhaps the Manchurian Incident was the opening round of World War II. In light of the subsequent events leading to the attack on Pearl Harbor, how realistic was the Hoover-Castle reliance on moral nonrecognition to check Japan's aggression?

Castle's key contribution to the U.S. response to Japan was his blunt May 4th speech, denying that economic and military sanctions would be used against Japan. Stimson, in fact, agreed with Castle that economic boycotts would lead to war. The difference was that Stimson wanted to retain the option of using the boycott to bluff the Japanese into compliance, while Castle felt bluffing a boycott was unrealistic and dangerous. Japan would, as he saw it, fight the United States rather than withdraw from Manchuria under economic pressure.[83]

Castle found substantiation for his caution in the reports of naval intelligence, which indicated that the United States could not win a quick war against remotely located Japan (although, given time and full mobilization, Pearl Harbor and the Philippines could become adequate staging areas for a naval attack on Japan).[84]

Castle, like most diplomats in a democracy, was well aware of the dangers of official policy attempting to go beyond what popular support would permit. Americans had always favored quick, high-reward, low-risk wars to advance widely popular foreign-policy objectives. Long, costly struggles were historically unpopular. Although China's independence had many vocal supporters, especially after Japan's Manchurian invasion and its subsequent invasion of Shanghai in February of 1932, the majority viewed official economic boycotts as too dangerous to world peace. Moreover, Castle was convinced that if more minority opinion leaders were aware of the link between economic boycotts and war, as well as the historic inability of boycotts to force the hand of foreign opponents, fewer would advocate their use. The demoralized and Depression-ridden citizens of the United States would not support a difficult, costly, and protracted war for a territory as remote as Manchuria.

In Hawaii following the end of the Hoover administration, W. R. Castle, Jr., took part in ceremonies preceding a June 25, 1933, baseball game between the visiting Kwansai University team from Japan and a local team called the Chinese. Castle was designated the honorary umpire while his brother Alfred, left, described by a sports writer as "the greatest pitcher ever developed at Harvard University," pitched the first ball with Japanese Consul General Kanekazu Okada batting. Sports promoter and Honolulu Stadium manager J. Ashman Beaven, right, was the announcer.
(Photo by Tai Sing Loo, courtesy of Donald F. Winslow.)

It would take a direct attack on U.S. soil at Pearl Harbor, and only after ten years of mounting Japanese aggression, to create a substantial consensus for a long war.[85]

As has been pointed out, foreign assistance for a U.S. war in Manchuria was far from certain. The League of Nations was virtually impotent without guarantees of strong, united military actions by the United States, France, and Britain. But each of these countries was suffering economically and afraid that further disruption of trade with Asia could topple governments in Europe. Moreover, under the pragmatist Foreign Secretary John Simon, England concurred with conservative thought in France and the U.S. that Japan was a barrier to Soviet expansion in Asia.[86] Without firm British support for unified action, the United States would have to suffer the consequences of war, including greatly diminished trade with Asia, alone. Britain's economic and diplomatic power could become paramount among all Western powers in the Far East. Suspicious of British imperialism and Britain's unwillingness to negotiate naval limitations in the General Disarmament Conference of 1932, Castle saw this as an unwelcome development.

Although Stimson later claimed that his concern for China's territorial integrity was more farsighted and "realistic" than Castle's reliance on Japan's civilian leadership to extricate itself from China without economic or military pressure, both men shared a suspicion of China's ability to support U.S. interests. Stimson's public defense of China throughout the Manchurian Incident rarely led to tangible assistance of any kind. Thus, his State Department refused to approve loans of military supplies or expert advice from American aviators for fear that Japan would be provoked.[87] Stimson was no more willing than Castle or Hoover to call a Nine Power Treaty conference, as China hoped, to bolster League action.[88] Privately Castle noted with some disdain that Stimson's regard for China was a regard for an imaginary ideal rather than for the Chinese as a living body of people with numerous interests, some counter to the valid interests of the United States.[89] Indeed, despite Stimson's sometimes legalistic calculations of world events, he was no more anxious than Castle to place faith or foreign aid in the hands of an unstable government in China. Chinese governments of whatever hue have rarely had reason to put much faith in the United States, and the Hoover administration was no exception to this long record.[90] Writing retrospectively in 1937, Castle observed:

> The thing to remember in this whole unfortunate episode is
> that it proved that the world was not going to war for the sake
> of preserving the integrity of China and that the United States

was one of the nations which would always hold back. It is unfair to assert that we were bound by treaty to fight for the integrity of China. The negotiations through these two years of warfare were always complicated and not always wise, perhaps, in that they often appeared to put the United States too far out on the firing line. Our somewhat futile attempts to cooperate more fully with the League of Nations were not of any value in the controversy; rather did they turn men's eyes away from the scene of conflict to a study of whether America might be planning to enter the League of Nations through a side door. The Secretary of State made too many protests to Japan, so that each succeeding protest, not followed up by force, was less effective than the one before. There were times when war looked dangerously close and it is fortunate that no hot-headed Japanese naval or army officer precipitated trouble as it was precipitated in Shanghai. There is no doubt, on the other hand, that the stand of the United States in the matter was intrinsically correct—that Japan was carelessly flouting the terms of treaties which she had signed. But correct or not, our influence was of as little importance in the end as was that of the League of Nations.[91]

If the essence of diplomatic realism is to recognize the limits of international action, alliance structures, ideologies, policy, and rhetoric, and then make a hardboiled assessment of national self-interest, Under Secretary of State Castle was a consistent realist. Attempting to protect and advance U.S. interests, which he defined primarily in terms of continued trade containment of the Soviet Union, the avoidance of war, and the retention of friendship with Japan's civilian leadership in extraordinarily difficult times, his diplomatic posture in retrospect seems sound. Castle's biggest shortcoming was his stubborn faith that Japan's definition of its own self-interests and those of the United States would ultimately coincide as they had in the 1920s. By the time of the Manchurian Incident, the period of Pax Americana had eroded, and along with it the ability of the United States to underwrite an Asian world friendly to its interests. The imposition of a renewed U.S. hegemony in Asia would occur only after World War II.

7

The Presidential Election of 1936

The political career of Kansas Governor Alf Landon brought him into contact with numerous members of the former Hoover administration. His relationships with these men and others in the Republican Party have been thoroughly studied. Less well studied, however, was the extent to which Landon would draw upon the advice of William R. Castle, Jr. The contact between these two men would have important implications for Landon's foreign policies during the 1936 election and in the direction the Republican Party would take in the years immediately after 1936. Castle's role as an advisor to Landon also testifies to his continuing role in public affairs while presaging his role as an anti-interventionist in the years prior to the attack on Pearl Harbor. The election reenergized Castle and reintroduced him to a substantial public role in advancing principles of diplomatic realism.

By November of 1936, Landon's foreign policy positions included a stress on international arbitration of disputes, avoidance of alliances, avoidance of membership in the League of Nations and World Court, and noninterventionism.[1] After the election, the Republican Party wrestled with the question of new directions in an attempt to become more attractive to American voters. The general lines of attack taken by the Republican National Committee during the critical years 1937–1940 were to forge a coalition with moderate Democrats and liberalize the GOP while continuing to oppose New Deal centralism. William R. Castle, Jr., and Landon, who had collaborated during the 1936 election, continued their association in attempting to render Republican opposition more compelling in a Democratic decade. As a presidential candidate and titular head of the party for four years, Landon presided over a turbulent but seminal period in the GOP's political history.

Meeting for the first time on May 27, 1936, Governor Landon requested that Castle submit a written set of suggestions and notations.[2] On May 30th, Castle wrote from his Washington, D.C., home detailing his recommendations for a foreign-policy plank. Castle immediately emphasized "the importance of the continuity of Republican American foreign policy." The essence of this was friendly relations with all nations and entanglements with none. The platform of 1936 should, he felt, stress the discontinuity perpetrated by a Roosevelt administration that had "substituted flattery for truth" in neglecting the interests of the United States to pursue the applause of other countries.

Secondly, Castle advised Landon to restore honesty and orderliness to the conduct of foreign relations. Most importantly, the Republican Party should promise to build up friendship through fair and equal treatment of all. Specifically, the 1936 platform should promise the pursuit of close relations and cooperation with the other nations in the Western Hemisphere. Common action between nations in meeting common problems would continue to be necessary. Specifically, Castle objected to the New Deal interference in the Western Hemisphere in defiance of the Republican Party's efforts to not interfere there. According to Castle's interpretation of New Deal Latin American foreign policy, Roosevelt had interfered in the affairs of this area more than any other president since Woodrow Wilson. Roosevelt, while not using Wilson's style of military intervention, had conspired to bring about

Kansas Governor Alfred M. Landon, Republican presidential candidate in 1936, drew on the advice of W. R. Castle, Jr., in developing his foreign-policy platform. (Library of Congress photo LC-USZ62-106389.)

revolution in Cuba (1934) in order to get rid of President Gerardo Machado. Castle argued that Machado might well have been voted out by the end of 1934 by Cuban voters.

To compound the problem, Roosevelt's administration had overreacted to outcries over Cuba by signing a treaty promising never, under any circumstance, to use force "diplomatic or otherwise" in the protection of U.S. rights. The vagueness of the language of the 1933 Pan-American Conference at Montevideo and the 1936 Inter-American Conference at Buenos Aires, Argentina, limited U.S. options to protect citizens from danger to their lives during periods of domestic strife in LatinAmerican countries. Such guarantees, Castle argued, compromised traditional American rights while sending a signal of confusion and weakness. Castle urged Landon to point out New Deal foreign-policy "errors" in Latin America.

Yet, another New Deal error that Landon could mention in speeches was, according to Castle, the 1936 treaty with Panama. This treaty, which recognized that nation's right to help operate and protect the great canal bifurcating the country, ultimately was rejected by the Senate. In the original treaty of 1903, the United States was given the right, in case the canal seemed to be in danger, to occupy certain islands and to take needed military measures. The new treaty changed this and provided for the necessity of consultation with Panama before protective measures were taken. The reckless measure, according to Castle, failed to see that the canal

> is not only a possession but a trust, that if it were injured though
> any negligence of ours, all the nations which depend on the canal would blame us. Fortunately, this Panama treaty was born
> dead, since the Senate of the United States was too patriotic to
> consent to its ratification even though the Executive urged its
> importance. It would seem as though the New Deal sought, in
> the negotiations of treaties to win the applause of the other
> party to the treaty, whereas the Republicans negotiate for the
> purpose of bargaining the maximum benefits for the United
> States. The moment you begin to kowtow to foreign nations,
> you are binding yourself to action which may, when the time
> comes, be unfortunate, if not disastrous. Furthermore, you are
> forfeiting the respect of other nations. Republican policy will
> always be to maintain through complete fairness, the respect of
> other nations, but this without giving up any American rights.[3]

On the important question of neutrality, Castle suggested that Republican leadership should make "every honest attempt" to preserve real neutrality. He also urged Landon to sponsor an international conference to formulate rules of neutrality that would be more responsive to modern conditions. On the one hand, the Republican Party must work to gain respect for U.S. rights in the international arena. On the other hand,

> we have no wish to demand for ourselves rights which we should deny others. We believe that all rules of neutrality should be international, that if we attempt ourselves to change the rules, especially during the course of a conflict, we are almost certain to be involved. We recognize the immense power of the U.S. in international affairs with due regard for the rights and interest of others.[4]

In a general way, Castle also urged Landon to attack the New Deal for making a mockery of neutrality. The traditional meaning of the word was that when two or more nations were at war, the neutral country treated the belligerents impartially, did not sell to one what it could not sell to the other, and insisted on its rights as much with one as with the other. Castle argued that the New Deal had tried to use what it mistakenly called neutrality for the purpose of influencing the result of the conflict. For example, the 1935 Neutrality Act, passed by an isolationist Congress, had provided for true neutrality. According to the act, if the president declared that war existed in the world, Americans could not ship arms or other weapons to any belligerent nation. In addition, U.S. ships could not carry arms to belligerents and Americans were to be warned that they sailed on belligerent ships at their own risk. When Mussolini's Italy invaded Ethiopia in hopes of reviving ancient Roman hegemony there, Roosevelt declared a state of war and invoked the 1935 Neutrality Act, as he was bound to do. He went further, however, and denied Americans the opportunity to travel in the ships of either belligerent. As Castle noted,

> This was a measure aimed at Italy, because everyone else knew that Ethiopia had no ships. He also urged Americans not to trade with the "belligerents," and this was un-neutral because the intention was to prevent goods going to Italy. Our trade with Ethiopia had always been negligible. Quite aside from the fact that the Administration was playing the League game, it was being palpably un-neutral. It was giving up American rights supinely, with the idea that surrender would make us safer, and actually, through it's lack of neutrality, was immeasurably increasing the danger that we should become involved. It pressed, unsuccessfully, to have given to the President the right to decide on the aggressor and, having made this decision, to discrimi-

nate as between the belligerents. This would have meant, without any doubt whatever, that the United States would have been involved in every war, whatever fought. The Republican Party, realizing that laws of neutrality are international, will strive to gain international agreement to the strengthening of these laws in every way which will serve to keep neutral nations out of the conflict. It will not tinker with local laws supposed to have world-wide application, as such laws are dangerous because insulting to other nations. We do not legislate for the world.[5]

Much of the rest of the letter of May 30th deals with Castle's basic belief that enlightened self-interest, tempered by moral concern for the rights of other nations, would foster world peace. He strongly sanctioned the position that the United States should avoid adopting the policies of the discredited League of Nations. In addition, he opposed the "meddling internationalists" who could do no good while at the same time opposing the isolationists who denied the increasing economic interdependence of a complex world.

Moreover, and not surprisingly given his work for the Washington Naval Conference (1921–1922) and the London Conference (1930), Castle strongly advised a proportional international disarmament. Further, he advised that any future disarmament conferences be held only after careful prior research, negotiation, and political persuasion. Disarmament conferences, correctly conducted, had the important result of increasing goodwill and cooperation. Incorrectly held, they promoted mutual suspicion and international tensions. Landon shared this faith in such conferences in promoting peace through the lessening of the tensions brought on by massive build-ups in lethal weapons.

Finally, Castle suggested that Landon's foreign policy include cooperating with the League of Nations or other competent international bodies in humanitarian, economic, and cultural areas. Furthermore, the Republican Party should seek to make the country a happier, safer, and stronger one. This would most likely happen if America was respected and admired by the rest of the world for its staunch integrity and its comprehensive understanding.[6]

That being said, Castle argued that the New Deal had done little to strengthen and extend the series of arbitration and conciliation treaties, which had bipartisan support in the past. Although some progress had been made in the various Latin American treaties, nothing had been done to advance the principle of arbitration in the far more important European and Asian sectors. Moreover, too much emphasis had been placed on Secretary of State Hull's reciprocal trade negotiations (beginning in 1934) and to "playing with the League of Nations." Thus, FDR had sent mixed signals about cooperating with the League of Nations in such trouble spots as Ethiopia while failing to create a domestic consensus for full cooperation with the League. He and Landon agreed that the Republicans should stand for complete noninvolvement with the ineffective and badly led League of Nations while also avoiding involvement with political problems in Europe. The Republicans would offer voters a clear choice. "The difference is that the New Deal would involve us in trouble without being willing to go far enough to cure the disease, whereas the Republicans would keep out altogether, being unwilling to flirt with danger, especially when the flirtation cannot possibly do any good and might lead the nation into serious trouble." [7]

Landon and Castle agreed that the Republican policy alternative was to seek the extension of arbitration treaties and realistic reduction of armaments to avoid, the "temptation of war." Castle urged Landon to remind voters of the substantial breakthroughs made by the United States at the Washington Naval Conference in 1921 and the London Conference of 1930. Both of these conferences had achieved results because, as Castle saw it, there had been clearly defined objectives and a carefully described agenda agreed upon by all parties before the conferences themselves were held. In contrast, the 1935 London conferences had started with vague expectation and an impossible set of assumptions. Although the grand rhetoric had gained points for Roosevelt at home, the American delegates had no practical suggestions to make. Roosevelt would have been well served to have said that naval reduction was impossible given international tensions and to have proposed a minor and temporary "naval holiday." Castle believed that Japan might have accepted a modest and brief holiday on the building of new ships but that FDR could not have. This reluctance was due to Roosevelt's desire for a naval buildup to be a poor form of public works project. With Landon, he despaired at any hope of Roosevelt's leading a call for disarmament and felt that the failure could lead to a disastrous war. [8]

For Castle, New Deal foreign policy had been a muddled failure, finally, because it had not defined what valid U.S. interests were. Roosevelt had, he claimed, alternated "between bluster and obsequiousness." To give up our rights for the sake of easy applause does not make us either liked or respected; it makes other nations say agreeable things to hide the fact that they despise us. They flatter and get what they can while flattery opens the pocket book and box of tricks." [9] Both Castle and Landon knew that a detailed critique of FDR's foreign policy would fail to change the outcome of the 1936 election. Domestic issues would predominate. Nonetheless, speeches, the Republican platform, news releases, and the like would need to include these foreign-policy issues. More importantly, the critique of FDR's foreign policy would, as both Castle and Landon saw it, need to become a regular part of Republican Party politics.[10]

Thus, although Landon drew more heavily on former Under Secretary of State J. Reuben Clark, Castle's recommendations were to a large extent in accord with them and were easily incorporated into the final 1936 platform. On June 9, two days before Landon's official nomination at the Republican convention, isolationist Senator Borah attacked the foreign-policy plank because it did not definitely oppose membership in the League of Nations and because it failed to support strict neutrality and embargo legislation. Only the last-minute maneuvering of former Treasury Secretary Ogden Mills, William Allen White, and others managed to save the essentials of the foreign-policy plank urged by Castle in May.

After the nomination, Castle wrote Landon congratulating him and making some general recommendations for his acceptance speech. Specifically, he advised that Landon stress the theme of constitutional imbalance caused by the usurpation of state and local functions by the federal government. In the area of foreign policy, Landon was urged to recommit the Republican Party to international understanding and the reduction of arms. Landon replied, thanking Castle for his helpfulness and indicating that both recommendations for the acceptance speech would be carefully considered.[11]

Once the campaign started, Castle's one major contribution, other than supporting Landon through fund-raising and regular party support, was to advise Landon to actively defend himself against Democratic charges that Republicans were nativists at heart. In the May 30th letter, Castle had advised Landon to campaign for the termination of unequal immigration quotas. By September, Landon had still not addressed the immigration issues in a separate speech, so Castle urged him to grant a private interview with the conservative Italian-American lawyer Edward Corsi.[12] As the former commissioner of immigration under President Coolidge, Corsi was considered a "safe interview." In addition, he had considerable credibility in the Italian-American urban press as well as in the national news magazines. Although Landon's tight schedule before his campaign departure on his special train, the *Sun Flower Special*, on October 8 did not allow him to grant this interview, Corsi wrote a Columbus Day message for Landon which weakened some of the continued attacks on Landon's "ethnic position." The message, which Castle transmitted to Landon by phone on October 7, read as follows:

> Honorable Nicholas H. Pinto, President, The Columbian League, 70 Pine Street, New York City. My Dear Mr. Pinto—Commissioner Corsi has called to my attention the celebrations that members of the Columbian League are planning in their respective communities for Columbus Day, and while it is impossible for me to be in the East on that occasion, I shall certainly be with you in spirit and wish you success. Columbus Day comes as an annual reminder to Americans of the great role played by Italy in the discovery of America . . . but Columbus Day reminds us also of the immense debt we owe to millions of immigrants from Italy whose contribution to our national life has enriched the patrimony of every American. The sons and daughters of Italy have helped build our cities, our roads, our homes; they have dug our mines and tilled our soil . . . they have brought to our shores the finest fruits of Italian civilization as evidenced by their achievements in music, painting, sculpture, and the sciences. America is proud of her citizens of Italian blood and welcomes their participation in our democracy." [13]

Such a message would not turn the tide of criticism of Landon's reputed anti-immigrant, anti-Semitic, anti-Black position but did reveal one weapon used to respond to these often hysterical charges.

Castle and Governor Landon met briefly on October 9 on the *Sun Flower Special*. They met for about a half hour and reviewed key points of foreign policy that the governor would reiterate in the many speeches made on the road in October.[14] For example, in Indianapolis on October 24, Governor Landon stressed the need to restore international faith in America, which he felt had been shattered by President Roosevelt's disruption of the 1933 London Economic Conference. In addition, he argued that the nation should continue the work of Republicans in the 1920s to reduce armaments while insisting on America's legitimate neutral rights. Reflecting the ideas of J. Reuben Clark and Castle, he also outlined the need for international arbitration as a means of avoiding war.[15] He repeated these themes until the last day of the campaign.[16]

Landon had known that "it was a desperate fight from the start" and the election results in November were perhaps not a surprise.[17] Castle wrote him immediately indicating his sadness with the results but indicating that the Republican campaign had been an important one in that it had raised important questions about the policies of the New Deal. He invited the Landons to visit him in Washington, D.C., and indicated his hope that their campaign friendship would continue.[18]

On November 7, Castle wrote Governor Landon again, reporting his letter to John Hamilton, Republican National Committee chairman. In the letter he proposed his support in the effort to rebuild the party. Indeed,

> I think we may have to make some pretty drastic changes. I am sure that something must be done to build up a real organization which will include the old time Democrats. I think I could be of use to John in the Washington Office as I know a good part of the people around the country on the National Committee and also a large part of the House and Senate, and I have had a great deal of practice in my life in this question of organization.[19]

After taking care of his most pressing postelection duties, Landon began functioning as the titular head of the party. To both Ralph Robey, former Landon staff member, and Castle, Landon wrote of his hope that the Republicans could become a vital opposition party. Its role would include educating the public, having a moderating influence on government policy, and, through investigation and publication, keeping the government's power in check.[20] In no case should the party be allowed to backslide into the condition it was in after the 1932 election. In a mid-December meeting with Castle before his Gridiron Club speech, these basic goals for the next four years were repeated.[21]

Although in the midst of moving out of office and the Topeka executive mansion, Landon wrote Castle, advising him to give direction to the policies and publication of *The Trumpeter*. The national committee had just taken over its publication under John Hamilton. Landon also requested that Castle keep him advised of news about foreign policy. Noting that he would give a short talk at the upcoming Lincoln Birthday Dinner in New York, he also urged Castle to consider him a friend rather than an acquaintance.[22]

In early 1937, Castle made important suggestions to Landon about how the Republican Party could regroup for the 1938 congressional election and 1940 presidential elections. Castle felt strongly that the party had to appeal to a larger number of voters. To accomplish this, the party had to be made more representative of a changing America. Specifically, the old-guard conservatives had to be subdued without being totally alienated. Men like Hamilton Fish would have to be made less obstreperous and less representative of the party in the public's eye. Further, he agreed with Landon that the party organization must be liberal-ized, westerners given a bigger part in the program, and the Black vote recaptured. In order to facilitate a possible coalition with "Jeffersonian" Democrats against a growing New Deal centralism, Castle suggested that a series of regional conferences be held that would bring together sympathetic Republicans and Democrats to discuss common problems and solutions. This would be particularly useful in the South, where the Democratic Party had important reservations about FDR. As Castle noted,

> I was talking with a man yesterday about Virginia. A live, young Democrat in the Virginia Legislature who bolted his party to vote for you. In the consequence, he lost his seat in the Legislature but is maintaining his interest in politics. . . . He says he is not coming out as a Republican . . . because he thinks this is not the way to treat the hide-bound Virginians. Instead he will be an Independent, although he was willing to help in any liberal movement fostered by the Republican National Committee. He says, for example, that he thinks that we could get up a long series of clubs through the South to be called as he suggested "New Southern Club No. 1," etc.— Clubs which would meet perhaps once a month and contain as many members, really people, Democrats or Republicans, and would discuss various matters such as Relief, Civic Service, Budget Balancing, etc. . . . There is no doubt in my mind that the reformation of the South must be a very slow process and on the other hand, I am convinced that in these days when we are trying to regenerate and reinvigorate the Party, we must look courageously ahead to an uphill road which we must climb and at the same time educate the American people all over again to what we know to be the fundamentals of American life.[23]

Castle concluded that this effort would have to be part of an ongoing and vigorous attempt to avoid dying "through dry rot" and finding the GOP "crowded out by a new and vigorous party."[24]

Increasingly, Landon, who looked to the Republican National Committee to coordinate the party's efforts, grew impatient with the inability of John Hamilton to originate new ideas and with his inability to muster financial support for the party. Thus, by March 1937, Landon had used his influence to obtain important staff positions for his friends on the National Committee. William Castle was named assistant to the chairman and quickly got to work with Landon's ally, Billy Hard, to achieve greater communication with the press. A continuing debate within the committee in the spring of 1937 was the correct strategy to oppose FDR's court reorganization, which would have allowed him to have created, through appointment, a court more receptive to the second New Deal. Since Roosevelt's announcement of the controversial plan on February 5, 1937, the Republican Congressional leadership had planned to allow Democrats to lead the Congressional opposition while supporting them quietly. Landon and others were persuaded not to speak out publicly for fear that this would unite Democrats behind the president's plan. By March, however, Republicans on the National Committee were growing restless in their desire to discredit the plan before the nation. Castle summarized developments to Landon on March 29:

> We have been getting speakers, for example, for the Senate Judiciary Committee and have been preparing speeches and giving advice to Democrats as well as to Republicans, but all that will never be known. Certainly we have no desire to make the Court in any way a partisan issue and I feel more and more strongly as the days go by that the time has come when we must not, as a National Committee, but as individual Republicans speak up with the utmost courage.[25]

Clearly, the 1938 congressional election would be critical to the advancement, if not indeed the very survival, of Republican hopes. The election would, according to Castle, provide an opportunity for the party to speak out clearly on key foreign-policy measures.

In a confidential letter Landon responded by saying that he too was secretly growing restless at not being able to take vociferous and public opposition to the effort to pack the Supreme Court. In any case, Landon felt that the hoped-for Republican–conservative Democrat coalition was at hand. His only concern was the leadership of such a coalition. Lew Douglas, Roosevelt's former director of the budget, had recently written him that the coalition, which would be fragile at best, should be brought under Democratic leadership. Landon strongly rejected the proposal, arguing instead that the parties should be co-captains.[26]

By June, Castle responded by detailing the activities of the Republican National Committee while the chairman, John Hamilton, was away. Castle, as assistant to Hamilton, had become active in soliciting information from state committee chairmen and federal political figures concerning the nation's attitude toward the New Deal. He found that the desire for a conservative Democrat-Republican coalition remained strong and that there was a growing business resistance to regulation and interference by the federal government. Once again, he stated his belief that such a coalition would be most successful in the South while also restating his hope that traditional Republican supporters would not be ignored in the effort to forge the coalition.[27] Most importantly, it would continue to be important for the party to retain its separate identity.

Landon agreed and further warned Republicans about ignoring the independence of their local organizations. Most importantly, he advised Republicans not to vote for conservative Democratic senators in the primaries; any sympathetic Democrats should be nominated "either on our own ticket, or endorsed on a third party ticket."[28] Thus, both men continued to dream of a coalition of anti–New Deal Republicans and Democrats that was never to be.

By the end of July, Roosevelt's plan to restructure the Supreme Court had died, and the Landon strategy of remaining silent on the issue in public had proven successful.[29] Thereafter, Landon and other party leaders spoke plaintively of Roosevelt's baneful threat to the Constitution.

In the fall of 1937, a startling rift had developed between Hoover and Landon over the wisdom of holding a full mid-term convention.[30] Both Landon and his former vice-presidential running mate, Frank Knox, feared that Hoover would use such a convention to control the party or begin a campaign to win nomination for the 1940 election.[31] Such a convention was urged by many Republicans as a means of defining Republican principles as well as publishing these principles to a public suffering from the recession of 1937. Although Landon favored a gathering, he wanted one that was fully representative of the party, particularly its progressive elements, one that was off the record, and one small enough to permit a candid discussion of party policies. A big, highly publicized convention open to domination by a clique such as the "reactionary old guard" was to be avoided.[32]

On November 5, the national committee created the Committee on Programs for the consideration of relevant policies of government. This compromise measure autho-

Frank Knox, Alf Landon's vice-presidential running mate in 1936, helped spearhead the opposition to Herbert Hoover's continuing influence in the Republican Party. (Library of Congress photo LC-USZ-6292897.)

rized the special program committee to determine as fully as possible the various views held by the rank and file of the Republican Party.[33] In an effort to obtain full support from Landon, Hamilton invited his nominations to the committee. Although nominating Fiorello LaGuardia, mayor of New York, Landon elected not to serve on the committee himself in order to retain freedom of action as well as party unity.[34]

On November 6, Castle wrote Landon at length expressing his desire that the newly formulated conference define basic principles without detailing specific implementations. Indeed, "without such definition I do not know how we can expect to attract to our banner the vast groups of unhappy and discontented Democrats. I hear them say all the time that they detest the New Deal but that they cannot support the Republican Party because they do not know what we stand for." The more representative the conference of Republican beliefs the better.

The letter then went on to criticize Landon for misestimating the ideological positions of Hoover and LaGuardia. In the case of LaGuardia, Castle felt, the Republicans had a man who was both charismatic and fundamentally conservative. Far from being radical, he was also a political figure who could and had drawn support from all shades of Republican opinion. Hoover, on the other hand, had also been misunderstood by Landon as a reactionary supported by the old guard. In fact, Hoover had much in common with Landon in that both were moderate progressives. As Castle reminded Landon,

> It was the forward looking elements of the party which elected Hoover and the so-called Old Guard never wavered in its dislike of him, with the exception of course, of certain among them who, because they worked in close contact with him, got to know him and were willing to forgive his progressive principles because they learned to appreciate the character and high purpose of the man.[35]

Castle went on to deny the bothersome rumor that Hoover sought to gain the 1940 nomination for the presidency. Instead, Castle claimed, Hoover merely wished to lend his valued experience in economics, management, and government to his party.

Landon responded by agreeing that Hoover was ideologically compatible with him but still insisted that Hoover's plan for a full midterm convention was poorly planned and timed. Landon also hinted of his continuing distrust of Hoover's future plans and of his unwillingness to fully accept Landon as the true leader of the Republican Party.[36] Clearly, Landon was now considering ways, other than public attack, of thwarting Hoover's potential future control of the party. After the Gridiron dinner on December 11, he quietly held private conferences with Republican Party leaders and urged opposition to Hoover specifically and the "retrograde" old guard in general.[37] One planning session was held with Frank Knox and others at a formal dinner party at the Castle home.[38]

Shortly after this dinner party, Landon announced his definitive decision not to run.[39] He and Knox had clearly decided that such a move would force Hoover's hand with respect to his own plans for 1940.[40] Thus, his definitive statement and other party opposition effectively blocked a possible attempt of Hoover to regain control of party leadership in the years ahead.

The last correspondence on public matters between Castle and Landon dealt with the 1938 congressional election results, which both men naturally found pleasing. In this election, the Republicans made substantial gains in both the Senate and the House. Even the defeat in New York of Thomas E. Dewey, who was running for governor, was only a narrow one. To Landon, it looked as if the nation was returning to a long-missing political balance.[41] Most importantly, the defeatism and indifference that had come to characterize much Republican thinking might soon change.

As the decade ended, both men were to go their separate ways. Throughout the stormy decade these two men, from different backgrounds and with different relations to Hoover, had become frequent correspondents and friends. Their association had a role in shaping Republican Party strategy and political thinking in one of the nation's most critical decades. For Castle, the association and his role in Republican Party politics gave him an outlet for his organizational energies while keeping him in the public eye. The Landon relationship had revived his career and helped him define an opposition to Roosevelt's foreign policy. That principled opposition, in the face of changing public attitudes toward intervention in World War II after the fall of France in 1940, would lead to his most controversial policy positions.

8 Opposition to Intervention in Asia, 1939–1941

In the wake of Watergate and Vietnam and the general concern about the heavy concentration of power in the executive branch, and its frequent abuse, historians have found new reasons to study the ideas of prominent noninterventionists prior to Pearl Harbor.[1] After the dominance of post–World War II "traditionalist" historiography, which stressed first the necessity of America's participation in a war caused by external threats to vital security interests and, second, the naive qualities of isolationists who opposed "entanglement" in the political affairs of other nations, a more complex analysis of groups opposed to entry into World War II has emerged.[2]

This friendlier assessment of the noninterventionists was preceded by skeptics like Charles A. Beard and Harry Elmer Barnes, who doubted that opponents to entry into the war were blindly obstructionist or ignorant of the realities of aggression on the part of Japan, Germany, and Italy. They viewed the major European powers as treacherous and their ideological justifications of their economic self-interest as shallow. For the revisionist historians of the 1940s and early 1950s, the so-called isolationists were legitimate heirs to the traditional American foreign policy of peace, commerce, and friendship with all nations.[3]

On another plane, Wayne Cole and Manfred Jonas later argued that noninterventionist groups, such as the America First Committee, had been more realistic about the nature of external challenges to American security in Europe and Asia than previously thought. Far from blindly obstructionist, many noninterventionists were very sensitive to the dangers that massive war preparation would have on traditional American liberties.[4]

Since the mid-1970s, attitudes toward many of the leading noninterventionists have continued to change. Studies focusing on Robert A. Taft, Charles A. Lindbergh, John T. Flynn, Herbert Hoover, Charles Beard, and Oswald Garrison Villard characterized these men as farsighted in their concern for traditional American democracy in an age of total war. Hoover and Taft were specifically cited as realistic and sophisticated for believing that the United States should not be, and ultimately could not be, an international policeman responsible for correcting every wrong in the world.[5]

Despite the rehabilitation of noninterventionist groups like the America First Committee, much research remains to be done. The focus of detailed studies of the America First Committee is largely on the European conflict. We now know a great deal about the primary thrust of the committee's opposition to military involvement in the European conflict during 1940 and 1941. We know far less, however, about its secondary thrust: the opposition to military involvement in Asia.

A leading opponent of intervention in Asia in the period from 1939 to 1941 was President Hoover's under secretary of state, William R. Castle. A chief organizer of the Washington, D.C., chapter of the America First Committee in 1940, he was among the most vocal of Roosevelt's critics. His focus on Japan was uncharacteristic of the noninterventionists, and no adequate description of his views currently exists.[6] The foreign policy positions of this former career diplomat are worth examining because of what they reveal about noninterventionist attitudes toward Japan. Neither a pacifist nor a rigid ideologue opposed to intervention under any circumstances, Castle feared the domestic consequences of modern warfare. Moreover, he believed Roosevelt's Asian policies were inconsistent, unrealistic, and needlessly provocative. Castle expressed his views in numerous public speeches and magazine articles in the late 1930s and early 1940s.

When the war in Europe began on September 1, 1939, Castle became a leading noninterventionist. In a key speech before the Annual Men's Mass Meeting in the Diocese of Rochester in October 1939, he urged a rational assessment of America's position in this conflagration. He reminded his audience that the European quarrel was caused mainly by strife over the division of territory and raw materials. Despite the ideological differences between the democracies and Hitler, the actual causes of the war were more directly related to economic, demographic, techno-logical, and material circumstances. Indeed, he stated that geopolitical realities drove nations more than self-righteous rhetoric.

Furthermore, Castle argued, the moral superiority of the major democracies was vitiated by the undemocratic aspects of their colonial rule. The United States, for example, had dealt on a regular basis with non-democratic Latin American nations. He noted that the United States had been misled during World War I by the dual promises that national sacrifice would "make the world safe for democracy" and that winning the war would end all future wars. He warned Americans to be sensitive to propaganda urging their participation in any armed conflict whatever its source.

If reason, rather than emotion prevailed, Americans would not confuse England's self-interest with the legitimate self-interest of the United States. The only valid reason for U.S. involvement, he argued, should be self-defense. As long as foreign laws did not endanger essential American property rights, U.S. citizens should not worry about how foreign laws were made. Under no circumstances should the United States become the moral policeman of the world or the arbitrator of material and ideological conflicts of long and distant standing. Castle wrote: "If we stay out we shall, after the war, be a beacon light for all the nations, the sanctuary where the lights of democracy and of religion have been kept alive." [7]

In touching on intellectual and diplomatic themes prevalent in the isolationist 1930s, Castle discovered a receptive audience for his beliefs. In late 1939, he further delineated the financial and political woes that normally accrued to any nation at war.[8] He stressed the duty of Americans to adhere foremost to their own national interests. In distinguishing European interests from our own, he struck a chord that had roots in the nation's early national period.[9] His interpretation of the European war also served as an interpretive framework for discussing the growing hostilities with Japan.

Like many noninterventionists, Castle insisted that the proposed repeal of the American arms embargo in 1939 would be unneutral because it would "change the rules of the game after the game had begun so as to help one side against the other." [10] Furthermore, he told *U.S. News* readers, the 1937 Neutrality Act had been ineffective in keeping the United States entirely out of war because it retained some clearly unneutral provisions such as extending favored treatment to nations with large navies and merchant marines—like Britain—that could take advantage of the "cash-and-carry" provision.[11] Castle also argued that preventing the sale of munitions abroad would mean that more resources would later be available for American defense.[12]

Although he opposed repeal of the arms embargo, he felt that the real threat of war arose not from the "rules and regulations" in dispute, but from the impact of "gradual and subtle propaganda." If local "grassroots" movements which insisted on rational deliberation and caution did not develop to counter the forces promoting intervention, he feared U.S. involvement might occur soon after the 1940 election.[13] Not only should informed citizens insist on government accountability and restraint, but, he explained to a meeting of the Delaware Bankers Association:

> we must prick the bubbles of sentimentality as well as those of untruth. When we hear that the war is one between democracy and dictatorship we must make people understand that it merely happens that way, that actually it is the old story of the conflict between those who have and those who want. If we do our duty to ourselves, we may have civilization.[14]

Castle's belief, in the Jeffersonian tradition, that "the informed people" were the best check on tyrannical centralism and his fear about the possibility of a war-induced domestic "dictatorship" were two important themes often repeated in his opposition to U.S. involvement in Asia.

Since Castle's experience as Hoover's under secretary of state had been mostly with Japan and he had served successfully as ambassador to Japan during the London Disarmament Treaty negotiations in 1930, it is not surprising that his major interest in the prewar period from 1939 to 1941 was Asia. He believed he knew much about this region, and he had profound respect for its people.

Joseph C. Grew. U.S. ambassador to Japan from 1932 to 1941, was a close friend of Castle's, held similar views regarding Japan's role in international affairs, and provided Castle much inside information about events in Japan even after Castle had left public office. (Library of Congress photo LC-USZ62-102349.)

Recognized by career diplomats such as Stanley K. Hornbeck, Hugh Wilson, and Joseph Grew as one of the nation's foremost Japanese experts, Castle's opinions about events in Asia carried considerable weight. Leading newspapers, magazines, and public organizations invited his comments. Not unexpectedly, noninterventionists tended to praise his judgment of developments, while interventionists and pro-Chinese public figures denounced them. The negative reception of his views intensified after the fall of France and the formation of the Japan-Germany-Italy Axis in September 1940.

Beginning in the fall of 1939, Castle vigorously defended his noninterventionist stance. A constant theme throughout his speeches was how anti-Japanese feeling had arisen because of ignorance and biased, unfair comparisons to China. Contrary to the belief of many Americans, China was not a peace-loving, unified state overcome by barbarous Japanese militarists. In fact, he reminded the audience of the Tuesday Forum, China had long been a disorganized, chaotic country where local warlords, rather than the government, had prevailed. Indeed, any depiction of China as possessing a government with popular following was problematic in light of decades of disorder. Furthermore, although Japan's 1931 invasion of Manchuria was illegal, China "had never had more than a shadowy hold on Manchuria and had never ruled the district." Prior to the invasion, warlords had attacked Japanese agents for their personal gain, and they remained provocative through the Shanghai Incident of 1932. On the whole, Japan had proven to be a "virile, almost progressive force" in an unstable area."[15] Americans who quickly condemned Japan without understanding conditions in Asia were warned to remember that the role of international policeman was dangerous.

America itself, Castle repeatedly proclaimed, was not without fault. The choice to fight aggressive nations meant, in all likelihood, perpetual war. America's legitimate role in China should be to protect American citizens and its immediate interests. No treaties mandated a military response to aggression in China, and official U.S. interference would be unwise. Private, humanitarian action, he told a gathering of the Jewish Community Center on International Affairs, would be understandable and justifiable, but in no case should the United States become involved in Manchuria, where U.S. trade had doubled and banditry had been reduced since the invasion of 1931.[16]

In any case, the United States was in no military position to "dam up" the expansion of Japan. Rather the United States could, if it maintained peaceful relations, guide Japanese expansion in ways acceptable to its national self-interest. Moreover, the likelihood of "guiding" Japan was certainly greater than guiding Russia, which would surely take advantage of a vulnerable China if Japan did not.[17] In an imperfect world, dealing with the lesser of two evils might be a more realistic choice than seeking to lead a self-righteous crusade to cleanse the world of every wrong. By late 1941, Castle's faith that the United States could "guide" Japan had proven a mistake. Yet he continued to insist that provocative moves by Roosevelt had played an important part in making impossible the American avoidance of Japanese aggression.

Castle was not overly apprehensive about Japan's proclamation of a "Monroe Doctrine" for Asia. In an article written for *Atlantic Monthly,* he objected to the Japanese use of the parallel but added that highly industrialized nations historically had tended to dominate less-advanced neighboring states. This had, for example, been the case with the United States and Latin America. Therefore, it was realistic to expect Japan to dominate China. If the term "Japanese Monroe Doctrine" (first used in 1934) really meant the blatant control of China, the United States might realize some advantages. Specifically, Japan would protect the area from outside (Russian) occupation, keep the peace, and foster international trade. Serious U.S. military opposition to such a doctrine would be expensive and perhaps unsuccessful. Such a stance would also endanger essential purchases of tin and rubber in the Dutch and British colonies.[18] Further, in a *Saturday Evening Post* article, he claimed that hostile threats of a trade embargo had damaged American chances of using the Japanese navy to help guard the Pacific from outside aggression, particularly Russian, since Russia had less to fear from Germany following the signing of the nonaggression pact.[19]

Between December 1939 and the summer of 1940, Castle made numerous public speeches denouncing the continued talk of an embargo aimed at Japan. His perception was that an "embargo is only useful if effective and if effective, it leads to war."[20] This theme had been stressed by both Castle and President Hoover during the Manchurian crisis in 1931, and it played a large role in preventing the State Department from mandating a punitive embargo against Japan at the time. Castle and other critics of the threatened embargo warned American voters that a decision for an embargo was ultimately a decision for war. He hoped an informed public could prevent obfuscation and irrational political choices. Furthermore, he argued, in a public address in Howe, Indiana, the imposition of an embargo on Japan had no guarantee of success, while at the same time it might drive Japan into an alliance with Russia. Although unlikely because of Japan's traditional antipathy for Moscow, it would be a foreign-policy disaster if it happened."[21] Emotional rhetoric and confused thinking about the embargo prevailed in part because of Roosevelt's reluctance to delineate publicly this important risk.[22]

A related objection emphasized in his speeches, and one shared by Roosevelt until the spring of 1940, was the risk that an embargo of oil would force the Japanese to obtain petroleum from the semidefenseless Dutch East Indies.[23] But beyond the obvious point that the Americans, British, Chinese, and Dutch were helpless to prevent such a contingency, Castle stressed constantly his faith that Japan had long been a friend of the United States and was only temporarily hostile. If the United States embargoed oil, it might lose whatever moderating influence it still had left over Japan; and if the United States went to war with Japan, the civilian liberal (antimilitarist) elements in the Japanese government would surely be driven from power. Moreover, such a war would be difficult because the United States could not successfully attack Japan in its home waters "without a fleet twice as large as ours is now, and this would mean years of desperate building."[24] Ironically, he argued, continued American possession of the Philippine Islands would not be endangered unless war broke out. Those Americans worried about the fate of that island chain were foolish to suggest that an embargo, an act usually preparatory to war, was necessary to protect them.[25]

The application of an embargo would also in all probability be perceived by Japan as an example of an inconsistent foreign policy. Specifically, the United States had not embargoed trade with the Soviet Union after it seized Latvia, Lithuania, and Estonia. Extraordinary measures on behalf of Chiang Kai-shek, hardly a reliable ally or a popular Chinese figure, would surely be viewed by the Japanese as needlessly provocative.[26]

Finally, Castle urged his audiences to avoid prejudice and emotion in judging Japan. The United States had its own unpleasant history of aggressive expansion, and Americans should carefully examine all sides of the issue.[27] In the last analysis, a rational assessment of national self-interest should prevail. As long as the United States presented Japan with realistic alternatives, war was not the inevitable consequence of events in China.

In the fall of 1940, Castle hoped to magnify his protest against intervention by affiliating with the newly formed America First Committee (AFC). Organized in September, its diverse membership opposed any measures that would involve the United States in World War II. The leading members included R. Douglas Stuart, Jr., General Robert E. Wood (national chairman), General Hugh S. Johnson, John T. Flynn, Chester Bowles, and Charles Lindbergh, who joined in April 1941. This group stressed the need for an impregnable American defense. They expressed fears about the danger to traditional American democracy from the centralizing, authoritarian measures many considered necessary to fight a modern war. To the AFC, democracy could be preserved only by keeping out of war; dictatorships were viewed as the products of war, not peace. Always sympathetic to the basic ideas of the organization, Castle created the Washington chapter on December 11, 1940.[28] The initial organizing meeting was held in Castle's home and included such notables as Captain Edward Rickenbacker, Johnson, and Flynn. One hundred people attended and Castle was named chairman. As he saw it, the AFC's real purpose was:

> to defeat hysteria; to make people think from an American point of view; to counteract as far as possible the pro-war propaganda of other organizations and individuals to work for sensible and complete preparation for defense; to do everything possible to maintain our American way of life.[29]

Members of the committee hoped the former ambassador to Japan would speak forthrightly on escalating tensions in Asia. They were not disappointed. Even before his formal affiliation with the national committee of the AFC, Castle had decided that he would expend all his energy in denouncing the drift toward war. From the early fall of 1940 until his serious, incapacitating illness lasting from May to November 1941, he was very active.

Decrying "wild rhetoric," Castle asserted that the only strictly American interest in the Far East was trade. Since most of that trade was with Japan, war would cause the United States to forfeit existing commerce and forego future commercial opportunities in Asia. This would occur because of Japan's ability to dominate Asia economically even by peaceful means. Repeatedly he reminded his audiences and readers that Japan was the only remaining large purchaser of U.S. raw cotton, "and we are rapidly alienating that last customer in a manner which seems to some to indicate that we are far less interested in the sufferings of our own people in the South than we are in China."[30] Indeed, as he reminded fellow Republicans at a rally in St. Albans, Vermont, the country's measures "short of war" had thus far irritated the Japanese and failed to help the Chinese. Even worse, these measures had failed to protect America's interests in the area.[31]

In a *U.S. News* article of October 11, 1940, he claimed Roosevelt's desire to aid England "short of war" was inconsistent with his hard-line, negative posture toward Japan.[32] If America were drawn into a world war because of developments in the Far East, it would be less able to help

Britain because the American navy would be committed to Pacific defense. The United States would have to keep its fleet in the Pacific indefinitely—or at least until the navy was doubled in size. Meanwhile, it would be nearly helpless, in a crisis, to support the British fleet in the Atlantic. Thus, fighting Japan would not help Britain but would very likely help Germany.[33] Moreover, he argued in a *Nation* magazine article the same month, if Germany honored the Axis agreement, the United States would be confronted with an unprecedented two-front war.[34]

The "cooked-up hysteria" of New Deal foreign policy also overlooked the obvious fact that the United States had no interests in Indo-China. This area had been seized by an imperialist nation, France, in the nineteenth century, and the United States had never shown much concern. He reminded an audience in Cincinnati that collaborationist Vichy France, which maintained possession of Indo-China, was itself controlled by Germany.[35] Consequently, the United States had no direct concern there worthy of dragging the nation into a bloody, dangerous, and costly war.

Castle asserted that Roosevelt's policies, without protecting America's legitimate interests, had alienated pro-American groups inside Japan. Instead of demonstrating flexibility and the ability to negotiate realistically in light of changed military and economic realities in Asia, Roosevelt had needlessly endangered the nation. Castle periodically exchanged diaries with Ambassador Joseph Grew, and both agreed that Roosevelt had failed to understand Japan correctly or to listen to experts who did.[36]

The irrationality and obfuscation of propaganda particularly disturbed Castle because it made decision making difficult and eroded the validity of political judgment. He faulted the Roosevelt administration for misusing words that confused the public. Among the most misused words was "democracy." When Americans were told to take all measures "short of war" to protect democracies, most probably assumed that the word applied to countries ruled by their own people. In fact, the word was applied to areas such as Indo-China and Greece that were clearly not examples of democracies. In reality, the word had come to apply to any area fighting the Axis powers. Anticipating George Orwell, Castle feared that "doublespeak" and other loose, careless speech would have a direct impact on the quality of public thinking. Debased language, he told the Rotary Club of Washington, D.C., debased the intellect and threw democratic institutions into question. Linguistic manipulation by the administration constituted a moral failing. Other words that Castle believed had been used in duplicitous ways included measures short of war, neutrality, patriot, strength, truth, inevitable, and moral superiority.[37]

Castle, along with Hoover, berated the "smear campaign" of "forces and groups" urging our involvement in the war.[38] Part of the problem derived, he asserted, from the fact that the press, radio, and motion picture industries were heavily influenced by interventionist groups.[39] Because much of the "Great Debate" between interventionists and noninterventionists focused on Europe, he was not personally victimized by the mislabeling that Lindbergh, Flynn, and Senator Gerald Nye were often subjected to. Since Castle was most concerned and vocal about Roosevelt's policies in Asia, many of the most active interventionists ignored him. Nonetheless, when the profascist magazine *Today's Challenge* misquoted a speech he had made about Japan, Castle temporarily broke with his practice of not addressing obvious smears. He made a public defense of his antifascist stance in the *New York Tribune*.[40] In one egregious case of false labeling and sensationalism, a reporter from the *New York Post* reported that the Castle home at 2200 S Street, N.W., in Washington had become the underground headquarters of subversion:

> To it go the leading advocates of appeasement when they visit Washington. Its dining room and study are the scene of many little informal gatherings at which broad strategy and specific tactics in the guerrilla warfare against the Roosevelt Administration's foreign policy are discussed.[41]

Castle did recognize and defend himself against rational criticism,[42] but he always felt that defending himself against smears merely lent legitimacy to charges best ignored. Other members of the AFC disagreed with this insistence on distinguishing between rational criticism and propagandistic, *ad hominem* attacks, but Castle rarely varied from his position.[43] Possessing a basic suspicion that rational thinking was too infrequent even under normal circumstances, he deplored any group that substituted emotion for reason and refused to allow himself to get into such exchanges. Thus, he always preferred responding to criticism in written letters, interviews, speeches, and radio broadcasts.

In May 1941, Castle fell ill and his public opposition to intervention ended. By fall, he had improved and was selectively answering correspondence. In mid-November, he summarized his continued opposition to Roosevelt's Asian policy in a letter to the editor of the *New York Herald Tribune*, which ironically was not published until December 7, 1941. In it, he repeated the claim that there was still no rational reason for war with Japan, that reopening our markets to Japan would minimize the danger of an attack on the vulnerable Dutch East Indies, and that Roosevelt had yet to offer creative alternatives to the "all or nothing" proposals of recent months. Indeed, Japan had no motivation for getting out of China until better relations were discussed. If the United States could avoid war with the Japanese, the Chinese would eventually "wear them down"and remove the invaders themselves. In any case, it was still an "Asian question" that should be solved solely by Asians.[44] After the Hull ultimatum of November 26, Castle fully realized that his worst fears about inept negotiations by the administration had been realized and that his guarded optimism about maintaining peace, as expressed in a *Tribune* letter, was both ill-timed and uninformed.[45]

The attack on Pearl Harbor by Japanese forces on the morning of December 7, 1941, carried a particular horror for Castle. He had been born and educated in Honolulu, and his brother Alfred and his family lived there. Although he had been prepared for the "inevitable war" following the November 26th ultimatum to Japan, he had not dreamed that the Japanese would strike an area so close to the continental United States. Like so many others, he believed that if war came, it would start with an attack on the Philippines or the Dutch East Indies. Writing Hoover soon after the attack, he expressed perplexity at the nature of the attack "except of course that the military may have felt that such an attack would frighten the U.S. into an immediate peace," but he believed they "were fools to think that." Even though the Japanese civilian government would not likely have issued the orders for such an attack, they had permitted it to happen and thus would have to pay the consequences.[46] Hoover, writing the same day, concluded that the war was the result of Roosevelt's ineptitude:

> You and I know that this continuous putting pins in rattlesnakes finally got this country bitten. We also know that if Japan had been allowed to go on without these trade restrictions and provocations, she would have collapsed from internal economic reasons alone within a couple of years.

He urged Castle to help him document the mistakes of the past two years (1939–1941) for future generations.[47]

Because of the necessity of unity in a national crisis, Castle welcomed the dissolution of the America First Committee in 1942. Nonetheless, he continued to make infrequent comments about events leading up to the Pearl Harbor attack.[48] Although expressing wonder at the United States being caught by surprise, he believed that any investigation into the mistakes that had left America's most important Pacific base unprotected would hurt morale and should not be conducted until after the war.[49] Later that year, he urged Americans to avoid indiscriminate hatred of the

Japanese people. The war, he told an audience at Choate School, was with a militaristic government that would be discredited by its actions and would, after the war, be replaced by a liberal civilian government with which the United States could happily live.[50]

After years of historiographical consensus that placed the primary blame for Pearl Harbor on Japan's desire to dominate all of Asia and its concomitant aggression, historians have in recent years reassessed American policy.[51] Although few have concluded that William R. Castle was correct in his analysis of the internal dynamics of Japanese society in the late 1930s and early 1940s, many recent studies are in agreement with some of his basic observations.[52]

As early as the 1950s, historians were beginning to doubt that the United States had interests in the Pacific strong enough to risk a war that might detract from more pressing interests in Europe. Furthermore, historians, among them George F. Kennan, criticized the Roosevelt administration for not recognizing the changed balance of power in Asia by 1939 and for failing to negotiate in a flexible way. Stimson, for example, has been criticized by Kennan and others for having established an intransigent moral posture in Asia that outran the resources available to impose it.[53]

Another thesis similar to Castle's *realpolitik* position is Paul Schroeder's account in *The Axis Alliance and Japanese-American Relations*.[54] Until July 1941, Schroeder argues, the United States had pursued two limited objectives in the Far East: splitting the Axis and halting Japan's southward advance. After July 1941, however, Roosevelt abandoned these limited goals and attempted to liberate China. Schroeder claims, as Castle did in 1941, that this goal was neither in the interest of the United States nor attainable using peaceful means. Ironically, then, the use of economic pressure on Japan to liberate China while maintaining peace had failed to do either.

Akira Iriye, Waldo Heinrichs, and James B. Crowley have argued that Japan was primarily seeking economic expansion and national security. The failure of the United States to recognize these ends as legitimate and its inflexible negotiating positions eventually aided in the triumph of militant elements within Japan.[55]

Finally, Castle's sense that a realistic appraisal of American and European power in the Far East would have revealed that there were basic limits on what could reasonably be expected overseas has received recent support from the works of Christopher Thorne.[56] The failure of the Western powers to understand that they could no longer exercise the same degree of control in molding the political and economic climate in

Asia rendered real negotiation unlikely. Relegating all of Asia to second-class status meant there could be little room for compromise. Any real appreciation of the limits of their power came to Britain and France only in the 1950s, and perhaps not to the United States until the last months of the Vietnam conflict.

Despite the fact that many of his friends and most members of the AFC overestimated Castle's understanding of Japan, he nonetheless anticipated in his critique of Roosevelt's policy many of the issues raised by historians of U.S. intervention in later years. His concern about the domestic consequences of waging perpetual war for peace has received a friendlier response from historians in the post-Watergate, post-Vietnam environment. His early warnings about the domestic consequences of excessive power in the presidency, the concealment or distortion of information to achieve policy ends, and the futile attempt to impose American values by sword in contradiction to the nation's self-interest are commonplace today.

9

Opposition to World War II Foreign Policy

The Japanese attack on Pearl Harbor was sad confirmation of William R. Castle's worst fears about American foreign policy gone wrong. His opposition to U.S. intervention in the Far East had made him unpopular with many Democrats, interventionist Republicans, and President Roosevelt, who labeled him a defeatist. The war years were difficult for Castle; his prewar identification with the America First Committee, and former president Herbert Hoover, made it awkward to affect Republican opposition to Roosevelt. Castle nonetheless used his friendships with Hoover, members of the State Department, and key congressional leaders to influence Republican Party policy.

After the attack on Pearl Harbor, Castle joined Hoover and other former anti-interventionists in expressing support for the war effort. Japan was clearly wrong in attacking Hawaii and would have to pay the consequences. While publicly in favor of disbanding the America First Committee, Castle privately felt that Roosevelt's provocative policy toward Japan in the months before the attack had led to war. He agreed with Hoover that the "constant sticking of pins in rattlesnakes" had provoked Japan and that, had the U.S. been patient, Japan would have collapsed from overexpansion.[1] Although calling for anti-interventionists to join ranks with Roosevelt for the duration of the war, Castle agreed that the mistakes leading to Pearl Harbor would one day be investigated and that the position of the noninterventionists would be vindicated.

Hoover spent the night of December 11 at Castle's Washington house and there confided that he had information about a Rooseveltian move and asked Castle to record it but not disclose it. Specifically,

The Japanese had a very friendly talk with Roosevelt not long before he went to the Warm Springs and he told them to take up details with Hull. They thought then that peace was assured. They agreed with the President that matters would be taken up in a five power conference to be called to keep the peace in the Pacific, a conference between the United States, Britain, Japan, China, and the Dutch. The Japanese agreed that Chiang Kai Shek's government should represent China. They agreed that matters would remain in status quo for six months, or until the conference should be concluded, in other words that they would make no move toward the Indies or Russia.

The United States was to study a new trade treaty and open trade on some basis immediately. It was generally understood, also, that the Japanese would withdraw back of the Great Wall immediately, keeping only certain garrisons in the ports. But when the President left something happened. Either Hull had word from Tokyo or the Chinese ambassador had over-persuaded him. At any rate he became very belligerent, would not agree to any such terms, insisted that nothing could be done until the Japanese got out of China completely, and really issued an ultimatum. It was clear that there was no longer any hope of a happy solution of the negotiations.

Cordell Hull, the longest-serving secretary of state in U.S. history (1933–1944), frequently shared information and discussed foreign affairs with the Republican Castle while serving in the Democratic administration of Franklin D. Roosevelt. (Library of Congress photo LC-USZ62-94179.)

Moreover, according to Hoover, Bernard Baruch had spoken with the two Japanese ambassadors, Kichisaburo Nomura and Saburo Kurusu, learned of their concessions regarding resumption of U.S. trade, and had visited the White House to urge the president to accept. Roosevelt dismissed any further effort as "too late." Hoover believed this was due either to Roosevelt's lax administrative discipline or perhaps even a "doublecross" by the Japanese.[2] All this reinforced a sense that the United States had been thrust into a dangerous war that would elevate the presidency, undermine the nation's economic strength, and endanger civil liberties. Hoping to persuade congressional leaders to challenge Roosevelt's foreign policy, Castle on December 12 hosted a dinner for Senator Arthur H. Vandenberg, and Congressmen Hugh Butler, Curley Brooks, and Bill Ditter. Hoover and the party leaders outlined future Republican opposition to Roosevelt's policy. Believing that many of the New Deal programs had been mismanaged and wasteful, all agreed that Republicans could remain an alternative to the Democrats if they argued the need for the war to be honestly and efficiently administered; that censorship be kept to a minimum; that the truth of America's unpreparedness at Pearl Harbor be investigated; and that the party serve as loyal opposition during the war and refrain from divisive attacks on the government. Behind these positions lay the assumption that Roosevelt would misuse the national emergency to usurp power and undermine civil and economic liberties. Dreading extension of the New Deal in the economy and diminished civil liberties, the group insisted on the right of responsible, if subdued, opposition. Moreover, feeling that the war with Japan would be long, they feared high taxes, a permanent military buildup, a militarized economy, and dominance for the Democratic Party. The expense of a long war might be great, and some Republicans, including Castle and Hoover, favored a negotiated peace. A settlement to split the axis would preserve Japan's territorial integrity, avoid reparations, resume relations with Japan's moderate civilian leadership, provide a barrier to Soviet expansion in the Pacific, and resume trade.[3] Clearly, they felt that survival of the party would influence the peace while downplaying the now unpopular position of Republicans before the war.[4]

Accepting his role as a behind-the-scenes advisor to Hoover and other Republican leaders, Castle made himself available as a sounding board, convener, editor, and strategist.

Castle spent the next six months exchanging critiques of Roosevelt's war strategy. One senses that he and other Republicans were struggling to define an alternative to the strategy in hope of preparing for the 1942 congressional elections. On February 11, 1942, Governor Alfred Landon, the editor Felix Morley, and Castle agreed that the United States should ensure that the Soviet Union did not sign a separate peace with Japan and Germany. Republicans, they felt, should remind America not to trust Soviet intentions regarding Asia and Europe. Although the Soviets had agreed to the January 1, 1942, Declaration of the United Nations, in which the powers at war with the Axis pledged no separate peace, Castle's supporters remained suspicious of actual Soviet designs throughout the war. Ever the realist, Castle felt that Republicans should be suspicious even of Britain's aims, particularly since the United States had little to gain from continuation of the British Empire's system of trade preference. If Japan should seize Singapore and other colonial holdings in Southeast Asia, Prime Minister Winston Churchill could lose control and Britain negotiate a separate peace.[5]

Castle argued that permanent peace would be best served by an economically restored and democratic Japan. Rejecting the scholar Owen Lattimore's contention that China was inherently more democratic and civilized than Japan, and hence a natural postwar partner, he retained his suspicion of China's ability to serve as a barrier to the expansion of communism.[6] He saw little hope in Chiang Kai-shek's leadership and predicted a long civil war leading to the triumph of a communist state.

Castle's sense of how the postwar world should look, as well as how Republican leadership could oppose the war, was sharpened by detailed advice to Hoover and the latter's close friend, Hugh Gibson. Hoover and Gibson submitted a draft of what was to become their book, *Problems of a Lasting Peace*. It sought to please both the Wendell Willkie interventionists and the Robert A. Taft noninterventionists. Hoover felt that the book manuscript, reviewed by Castle, could unify the party and assist in the fall elections.[7]

Hoover and Gibson's manuscript diagnosed the forces that had led to the collapse of peace. Among them was the inability to deal with cynical European politics during World War I, the assessing of guilt for the war to Germany by the United States, maintaining a postarmistice food blockade against Germany, allowing a $430 billion bill for reparations to bleed Germany's economy, changing borders to divide German-speaking peoples, and allowing the dream of open diplomacy and open covenants to die. President Woodrow Wilson, earnest but callow, was doomed from the start by European politics. His error was not to realize how such forces as economics, ideologies, imperialism, militarism, nationalism, and fear drove diplomacy.

The remainder of the book dared to prescribe steps to influence events after the war. Decrying high ideals, Hoover and Gibson believed in a realist approach. They argued that there should be no formal peace conference. The United Nations, they felt, should make agreements in advance of a settlement. Any foundation for peace would need democracy, representative government, and free enterprise. Moreover, disarmament should be for the victors as well as the defeated. Economic blockades should be lifted after the war and trade reestablished. Military and government leaders who had started the war should be punished, but reparations avoided, as should collection of debts. The victors must provide economic aid to the vanquished and deal with the suffering of displaced persons. As to borders, the book called for regional commissions of representatives of the allies. Only after these steps could a world organization—a United Nations—be created.[8] Knowing that the book was part of an emerging Republican opposition, as well as a basis to unite a party divided by debate over intervention before Pearl Harbor, Castle read the manuscript carefully. Although he agreed with the historical sections, he criticized the authors for being less than completely realistic in imagining what a postwar world would look like. His most important objection was to the recreation of "all the little nations of Europe" to ensure that every nationality had its country. Castle saw this as an invitation to future wars as small nations competed for resources.

> It would seem to me in distinction from this that the whole tendency of the war was to do away with these endless independent units in favor of larger economic blocs. It seems to me that if you had retained, after the last war, the Austrian Empire with a very large measure of autonomy for the different races, these races would have come to realize that the working together of the whole as an economic unit was their only salvation. Whether such a plan could be carried into effect now I very much doubt, because these little nations have tasted the horrors of freedom, and instead of being willing to cure the ills they have run into by some kind of confederation, I am afraid they are much more likely to want to cure these ills by trying to conquer their neighbors. Although you could not create empires in this way, I am not at all sure that you could not create economic blocs in which some one nation would be pretty sure to be the directing force.

Moreover, Castle had, since the 1920s, been an advocate of allowing regional economic blocs to "police" their regions to guarantee peace and stability. Although agreeing that it was not an ideal solution for world peace, he looked favorably upon the U.S. economic domination of Latin America and the resulting relative stability. In the late 1920s, he had despaired of French economic domination of Europe and had held out hope that a restored post–World War I Germany might serve as a regional policeman for Europe.[9] Indeed, he had also argued before Pearl Harbor that Japan should be recognized by the United States as having a regional interest in Asia, similar to the dominance of the United States in Latin America.[10] Regional blocs, operating out of self-interest, would likely avoid wars, facilitate trade, and police the smaller states that they dominated economically to provide order. Castle suggested that Hoover and Gibson's idea of equal access to raw materials would be a force for peace. If the regional economic blocs could agree that it was in their own interest to grant equal access to raw materials under their control at market prices, an important temptation for war would be removed. Britain, with its colonial trade restrictions, had caused great mischief in the past and must, he felt, be part of any such agreement. For Castle, self-interest was, correctly organized, an ally of peace and was not fully or squarely faced in the book. Idealistic solutions to the problems of a fallen world would never work. Indeed, for the self-described "hard-boiled" realist,

> if anything at all is going to be saved of civilization we shall have to call a halt somehow, even if that halt shall be only a truce. It is worth remembering that there are truces which, in the course of time, develop into lasting peace, perhaps not the kind one would long for, but nevertheless something better than war, just as much as there are truces which are only breathing spaces to prepare even more lethal weapons. Furthermore, I find it, myself, difficult to envisage a very happy world if the United Nations win, because, so far as Europe is concerned, it looks as though that would be a domination by the Soviets and people who believe that Stalin is more noble than Hitler are just crazy. I quite see, on the other hand, that in writing the book you have to make that assumption. You have to do that because otherwise you would be totally out of temper with current thinking and would be held up to scorn as a defeatist.[11]

Although the authors were unwilling to accept the regional bloc concept, the three were in broad agreement about the course Republican opposition should take. All were opposed to Willkie's idealistic plans for "one world" as well as Roosevelt's manipulation of the truth and "mismanagement" of the war, wartime censorship, and hysterical propaganda aimed at promoting hostile public opinion toward Germany and Japan. All three deplored the liberal, internationalist wing of the Republican Party, led by Willkie, which advocated purging or marginalizing those who had become "ostriches" and "turtles" in the face of fascist aggression. All three sought a resumption of normal debate, the resurrection of a viable Republican loyal opposition to Roosevelt, and the renewed vigor of the conservative wing of the party under the direction of Robert Taft and perhaps Hoover himself.[12] Castle's role would be to quietly advance this agenda as a valued advisor to Hoover, Taft, Congressmen Joseph Martin and John Vorys, and other leaders of the conservative wing. His advice would be listened to, if not always followed.[13] Castle was a staunch opponent of wartime censorship.

In May 1942, preparing for his first speech on the war, Hoover asked Castle to discuss with Charles Evans Hughes (for whom Castle had great regard) the themes of his book. Hoover was frustrated that his May 20 speech in New York had been refused radio coverage because of possible controversy, and he wanted an endorsement from Hughes, the former chief justice of the Supreme Court and former secretary of state, for his peace plans. To Hoover's disappointment, Hughes thought the book ought not to be published. With the war going badly and Russia's ability to survive in question, Hughes felt plans for peace were premature. Moreover, if Russia were successful in driving Hitler out, it would demand a larger role in any peace.

With incompatible ideologies, the United States and Russia would have different ideas for a postwar world.[14] The themes for Hoover's radio speech included the need for limited dictatorial powers for a wartime president, the need for debate about the conduct of the war and the postwar peace, the necessity of avoiding social "engineering" or experimentation during the war, the need to avoid intolerance of dissent or blind hatred of current enemies of the United States, and the need to plan for the efficient sharing of food after the war among friends as well as enemies.[15] When political commentators praised the speech, Castle, Landon, Hoover, and Gibson felt the tide might finally be turned in their favor and the basis for a solid Republican op-

Charles Evans Hughes, the first secretary of state for whom Castle worked, remained a friend and confidant for life. Castle regarded him as a moral exemplar comparable to his own father. (Library of Congress photo LC-USZ62-103904.)

position laid.[16] Subsequent speeches by Castle and Landon repeating the themes of *Problems of a Lasting Peace* were also well received by special audiences.[17] These addresses were conciliatory to Roosevelt in that all three speakers granted that FDR had the right to infringe on the free-enterprise system and to censor selectively during a national emergency. By extending the olive branch to the Roosevelt administration, Landon, Castle, and Hoover felt that they could be "more hard-boiled" later while gaining access to valuable press coverage and media approval.[18]

A theme in the Castle-Hoover conversations and their communications with Republican leaders was the Roosevelt administration's failure to conduct the war efficiently. Both blamed many of the 1942 military setbacks on waste and confusion in the administration, and they distrusted Stalin's desire to stay in the war. The delays in equipping the army and building adequate shipping would, they felt, reduce U.S. chances to dictate the terms of the peace and enlarge Stalin's influence. In addition, the alliance with Stalin, and to a lesser extent with Britain, detracted from American ideals. Indeed, these allies, particularly Stalin, "confused" Americans, who perceived the war as a crusade for liberty and were not likely to commit lives and resources to perpetuate the British Empire in India, Singapore, Hong Kong, and Malaysia and the Soviet empire.[19]

Contemptuous of talk that the end of the war might come soon, Castle and Hoover, by the summer of 1942, had reached what they felt were more realistic appraisals of war strategy. Both believed that Japan, with interests at stake in Asia, would not likely come to the aid of Germany in Europe. Japan would, if the war continued long enough, wear out its welcome in Asia and face unprecedented wars of national liberation in Southeast Asia. Facing continued war with China and the consequences of an overextended empire, Japan might be persuaded to retreat to the more modest borders of Korea, Manchuria, and Formosa. With respect to the Soviet Union, it was not likely that this hidebound totalitarian empire could survive the German assault. If this assault could be achieved at great price to Germany, both felt it could weaken the primary enemy of the United States while eliminating the baneful influence of a communist country. To that end, Castle and Hoover called for a war of attrition, avoidance of a second front in Western Europe, and the continuation of aid to the staggering Soviet Union. Nothing would be worse than the "useless slaughter" of American youth for the salvation of the Soviets.[20] The two differed only on the likelihood of a separate peace. Hoover was convinced that Russia would, as it had in 1918, suddenly declare a separate peace; Stalin could not stand up to mounting criticism by his own people who were suffering, due in part to his incompetence. Castle, however, felt that Stalin would not sue for an independent peace because he needed the war to rally his subservient subjects behind him. Besides, too many lives had been lost in the brutal, bitter fighting for either side to back down.[21] Both men realized, however, that their influence over military strategy was nonexistent; their real agenda was to question FDR's efficacy and to prepare the Republican Party to resume a viable opposition to wartime policy.[22]

Confirmation of his marginality to the war effort came in the late summer and early fall of 1942. A surprised Castle was invited by the Office of War Information to write a series of scripts for five-minute broadcasts to Japan. Robert E. Sherwood, director of overseas operations for the OWI, believed that Castle's reputation in Japan and contacts with leading Japanese moderates before the war made him a good candidate for broadcasts aimed at undermining Japanese militarism. Despite knowing that his words would have little impact in Japan, Castle was delighted to have a useful, if limited, role in government. His strategy was to appeal to Japan's moderates, for whom Castle still had considerable goodwill, while attempting to review the long and basically friendly relations between the two countries before 1931. His broadcasts appealed to Japanese civilians to reassert their authority and end the "futile" war with the United States. Castle had always deplored the racist assaults on the Japanese that had accompanied the Pearl Harbor attack. Refusing to condemn all Japanese for what he considered the wrongs of the military leadership, he hoped his broadcasts might one day be made available to the American press. Alas, in September, a reporter for the *Times-Herald* discovered the broadcasts and decried Castle as "an appeaser" and associate of Hoover. For reasons unknown to Castle or his friends in the OWI, Robert Sherwood ordered that the broadcasts be discontinued at once. Appeals by Arthur Krock to restart the broadcasts were ineffective with Sherwood, who would only say that the order came from the top and that OWI policy required a blanket condemnation of Japan.[23] Clearly the stain of active opposition to Roosevelt before the war had not been removed.

The elections of November 1942 were promising for the Republicans, who gained ten Senate seats and forty-seven seats in the House of Representatives. The electoral victories, though not definitive, indicated to Castle that Hoover's strategies for peace and criticisms of how the war was being conducted would be taken seriously by the press. To promote more efficient management of food resources in the United States, massive aid in food to the occupied democracies, and his outline for peace in *Problems of a Lasting Peace,* Castle convinced Hoover to meet with key new Republican senators. On February 7, 1943, Hoover met privately with nine senators in Castle's house and reviewed with them his hopes for the Republican Party. Castle briefed Hoover before dinner on the background of the new senators, their strengths and weaknesses as he saw them. As had often been the case in the past, Hoover looked to Castle for an honest (often brutally so) assessment of personalities, which Hoover would use to further his agenda for the party.

At dinner, Hoover urged the senators to support his critique of the war and to work to establish credibility from a strong loyal opposition. Specifically, he called for Republicans to take political advantage of the meat and milk shortages in the United States, which were due, as Hoover saw it, to mismanagement by the Roosevelt administration. As opposed to government regimentation and ration cards in World War II, Americans had experienced no food shortages and relatively little coercion during the cooperative days of the Great War. The proper organization for Hoover was the division of civilian activities under functional groupings, each headed by a single administrator responsible for all functions of government related to his group of activities. Where possible, decentralization could avoid bureaucracy if state agencies were employed in a cooperative administrative arrangement. He also called for a limit on the military draft and the deployment of one million workers for farming, mining, and oil drilling. To add to production, he urged Republicans to fight Roosevelt's farm-price policy and to create free-market incentives for farmers to maximize output. He finally asked the senators to advocate for his peace plan, which featured protection of American interests, cooperation among sovereign states, the avoidance of a world state, and a careful transition and cooling-off period before permanent postwar borders were redrawn.[24] Castle's role was to assist this agenda further by serving as a liaison, a speech writer, a sounding board, and a source of information for Hoover and like-minded Republicans.

In March, Harrison Spangler, GOP national chairman and ally of Hoover, asked Castle to rewrite an address by Landon on foreign relations. A poor writer, Landon intended to speak out on behalf of Hoover's agenda; Castle, who was familiar with the nuances and origins of that position, was a natural to refine Landon's ideas. The speech warned against believing too easily the idealistic schemes for the future of Europe and called for maintaining a free hand for the United States after the war. At the request of Representative John Vorys, Castle set up a dinner for Hoover to advance his cause with new Republican representatives. Repeating the points he had made with the freshman senators, Hoover asked Castle to use every influence he had to undermine Willkie's influence in the Republican Party by exposing the flaws in his "vague internationalism."[25]

While meeting with senators and representatives to explain and advocate Hoover's proposed policies, Castle was also, in conversation with current and former State Department officials such as Joe Green and Gene Dooman, refining his views on the Soviet Union. Castle's suspicion and dislike of the Soviet state was intensified when he learned from Dooman that the Russian people were not being told about the extent of American lend-lease aid. This secrecy, as well as the apparent ineptitude of America's lend-lease representatives in Russia, had fed suspicions among the populace that America was not contributing to their war effort. To make matters worse, contacts in the American Red Cross found that $15 million worth of damaged supplies had been confiscated by the government and placed on sale in ships in Moscow and St. Petersburg.[26] Castle warned Republican leaders and sympathetic State Department professionals that Russia's war aims were radically different from those of the United States. Driven by motives of aggrandizement, Stalin had "made up his mind what he wants territorially and knows that neither England nor the U.S. will fight to prevent it. His voice will be the principal voice of the peace conference. He fully intends to dominate Europe and beyond that is not particularly interested."[27] Castle felt that any definitive peace plan was academic because Stalin, by dominating much of eastern Europe and perhaps China, would be able to dictate peace terms. Such terms would have no reference to the Atlantic Charter.

With respect to Asia, Castle found that it was in the interest of the Soviet Union to prolong America's war with Japan as long as possible. This was made more likely by what he saw as the fatal mistake of demanding an unconditional surrender of Japan. He predicted that the Japanese would fight to the end if conditions to protect the emperor's throne and some minor territorial concessions were not made. With the United States tied up in a costly and endless war, the Soviet Union would consolidate its position in China. Chiang Kai-shek was not likely to deal effectively with Mao and the communist insurgents. Indeed, Chiang could barely deal with his allies among the warlords. Roosevelt did not seem willing to realize "that the Russians are Asiatic, as different from us as are the Japanese, and simply laugh at all our idealism which they consider mere sentimentality, as often it is."[28]

A primary activity for Castle during the war years was using his contacts to defend Hoover from allegations that he had been an appeaser of

Germany and Japan before the war. After Hoover gave a speech in the Senate warning of a possible domestic food shortage, Senator Green attacked Hoover as a defeatist and alarmist who had warned of huge food shortages during World War I which had never materialized. Further, Green had claimed in an April 1943 attack that Hoover had tried to prevent the War Department from sending a large army overseas for fear that the nation would starve without adequate farm labor. The speech clearly did not represent Hoover's views, and Castle privately asked Representative Dewey Short to object to the treatment in a speech before the House. Short later extracted an apology from War Department officials who had provided incomplete and incorrect information to Senator Green.[29] Hoover's standing as an expert on food policy was a key to his visibility during the war and also a critical component of responsible opposition by the Republican Party.

In the spring of 1943, the highly respected English author and political analyst Rebecca West wrote an article for the *Atlantic Monthly* describing *Problems of a Lasting Peace* as "an illiterate and ignorant book." Her article renewed questions of Hoover's affinity to those who most opposed intervention before Pearl Harbor and criticized his willingness to win the war, his desire to ship food to the conquered allies, and his lack of appreciation for the contributions of the British Empire.[30] Not wishing to respond directly, Hoover urged Castle to send a sharp private rebuke to the editor and write a strong public response. Castle's theme in his response was that West had misrepresented Hoover's position and that the timing of her attack might hurt the Allies' efforts to win the war. No friend of the British Empire, Castle saw the article as an example of the British putting their colonial holdings above the interests of the United States.[31] Clearly, in his loyalty to Hoover, Castle (who himself had questions about the book's argument) overreacted to West's legitimate analysis of a flawed book. Castle and Hoover were sometimes narrow in their views and unaccepting of criticism. Rather than attack the substance of an opponent's argument, both tended to suspect the personal motives for positions opposed to their own. This was particularly true where New Deal advocates were involved. Perhaps to different degrees, both were victims of their own sensitivity to and awareness of the extent to which organized propaganda had come to erode the vitality of public discourse. Both had grown up and had productive professional lives at the very time that behaviorist psychological theory and organized modern advertising, combined with massive government manipulation of public opinion, had changed the way people regarded public speeches and official pronouncements.[32]

In October of 1943, Secretary of State Hull obtained a "declaration" in Moscow which became the object of considerable scorn by Castle and like-minded Republicans. At the Moscow Conference the Soviets, British, and Chinese pledged to cooperate in creating a postwar international organization. An overoptimistic Hull subsequently reported to Congress that the declaration would render needless spheres of influence and alliances to achieve a balance of power. If true, this would indeed have represented a radical break with the Euro-American diplomatic past. The interest of the declaration was to force an open, democratic, and cooperative world in eastern Europe. Hoover was more enthusiastic about the Moscow Conference than Castle, in part because Hull attributed the impetus for its declaration to Hoover's own thinking about peace.[33] The Moscow Conference had gotten Hoover's idea of a transition period before permanent borders were redrawn and an international peacekeeping entity established. In addition, Hoover approved of the degree of consultation and cooperation promised by the conference and the protection of sovereign equality in a prospective world peacekeeping body.[34]

Castle and Landon, however, were more cautious in their understanding of the conference. On December 3, 1943, Castle hosted a small press briefing with Landon in his home. Meeting with notable newspapermen, including Bert Hullen, Fred Simpich, and Larry Sullivan, Castle and Landon agreed that it would be impolitic for the Republicans to endorse the Moscow declarations before determining how Stalin interpreted the informal agreements. Although a step in the right direction, both told newsmen, if Stalin got to Berlin first, he would ignore the declarations and dictate his own terms for eastern Europe. In any case, both felt that Hull's exuberant claims that the need for divisive spheres of influence had ended was inane and represented a continuing inability of the Roosevelt administration to separate Stalin's manipulative talk from reality.[35] When Landon repeated his reservations in the *New York Herald Tribune* and the *New York Times,* Hoover was caused some embarrassment. The latter moved quickly in fact to interpret Landon's public objections to a natural caution and not to any political split that rival Willkie might exploit.[36] In retrospect, the United States would develop a sphere of influence in Italy and western Europe which would be opposed by Stalin's sphere in eastern Europe. The realist Castle was prescient in this instance.

In the fall of 1943, Hoover and Castle expressed interest in the administration's proposed United Nations Relief and Rehabilitation Agency (UNRRA). Although Churchill remained opposed to U.S. food relief to the occupied democracies, FDR had become convinced that such relief was necessary to stabilize postwar Europe. Indeed, as early as May of 1943, a resolution sponsored by Senator Taft called for hearings before the Foreign Relations Committee. The hearings on Resolution 100 would determine whether ample reason and a sufficient constituency existed for an immediate extension of food relief to the occupied territories. A growing number of organizations and legislators had come to support the resolution by November of 1943. Both Castle and Hoover saw the popularity of the resolution, which was largely based on Hoover humanitarianism even in the face of the existing Anglo-American blockade of the occupied territories. To assist Hoover, Castle wrote friends advocating a greater role for Hoover as an expert for food relief.[37] Moreover, Castle echoed Hoover's advocacy for preventing the consumer nations from determining the prices of food to American farm suppliers.[38] Castle argued in numerous informal talks with Republican congressmen that food supplied should be sold on credit rather than being given as an outright gift. Loans of food would, it was hoped, stimulate productivity and conservation while restoring commercial agricultural relations in the recipient countries.[39] Visiting with Representative Vorys in December of 1943, Castle urged a speedy consideration of the bill before Congress. Part of the strategy they developed to obtain an appropriation for UNRRA was to prevent the funds from going to the president, where they would be spent without congressional review. Furthermore, both concluded that a limited appropriation which would not continue beyond the war would prevent the UNRRA from exercising automatic and protracted influence. With this strategy the noninternationalist wing of the Republican and Democratic parties would be more likely to support the measure.[40] The strategy, which also stressed the need for congressional independence from undue presidential interference, was successful. The UNRRA, however, would not itself be effective until after World War II due to Churchill and Roosevelt's reluctance to alter the blockade of Europe.

The year 1944 opened with Castle seeking to be of use to Hoover and the party as it prepared for the November elections. Active with the U.S. Chamber of Commerce Committee on Postwar Planning, he visited Secretary of State Cordell Hull to find out FDR's plans for Europe and Asia. Hull, whom Castle liked as much as any of the war-time cabinet, confided some of the details of the Moscow Conference. At a January 27th meeting, Hull told Castle of his frustrations in getting Stalin or Molotov to reveal their battle strategy against Germany. Nonetheless, he felt Stalin would enter the war against Japan after Germany was defeated. Castle had always feared Russian involvement with the United States against the Japanese, as it would mean an expansion of Russian power in the Pacific after the war. The ease with which Hull could accept Russia's engagement with Japan disturbed him. Moreover, the fact that Hull had overlooked Stalin's reluctance to permit U.S. veto power over Soviet actions in eastern Europe at the Moscow Conference led him to conclude that "when you come down to bedrock Hull does not know the Russians; they probably both liked and flattered him and he believed a lot more of what they told him than I should have." [41] Though he found Hull completely honest (unlike FDR), Castle came away from the meeting feeling that Republicans could make political headway by charging the Democrats with vague internationalism and credulity when it came to the devious Stalin.[42]

In anticipation of the November 1944 election, Castle joined Hoover in the winter and spring of that year in advocating their view of an international organization. Specifically, both were concerned that the Republicans might rush the formation of a collective peacekeeping body in order not to lose the initiative to FDR.[43] Hoover continued to warn that permanent peace arrangements should not predate the end of fighting, when the actual strength of the Allies would be known. Further, a transition period in which wartime passions cooled would permit a more judicial assessment of permanent arrangements for postwar organization. Any commitments made by the United States before the war ended would tie the hands of the country and preempt important revisions in strategic thinking. Indeed, like Castle, Hoover blamed the failures of the League of Nations on a combination of Wilsonian idealism and the founding of the League before actual order had been restored to Europe.[44] Castle, more convinced than Hoover that Hull and Roosevelt had been seduced by Stalin at the Tehran and Moscow conferences, argued that the transition period advocated by Hoover should be limited to six months, as a longer period would open the door to Soviet meddling in western Europe.[45] Moreover, Castle worried that giving Stalin a role as a peacekeeping trustee during a prolonged transition period would consolidate his control of eastern Europe while strengthening his hand in a permanent United Nations.[46]

By the summer of 1944, Castle agreed with Hoover that Thomas Dewey, a moderate internationalist, was the best chance the Republicans had to defeat FDR. Although both had rejoiced at the withdrawal of Willkie from the race in April, neither was enthusiastic about Dewey's experience in foreign affairs or the likelihood of his adhering to a foreign or domestic policy sufficiently distinct from FDR's. Although both would have preferred John Bricker as the candidate, they felt FDR was not likely to lose the election given the continuation of the war. Hoping to influence the Republican platform, if not the actual policies of Dewey, Hoover had Castle review and make suggestions on his proposed foreign-policy speech to the Republican convention.[47] Warning Hoover that it would be condemned as "isolationist" by detractors, he could recommend no changes in the "courageous speech" and urged that it be made as a bold challenge to FDR's variant of internationalism. Hoover and Castle agreed that if Dewey adopted the main outline of the speech, American voters would have a clear choice in the November elections. On June 27, the elder Republican statesman delivered his speech at the convention. Echoing now-familiar themes, Hoover called for a realistic appraisal of the emerging postwar world. Nationalism had rendered otiose the idealistic calls for a supergovernment to keep a lasting peace. After an indefinite transition period, peace would be based upon cooperation between independent sovereign states. Specifically, three or four great centers of power—the United States, perhaps China or France— would police their own geographic areas and be responsible for peace. After a transition, a world organization with divisions for Europe, Asia, and the Western Hemisphere would maintain peace through cooperation between the powers. Hoover criticized FDR for engaging in a vague "balance of power diplomacy" and for playing the role of broker between Russia and Britain. Roosevelt, Hoover maintained, looked foolish appearing at summit conferences and should remain at home.[48] The Republican platform was clearly influenced by Hoover's advocacy, and both he and Castle were pleased with the speech's reception. Specifically, the foreign-policy platform called for postwar peace through "organized international cooperation and not by joining a world state." Furthermore, while calling for some form of participation in a world state, it called for caution in proceeding.[49]

Despite Hoover's apparent influence on the platform, Dewey and Herbert Brownell, the new chairman of the Republican National Committee, had no plans to use him or Castle in their campaign. Indeed, Dewey and his campaign staff went out of their way to avoid associating with the "Hoover crowd" for fear of being tainted by their prewar opposition to FDR's policies and war preparations. Dewey's campaign also featured a moderate Republican position with respect to New Deal reforms and downplayed specifics regarding what he would do if elected.[50] After the expected defeat of Dewey in November, Castle analyzed the foreign-policy consequences of the election in a letter to Hoover:

> My friends in the State Department are terribly worried as to what is going to happen there. Everyone seems to feel that Hull is just about finished. Even though he does not always know

what it is about, he is an honest fellow and seems to hold the Department more or less together. Ed Stettinius has evidently proved himself a failure on organizational matters, and it may be true that nobody could do any good in a place where conflict is as rife as it is there. Of course, there are all kinds of rumors. The fact that Roosevelt said at a Press conference recently that he considered [Henry] Wallace the man in the country best qualified on foreign affairs might be a build-up to make him Secretary of State. And that would be a tragedy. A good many people seem to think that Ball has a chance. That would be fantastic because he knows nothing and, of course, the only possible explanation, if it happened, would be that he had been bribed with that offer to desert Dewey. I don't at all like the outlook.[51]

Castle and Hoover could find small consolation in the fact that FDR would not likely be around in 1948 and with the reduction of his vote in 1944 from the 1940 election, he might be more restrained in domestic and foreign policy.[52] Still, both knew that conservatives had a major task ahead of them and future success was far from guaranteed. The forces of collectivism were ascendant and the virtues of individual responsibility and individual freedom seemed increasingly abstract to the world population. Nonetheless, Hoover urged Castle to "push the stone uphill again" and continue his critique of the disastrous New Deal foreign policy.[53]

This critique, urged by Hoover, was continued with Castle's detailed analysis of the recent Dumbarton Oaks proposals. From August 21 to October 7, representatives from the United States, Britain, China, and Russia met in Washington to plan for a new peacekeeping organization. Its draft proposals became the basis of the United Nations Charter, which would be considered at the San Francisco Conference in April of 1945. In the December issue of the journal *World Affairs,* Castle wrote an article detailing his reservations regarding charter provisions for the UN. Although praising the efforts of the leading allies for showing a willingness to work together for peace, he cautioned U.S. policy makers not to commit the country to any irrevocable agreements until the nature of the peace to be won was known. In brief, Castle found the charter deficient for three reasons:

(1) The proposals failed to provide adequately for regional considerations. With the permanent members of the Security Council to come from the Big Four, the council might not fairly represent the interests of smaller nations. Castle strongly endorsed direct representation of all important regions at all times and feared that the consequence for lack of

such representation would be unrest. Thus, the nonpermanent members of the Council should be elected from definite regions (Far East, Latin America, Near East, and Africa).

(2) The UN should, as a condition of membership, require small, economically dependent countries to form economic blocs without tariffs or other hindrances to trade. Had this been done after World War I, as Castle had urged, the smaller European nations would have been less threatened by Hitler in the 1930s. The UN could be the proper lever to effect this kind of collaboration.

(3) The U.S. Constitution was the law of the land and the right of Congress to declare war must be protected. Since the delegate to the Security Council would be the president's representative, he would be able to authorize punitive or "sanitary" expeditions with narrow and limited goals. However, any significant, protracted conflict with a major power authorized by the UN would need authorization by Congress.

Castle also criticized the lack of power given the proposed assembly where every nation would be represented. The disproportionate power of the Security Council made the UN less democratic than the covenant of the League of Nations. This limitation on democracy was ironic in light of the Atlantic Charter of professed goals of the war.[54]

Subsequent to this public critique, which had held out hope for the cooperative venture at Dumbarton Oaks, Castle met with Hoover to discuss their private assessment of the war and the prospects for peace. As Castle noted in his diary,

> Hoover believes in going ahead in the attempt to form some kind of international organization to keep the peace but thinks, as I do, that it is more or less academic for the reason that there is little sign of peace in Europe outside of England and not much sign there so long as Churchill is in control; also because he knows that peace depends on really good relations between the three great powers and does not believe that will be possible for any length of time. He wonders why the Russian advance has been so rapid, or rather says that it is because there has been little opposition, the Germans retreating as fast as they can. The Army people with whom he has talked believe it probable that the Germans will soon make a firm stand which will slow things up for a time, but they are afraid, just as Hoover is, that if Stalin has gone far enough into Germany to make it certain that he is victor he may listen to peace overtures.[55]

Both men were discouraged with the prospects for peace and Roosevelt's ability to handle Stalin at the upcoming conference in the Crimea. Hoover confided in Castle that he had not wanted the United States to intervene in the war in Europe in the period 1935–1941, primarily because he felt "Stalin would take control of matters, Britain would almost have to play ball with him, and our role would be largely to pay the bills and dance when they pulled the strings." Both men also felt that Stalin, frustrated in his prewar plan to acquire the Baltic provinces and perhaps part of Poland, had made his alliance with Hitler in 1939 in part to obtain them and, despite the surprise attack by Hitler in 1941, had managed to acquire even more of eastern Europe than he had originally hoped for. Both also believed that FDR would come back from Yalta with "all sorts of agreements signed by Hitler," declare a diplomatic victory, and later be betrayed by a scheming Stalin.[56]

Hearing a speech by Thomas Dewey pledging Republican support for the Dumbarton Oaks draft, Castle wondered whether Dewey really believed his own optimism. A darker assessment revealed that

> We have been extraordinarily foolish in our treatment of the Soviets because we did nothing to look after our own interests and our own ideals when we held all the cards. Had we done so, the situation today would have been far more hopeful. Now we have comparatively little to bargain with and if the Russians take Berlin in the immediate future even that little will disappear. We seem to have started a real push on the western front and that should materially help the Russians but whatever we do we shall not reach Berlin as soon as they—unless they stop—and when they are there the peace terms are in their own hands.[57]

By mid-February the details of the Yalta agreement were released to the public. Provisions included Stalin's secret promise to enter the war against Japan two to three months after the defeat of Germany. The Soviet Union also received concessions in Manchuria and in the territories that it had lost to Japan in the Russo-Japanese War of 1904–1905; Stalin recognized Chiang Kai-shek and promised to urge Mao to end the civil war; Stalin dropped demands for stiff reparations from Germany, accepting a temporary partitioning of Germany with future discussions by a reparations committee; Stalin agreed to plans for a UN conference to be held in San Francisco in April to establish a permanent collective security organization; agreement that Stalin would remain dominant in eastern Europe with vague promises of democratic elections to be held after the war in occupied countries such as Poland. Reviewing the results of the conference, Castle concluded that Stalin had gotten every important objective he had in 1941 and that the would never uphold the vague promises regarding Poland and eastern Europe. Indeed, "in the pictures of the three great men, he [FDR] looks like a senile old man with Churchill and Stalin buttering him up so that he will agree." [58] As to reports that Stalin had reached an agreement on Soviet voting rights in the proposed UN Security Council, Castle dismissed the concession as virtually meaningless. He continued to view the UN as a secondary agent of international peace. The ability of the United States and other major powers to reach realistic accord out of self-interest was the key to peace. [59]

To Castle's surprise and disappointment, Hoover issued a press statement expressing the belief that "it comprises a strong foundation on which to rebuild the world. If the agreements, promises, and ideals which are expressed shall be carried out, it will open a great hope to the world." [60] A number of astonished conservative opponents of Yalta, including the Polish ambassador, Jan Ciechanowski, demanded that Castle explain what the former president meant. Afraid that Hoover's apparent endorsement would preempt a full and public Republican critique, he asked for guidance in explaining and, if need be, defending the public endorsement. [61] Hoover responded immediately, saying it was too late to protest a bad conference and that the compliant agreements made by FDR were necessary to hold the shaky coalition together until Germany was defeated. [62] He asked Castle to review his private letter to Alf Landon and to comment on it. In the letter, Hoover opined that

> The Atlantic Charter, the Moscow Pact, Dumbarton Oaks, the Yalta Declaration, etc. all reiterate certain ideals and principles which, if carried out in good faith, comprise a foundation for such an organization. The odds are they will not be carried out in good faith. And in that case these promises come to nothing. But at least we can hold up the ideals and promises as a basis of real peace and then hold them to carrying them out.
>
> In sum my idea is: to try to build on what we have to support the broad purpose of Dumbarton Oaks; to seek amendment to its weaknesses and ignorance of human experience; to insist that the enunciated ideals and principals be lived up to. We probably will not succeed in this, but we will have acted constructively and be in a better position for remedy in the future. If the setup finally proves weak, false and immoral, then we will have to oppose it for our own conscience sake. Put an-

other way, I am for helping design an experiment. If it has the elements of success, to support it: if it is hopeless, then to damn it. And I want to see it succeed.[63]

Castle reviewed the letter, found it to be in accord with his own thinking, and urged Hoover to publish it. He admonished Hoover that he should have qualified his public support of Yalta while not presenting a futile oppositional front. In any case, FDR's health problems might bring a new approach to peace.[64] He confided to his diary that Hoover should have scrapped the entire public statement and used the substance of the Landon letter instead.[65] The split with Hoover on the public statement's content indicated that Hoover had changed his mind about an international organization. Some time before Pearl Harbor, both had held that no such organization could amend bad peace treaties or be based on flawed treaties. Whereas Castle continued to hold to this position, Hoover had been forced to fall back upon the proposed United Nations for the correction of bad treaties, such as Yalta, much as Wilson had been forced to at Versailles.[66]

Like Hoover, Castle welcomed the change in leadership upon the death of Roosevelt on April 12, 1945, and indeed questioned why FDR's physicians had allowed him to run in 1944 with his health deteriorating. Although he knew little about the new president, Harry Truman, he believed that the man from Missouri would be more skeptical of Stalin. Castle feared, however, that Truman knew little about foreign affairs and was therefore likely to make errors at a crucial time in the war. Moreover, Truman's former ties to the Pendergast machine in Kansas City cast some doubts as to Truman's honesty.[67] Despite his ambivalence toward Truman, however, Castle found his feisty disposition refreshing. As he wrote,

The atmosphere in Washington is infinitely better since Roosevelt's death, and I find that many people, such as General Robert Wood, who know Truman well seem to feel that he is a straightforward, honest man and that we can expect good things of him. I think Fulton Lewis was right yesterday in saying that he made his first political mistake in coming out with a statement supporting the conduct of the CPA, but he is bound to make some mistakes. We cannot really tell, I suppose, what he is good for until he makes more important appointments. If he leaves a man like Ed Stettinius in the State Department it will certainly show that he lacks imagination, and I hope to see several changes in the Cabinet. I wish more than ever, at this particular time, that you could be at the head of UNRRA because that organization can do more than any other to smooth the way for the rehabilitation of Europe, and it ought to have at its head someone who understands the different countries. I think everybody in Washington feels that something of this sort is vitally important, especially when UNRRA is getting in a very bad position from the dishonesty and disorderliness of its operations.[68]

In the late spring and summer of 1945, Castle's primary concern was advocating a conditional peace with Japan. Along with Hoover, he was adamant that peace with Japan be made as soon as possible after VE Day. Hoover, in conversations with Joseph P. Kennedy and Stimson, argued for a quick peace with Japan based on restoration of all Chinese territory and Japanese disarmament for thirty to forty years. Japan should, Hoover felt, be allowed to retain Formosa and Korea in order to "save face" and to recover economically from the devastation of war. The reason for this was the need of British and American business to have access to markets and raw materials in "Asia outside of Russia." With the dominance of the Soviet Union in eastern Europe, fewer trading opportunities existed there. A slow, costly war of attrition against our former trading partner would waste a million more lives while assisting Russia with its penetration of China, Manchuria, and Korea.[69] It was Hoover's private opinion that Korea had never been decently governed and that the Japanese occupation had actually improved life there; Japanese "law and order" had given the average Korean a bit of safety. Castle agreed that Korea had been badly governed but argued that the matter of Korean independence was important to Korean-Americans and was of symbolic importance to many Americans, particularly those who had long felt a special empathy for Korea as a partly Christian country. To make a public offer to Japan promising them Korea would cause controversy and might debunk Hoover's bold proposal for a peace initiative. Moreover, unlike Hoover, Castle felt that the average Japanese would be very responsive to such a reasonable proposal, as only the militant had wanted war. "It was perfectly clear," he noted, "that large sections of the population had not wanted war, including the Emperor, and I felt they were looking for a way out that could be labelled something other than unconditional surrender which their own propagandists had made . . . seem like extermination."[70] Both Hoover and Castle agreed that Truman's advisors, most of them holdovers from the previous administration, would advise against such a proposal. The inability of the United States to make a new, realistic appraisal of its relations with Japan was a result of wartime emotions, anti-Japanese propaganda, residual racism, the desire to avenge the Pearl Harbor attack, and sheer stupidity. For Castle, Asia would be more important to the future economic health of the United States than Europe. With a free Japan as a bulwark against communism, the United States could resume normal trade relations and fulfill the hope, which went back at least as far as Theodore Roosevelt, that Japan could guarantee the kind of peace in Asia which would best serve U.S. interests.[71] Moreover, the United States should be skeptical of British cries for a total victory in Japan. It was not in the interest of the United States to sacrifice "lives or dollars in the Far East to restore to the Dutch and the British colonies they had seized when they were strong enough to do it."[72]

Any hope for a quick, conditional treaty with Japan was crushed by news of the Potsdam Conference and the renewed call for unconditional surrender. Castle saw the ultimatum to surrender or face a war of mass destruction similar in its lack of face-saving alternatives for Japan to Hull's ultimatum of November 26, 1941. With no motivation to surrender and with the office of the divine monarchy under dire threat of being ended, Castle saw another year of wasteful fighting to the bloody end.[73] Castle, not knowing of the secret commitment of Stalin to enter the war against Japan after the defeat of Germany, also wondered why the dictator was allowed to issue such a joint proclamation. He attributed the blunder to Truman's inexperience in dealing with totalitarianism. Churchill was defeated for reelection and replaced at the conference by Clement Atlee. Churchill, whatever his drawbacks, had been tougher on Stalin than Roosevelt. The left-leaning Atlee was not likely to oppose Stalin, and Castle gloomily predicted the worst. Should Russia get into the war, at the late date of July 1945, the Soviets would demand territorial concessions in China and the Pacific, making it difficult for the United States to obtain strategic military bases there, while preventing American economic penetration of their occupied territories.[74]

The Potsdam Conference also confirmed for Castle, as it did for Hoover, that Stalin intended to forcefully annex the Baltic states, east Finland, Bessarabia, and Poland. Large portions of the rest of eastern Europe would have Communist-controlled governments. The elections promised for Poland would be a fraud. Finally, Germany would be so weakened by Soviet dominance in the eastern half of that diminished country that it would not recover for decades. A weak Germany meant instability and economic problems for Europe and the lack of a countervailing power to counter Soviet imperialism.[75]

The shocking and unexpected use of the secret atomic bomb took Castle by complete surprise. Although Hoover had been informed of a major secret project to develop a nuclear weapon in late 1944, he had not shared even a hint of this information with his close friends. Although agreeing with Truman's position that the use of the bomb would hasten Japan's surrender, he felt that due to conventional bombing of Japan starting in March of 1945 and Japan's defeats in the Pacific, the end was hastened by only a few days. The tragic use of the bomb, which he felt was immoral, was a miscalculation of Truman brought on by the unwillingness of Roosevelt and Truman to negotiate a realistic end to the war. At a minimum, the Japanese should have been guaranteed that their form of government would not be interfered with.[76] The consummate skeptic, he also mocked those who "say it [the bomb] will prevent war [in the future] because it will make war so awful. . . . Possibly, this might be true if we could keep the secret entirely in our own hands, but this is impossible. Russia will get the secret, perhaps has been given it already . . . , and Russia will use it for her own purposes, just as Germany would."[77] He was shocked to hear, further, that many Americans felt the Japanese had deserved such a fate because of their supposed subhuman racial characteristics and their sneak attack on Pearl Harbor. Castle had, throughout the war, been alarmed at heated racial rhetoric aimed at the Japanese and had feared that these feelings would make it difficult to negotiate a rational, self-interested peace with Japan.[78] The savaging of Japan during the war had made the immoral and unnecessary attack on Hiroshima and Nagasaki possible. Reestablishing normal relations with an old ally might also be more difficult.

After the bombing of Nagasaki, which he found more outrageous than the first bombing at Hiroshima, Castle joined a host of critics who deplored Stalin's "last-minute" entry into the war on August 8. With Soviet troops approaching the home islands and sure to demand a role in any peace with Japan, Castle criticized Truman's failure to immediately offer peace terms allowing Emperor Hirohito to remain as a symbolic head of state. He was particularly appalled that Secretary of State James F. Byrnes had played with the idea of humiliating the emperor by restricting his powers while allowing him to keep the throne. From August 10 to August 14, planes hammered Japanese cities with conventional bombs and thousands of civilians died. When the emperor seized the initiative, overruled militants who would still fight to the end, and accepted surrender with the condition that the office of emperor be retained (August 14–15, 1945), the tragic, and perhaps needless, ordeal was over. The world would never be the same and the United States never in more peril.[79]

Marginalized by his unpopular opposition to U.S. interventionism before Pearl Harbor and suffering the fate of many of Hoover's close advisors, Castle could only observe, analyze, and criticize World War II diplomacy as an outsider. Nonetheless, he used his network of influential friends in and out of government to advance his view of a realist opposition to FDR and Truman. To a large extent, his positions were close to Hoover's, and he was of considerable assistance in defending and interpreting the former president's presence in foreign affairs. Forced to choose an indirect and behind-the-scenes role in opposing wartime policies that he felt lacked the proper realism and skepticism of Soviet and to some extent British power, Castle would continue this role beyond the war. His conviction that a rebuilt, disarmed, and prosperous Japan was a key to future U.S. economic penetration of Asia as well as the containment of Soviet and Chinese communism became part of U.S. Cold War policy.[80]

10 Diplomatic Realism and the Postwar Transformation of Japan

No event since 1941 has played a larger role in determining the course of relations between the United States and Japan than the postwar occupation that followed four years of savage fighting. Having at last defeated the Japanese, the Allies were determined not only to revise Japan's political and economic systems but also to redeem the very soul of the nation. Under the aegis of General Douglas MacArthur, supreme commander for the allied powers (SCAP), Japan was to be democratized as well as demilitarized. A new constitution was written and enacted; the old militarists were purged; offensive war was renounced; women were given the vote; labor unions and land reform were encouraged; and a start was made on dissolving the great corporations (*zaibatsu*) that had provided the muscle for Japanese aggression. All of these dramatic changes occurred within eighteen months of Japan's unconditional surrender in September of 1945. And yet, by 1947, MacArthur's occupation policy was under relentless attack by the press and powerful business and diplomatic leaders in the United States. Within the space of a few years, the occupation policy had been reversed, the *zaibatsu* were reestablished, and a revivified Japan was enjoying access to the lucrative U.S. market and to raw materials in much of the non-communist world. It was an astonishing reversal of policy, the effect of which was to ensure Japan a share in the world economy as great as if she had won the war.

Explanations for this profound reversal are varied, but mainstream analysis sees it as an outgrowth of the emerging Cold War. With the increasing aggressiveness of Stalin and the successes of Mao in the ongoing revolution in China, wartime plans to reconstruct Japan along democratic, nonmilitarist lines were abandoned in order to rebuild a Japanese economy tied to the U.S. economic orbit.[1] Reform in Japan, according to this explanation, would be less important than the partial remilitarization of the country combined with quick economic reconstruction.[2] Winning the Cold War would require a strategic sphere of influence within the Western Hemisphere, domination of the Atlantic and Pacific oceans, an extensive system of outlying bases, the maintenance of nuclear weapons, and support from the Truman administration for a resurrected Japan and West Germany.[3] Other historians view the change of course in terms of the changing domestic needs of Japan, most importantly the need to halt the inflationary price spiral of the postwar period, which endangered MacArthur's original reform effort.[4]

The leading revisionist challenges to this interpretation of postwar policy come from Joyce and Gabriel Kolko, John Dower, and Walter LaFeber. In their view, the driving force in reversing the Japanese occupation policy lies in the domestic economy of the United States. Troubled by the continuing crises of inflation and a surplus of manufactured goods, the revisionists argue, Truman's administration called for the restoration of West Germany and Japan in part because they would become important buyers for America's burgeoning industries. Programs of demilitarization, democratization, and land and labor reform would only slow the incorporation of these key countries into a world capitalist order that would exclude the Soviet Union and China and would be dominated by the United States. For the revisionists, no military threat from the Soviet Union or China was deemed as great by Truman and most of his advisors as the threat of economic stagnation and unrest in the United States.[5]

More recently, a few historians led by Howard Schonberger and John G. Roberts have focused on the extent to which unofficial pressure groups as well as influential business and past diplomatic leaders were important influences on Congress, the Truman administration, and public opinion.[6] Schonberger's work has been critical in shaping my and other historians' research on occupation policy. The most important of these groups was the American Council on Japan (ACJ), the organizational umbrella for the so-called Japan lobby. Largely forgotten or ignored today, the ACJ operated behind the scenes and represented a loose-knit group of influential "Japanists" who, in their capacities in the Foreign Service and the U.S. Department of State, consistently promoted American-Japanese cooperation from the end of World War I to the early 1950s. Trained as European specialists, most of them viewed Japan in the larger context of U.S. relations with Europe and the Soviet Union. Their willingness to use their substantial influence to redirect occupation policy in the emerging Cold War to serve their view of America's future position in world affairs was poorly understood at the time and is only dimly remembered today.[7]

The ranks of the powerful Japan Lobby included William R. Castle, Joseph C. Grew, Hugh Wilson, Jay P. Moffat, Hugh Gibson, Joseph W. Ballantine, Eugene H. Dooman, Edwin L. Neville, John Curtis, Thomas C. Hart, James L. Kauffman, Harry F. Kern, Kenneth S. Latourette, Clarence C. Meyer, Compton Pakenham, William V. Pratt, Antonin Raymond, John W. B. Smith, Henry St. George Tucker, Langdon Warner, and Charles W. Wood. This diplomatic elite shared a common background of family wealth, private schools, and an Ivy League education.[8] Socially and professionally homogeneous, these men also shared a common European orientation and aggressive anticommunism. Their vision of Japanese-American relationships helped shape foreign policy under the administration of Herbert Hoover, criticized Franklin Roosevelt's Asian policies in the 1930s, influenced wartime planning for the surrender and occupation of Japan, and reappeared in the late 1940s to alter MacArthur's early occupation policy. Throughout the period from 1918 to the 1950s, the Japan Lobby tended to call for a Japan aligned with the United States. Such an alignment, they believed, would block Soviet expansion, stabilize East Asian relations, and prevent the need for American military commitments on a global basis. The Japanists believed, moreover, that the United States could exist peacefully in a prosperous world of independent economic spheres.

As national cochairman of the American Council on Japan, William R. Castle, Jr., would help to represent the interests of the Japan Lobby and powerful Japanese economic interests. Although not the most important leader of the lobby, he symbolized the continuity of the postwar Japan Lobby with the prewar forces that had urged cooperating with civilian moderates in Japan, moderating the Chinese revolution, containing the Russian Bolsheviks, and keeping the Far East open to American commerce, investments, and democracy. Although overlooked by many historians of postwar Japan, Castle played a role in the success of the ACJ's efforts to revise occupation policy.

Castle's interest in policy, which had lagged in the eighteen months immediately after the war, was renewed in early 1947 when MacArthur announced his intention to purge Japanese business leaders in order to facilitate the transition to peace and a wider distribution of income and ownership of the means of production. Castle's close friend Harry F. Kern, foreign affairs editor of *Newsweek*, had initiated a public attack on MacArthur's policy with the support of part-owner of the magazine Secretary of Commerce W. Averell Harriman.[9] Throughout 1947, Compton Pakenham, *Newsweek*'s bureau chief in Tokyo (and later a founding member of the ACJ), and Kern criticized MacArthur's handling of reconstruction and the emergence of a left-wing domestic labor movement causing, as they saw it, high inflation and economic distress.[10] Moreover, they feared that a lack of realism in planning for Japan's long-term integration into the economy of the United States threatened peace and prosperity in the region.

Kern received substantial support for his position from former President Hoover, then head of the Famine Emergency Committee, and from his former under secretary of state, William R. Castle. Both men encouraged Kern to continue his journalistic crusade against MacArthur's *zaibatsu* policies. Castle stressed his prewar claim, shared by Hoover and other Japanists, that if Japan could be rehabilitated along democratic capitalist lines, the country would become a strong bulwark against Soviet expansion. A peaceful, capitalist network would be an effective "safeguard against Russian domination" without the United States having to serve as the sole policeman of Asia.[11] In short, a strong Japanese economy would provide for economic containment of Russia and obviate the need for expensive, long-term U.S. military containment. These themes were consistent with Castle's prewar faith that a realist stance in U.S. policy required a partnership with Japan in stabilizing Asia.

By the winter of 1947–1948, Castle was in frequent contact with sympathetic members of the Japan Lobby. These included his close friend Joseph Grew, ambassador to Japan from 1932 to 1941; James Lee Kauffman, an attorney who represented American investors in Japan and one of the few foreign attorneys practicing in Japan during the period 1914 to 1938; retired Adm. William V. Pratt, a close friend of Herbert Hoover; Kenneth C. Royall, secretary of the army; James V. Forrestal, secretary of defense; William H. Draper, assistant secretary of defense; Joseph Ballantine, special assistant to the secretary of state and former head of the Far Eastern Division of the State Department; George F. Kennan, director of the State Department's policy planning staff; and Eugene Dooman, former counselor in the American embassy in Tokyo and long an advocate for the retention of the emperor's office and Japan's fundamental economic system. In constant contact, and in periodic consultation, with Kennan, this group had formulated an alternative peace treaty for

Japan by the fall of 1947. Its main features included the fundamental premise, long advised by Castle, that the long-term economic interests of Japan and the United States coincided. Moreover, since Japan could not change its "aristocratic social organization," misplaced economic idealism would only destroy Japan's economy without providing for viable alternatives. Japan should not be forced to accept a stripped-down version of its former economy nor to become a strictly agricultural nation. Rather, the Japan Lobby believed, Japan should be allowed to develop a powerful industrial base with a minimum capacity for self-defense.[12] A rebuilt, prosperous Japan could, the realist Castle argued, serve U.S. strategic interests in Asia and assist in the containment of communism while furthering America's economic needs for markets.

Significantly, the ACJ was in tune with the growing consensus within the Truman administration that the economic rehabilitation of Japan was critical to American policy in Asia, especially in light of the collapse of the Nationalists in China and the Soviet threats to an economically weakened western Europe. The December 1, 1947, issue of *Newsweek* summarized Castle's position as well as the developing positions of the "Japan Crowd." Indeed, Kern, before preparing the issue, had transmitted a draft of his thoughts to Castle for comment. As was his wont, Castle circulated the draft among members and obtained a basic consensus. When the issue appeared, Kern could be certain that the ideas expressed were those of the Japan Lobby.[13] Indeed, the *Newsweek* issue was a summary of Castle's ideas as expressed in his private diary on January 9, 1948. The vast majority of Japanese did not want socialist solutions to their economic problems; the well-meaning but muddled ex–New Deal bureaucrats who made up much of MacArthur's staff had gone too far too quickly in their efforts to shape Japanese society to conform to an abstract ideal of a "democratized economy."[14] *Newsweek* also quoted from the scathing Kauffman report, issued earlier in 1947, which found that the extremists within MacArthur's bureaucracy had discouraged traditional Japanese business leadership, pampered labor, and undermined America's economic bastion against Far Eastern communism.[15]

When MacArthur remained adamant and urged the Japanese Diet to pass the SCAP industrial deconcentration bill that would effectively break up Japan's largest corporations, Castle assisted Kern and other like-minded leaders in organizing special missions to Japan. One of these leaders was Castle's acquaintance George F. Kennan. In contact with Castle, Grew, Dooman, and Ballantine, Kennan impressed MacArthur with the broad views of the Japan Lobby, the congruence of their ideas with changing official policy, and the necessity of placing Japan's future in the context of the long-term containment of communism.[16] Kennan was soon followed to Japan by William Draper and five representatives of America's most powerful corporations, led by Percy Johnston of the Chemical Bank of New York. Draper and his associates argued the familiar theme that the further dissolution of the *zaibatsu* would weaken Japan and delay its economic recovery and reintegration into a new capitalist order in the Pacific.[17] These missions, as well as changing policy in Washington, were enough to pressure MacArthur into moderating his position.

Delighted with this success and convinced that a more formal lobby would be needed to continue the work of implementing programs in Japan that would foster social and political stability, stem inflation, reduce dependency on U.S. aid, boost exports and production, and speed peace, Castle agreed on June 28, 1948, to Kern's suggestion that he and Grew cochair the American Council on Japan.[18] The appointment of Castle and Grew served to link the group to the important prewar pro-Japanese lobby, which had stressed the realists goals of cooperation with Japan, mutually compatible spheres of economic influence, anticommunism, and keeping Asia open to American goods, investments, and liberal democracy. Further, the social and economic ties between members of the ACJ, various business groups, quasi-official policymaking bodies, and the highest-ranking groups within national government would give the ACJ unusual influence over the Truman administration's handling of Japan.[19]

Throughout its short existence, the ACJ also served as an important source of contact with Washington for top Japanese business and political leaders. Prevented from maintaining representatives in the United States, powerful Japanese officials, bankers, and industrialists sought the assistance of Castle and other ACJ members in efforts to bypass SCAP officials and to influence potential allies in the United States. Castle, as a former ambassador to Japan (1930), was a major channel of communication largely because of his prestige in the Japan Lobby and his important contacts among Japan's prewar civilian leaders. Castle's private diary reveals that throughout the period 1947–1956 he was in periodic written and personal contact with such dignitaries as Prime Minister Shigeru Yoshida, Foreign Minister Hitoshi Ashida, and Tadakatsu Suzuki, director of the influential Central Liaison Agency. From the study of his spacious home at 2200 S Street, N.W., in Washington, Castle frequently interpreted U.S. policy to Japanese leaders seeking his opinion. Additionally, he served as an intermediary between Japanese officials and key congressional leaders, such as California Senator William F. Knowland and New Jersey Senator Howard Alexander Smith, a powerful member of the Foreign Relations Committee.

One of Castle's most valued Japanese contacts was the aristocratic former admiral and foreign minister, Kichisaburo Nomura. Serving as ambassador to the United States at the time of the attack on Pearl Harbor, Nomura had been in frequent contact with Castle, seeking his advice concerning Roosevelt. By 1947, Castle had resumed his correspondence with Nomura, believing him to be a key to the future of a rebuilt, capitalist Japan.[20] Despite the purge of Nomura by SCAP in 1946, Castle recognized his friend's importance to Japanese-American relations. Nomura provided information about the activities of Japan's old ruling circles as well as officers of the Imperial Navy right-wing nationalist rearmament organizations. He was a friend of the prime minister and other top Japanese officials. Further, Nomura's friendships with top U.S. officials such as Special Ambassador John Foster Dulles, Admiral Turner Joy, and Admiral Arleigh Burke were either initiated or fostered by Castle. For Nomura, Castle was a reliable source of advice and one who could assist him in his efforts to partially restore the Japanese naval establishment to respectability. More importantly, Castle's view of Nomura as being a "moderate" helped to make him respectable in the eyes of Washington officials. Because Nomura's view of Japan coincided with that of most members of the ACJ, he would continue to serve as a key link to Japan throughout the remainder of U.S. occupation.

Other prominent officials saw Castle as a vital link to Washington and American business leaders. Castle, well known to most of Japan's prewar economic, civilian, and business leaders, took a hand in shaping the ACJ's recommendation that American private investment play a major role in Japan's economic recovery. Castle joined other ACJ leaders in calling for a uniform and fixed exchange rate for the yen. Such an exchange rate would also help Japan expand its exports, which was critical to its becoming a self-supporting nation.[21] Moreover, Castle, in private conversations with Japanese officials, came to believe that to encourage U.S. investment in Japan, the United States should guarantee the principal and interest on loans to Japanese industrialists. Castle also urged, through his private conversations with congressmen and State Department officials such as W. Walton Butterworth, director of the Office of Far Eastern Affairs, the revision of tax liability laws to allow American corporations to repossess their Japanese properties lost during the war. Castle believed that Washington could also tie Japanese development to U.S. economic interests if it served to pressure the Japanese government into repealing moderate Japanese tax, patent, and antitrust regulations unfriendly to foreign investors.[22] This position would help ensure the continued public activity of the ACJ by surveying business opinion and by openly lobbying for favorable tax legislation in order to facilitate the interdependence of the U.S. and Japanese economies.[23]

An example of Castle's behind-the-scene activities on behalf of the ACJ's political and economic positions was his relationship with Takeshi Watanabe, a former viscount who was deputy chief of the liaison office of the Finance Ministry under Takeo Fukuda. As the government's intermediary in questions concerning both national and international finance, Castle arranged for the bilingual Watanabe to be invited to join the prestigious Metropolitan Club in Washington.[24] Like so many Japanese business leaders and officials, Watanabe was introduced to key ACJ members and sympathizers after being referred to Castle by Prime Minister Yoshida.[25]

Through Castle, for example, Watanabe met Kern, Pakenham, Draper, and Kauffman, who would promote his later career in the United States with the International Monetary Fund and the World Bank before he became president of the Asian Development Bank. Through Castle and other ACJ leaders, Watanabe provided justification for SCAP to dispatch financial experts empowered to straighten out Japan's economy. On February 1, 1949, Joseph M. Dodge, a prominent Detroit banker and Marshall Plan financial expert, arrived in Japan as an advisor to SCAP. A friend of Castle and Watanabe, Dodge sought to implement the position of the ACJ. In March of 1949, he applied the occupation's "reverse course" economic program into an austerity budget which the Japanese Diet immediately passed.[26] Dodge also began the U.S. Counterpart Fund Special Account, which pooled the proceeds from the sale of American aid commodities for investment to boost industrial production. This would, in turn, enhance the fortunes of political leaders selected and nurtured by the ACJ.[27]

In addition to assisting influential Japanese business and government officials to make contacts in Washington, Castle played a key role in ensuring that ACJ policy became intertwined with official policy. No clearer example of this exists than George F. Kennan's reliance on him for suggestions and comments on Kennan's famous National Security Council (NSC) Document 132, which was approved by the president in October of 1948.[28] This document, which represented an official turning point in policy toward Japan, closely paralleled long-held ACJ positions. Castle, who had long respected and valued Kennan's work, maintained the fundamental position that Japan should be restored to independence and economic self-sufficiency. Japan would become a loyal ally if SCAP would phase out its regulatory activities and end the purge of "natural" prewar civilian Japanese leaders. Castle felt, and the NSC report agreed, that the pure objective should be to terminate reparations, eliminate most restrictions on Japanese industry, and promote export-oriented production. Moreover, SCAP and the Japanese government should be forced to allocate raw materials in ways that promoted export production over domestic consumption while limiting social welfare spending and forcing workers to accept a reduced standard of living. Along with Ballantine, Grew, and General Robert Eichelberger, with whom Kennan shared his draft of the critical document, Castle urged that as a strategy of containment, Japan must quickly become the economic hub of a revived Asian trading network.[29]

Most significantly for official policy, President Truman used the mandate of his election in November of 1948 and the success of the Democrats in regaining control of Congress to implement the document's recommendations. On December 10, 1948, he issued a nine-point directive to SCAP and appointed a special emissary, the conservative banker Joseph Dodge, to ensure that the "reverse course" policy was acted upon. Despite denunciations from MacArthur and delays in implementation, SCAP ultimately surrendered. Promoting a far more conservative economic and social agenda, SCAP turned its attention to suppressing left-wing labor and political groups while simultaneously opening new dialogue with traditional Japanese conservatives. Indeed, as SCAP drifted to the right, unions composed of some government workers, communication workers, railroad workers, and educators led strikes and demonstrations against the new policy. By late 1948, much to the delight of the ACJ, MacArthur stripped all government workers of their right to strike or bargain collectively. Privately, MacArthur claimed that his measures had split the Socialist Party and set the example for private employers to check the labor movement.[30] As Castle contemplated the new decade of the 1950s, he had reason to feel optimistic as the old ruling elite stood ready to displace the SCAP bureaucracy and Japan appeared poised to become a revived regional power. As he saw it, such a Japan would exchange its manufactured products for Southeast Asian raw materials, thereby ensuring that this strategic area would, as it achieved political independence, become linked to Japan's economic orbit.[31] Moreover, most of Japan's exports would go to the United States, ensuring close relations for years to come.

With the beginning of the new decade, Castle shared with Kern, Grew, and other ACJ leaders the concern that the State Department was too slow in granting Japan a peace treaty. In a private meeting with Judge Kuriyama, a Japanese Supreme Court judge sent to Washington by Prime Minister Yoshida, Castle was told that a delayed peace treaty would embitter the Japanese at the very time relations with Japan's ruling elite had improved. Such a position was reinforced by notes sent to Castle by Yasumasa Matsudaira, a member of the imperial household, Renzo Sarada of the Foreign Ministry, and other top officials.[32] Castle felt that the delay in a final peace treaty was the result of the State Department's preference for an indefinite perpetuation of the occupation to guarantee American pre-eminence in Japan. Particularly upsetting was the fact that Russia was "bribing" Japan with the promise of returning the Kurile Islands to Japan if Russia were allowed to participate in a multilateral peace conference. Prolonged delay seemed to open the door for Soviet penetration of Japan.

To help move the peace process forward, the ACJ, led by Kern, produced a position paper on the "ideal peace," which stressed the need for Japan to partially rearm and ready itself for possible future combat with Russia, the development of an adequate internal police force and coast guard to deal with internal radical subversion, the right for Japan to repeal SCAP reforms that lacked the support of the ruling elite, and a self-supporting, productive Japanese economy through the encouragement of private investment and free enterprise. The policy report, which had been reviewed and approved by both Castle and Grew, was distributed to key policy makers together with a detailed report written by Castle, Dooman, and Admiral Thomas Hart which further argued that the State Department should permit an enlarged Japanese merchant fleet in the final peace treaty.[33]

The Japan Lobby received a major breakthrough in May of 1950 when President Truman appointed

John Foster Dulles, appointed in 1950 to negotiate a peace treaty with Japan, had close ties to W. R. Castle, Jr., and the American Council on Japan through Dulles' brother Allen, who would later direct the Central Intelligence Agency. (Library of Congress photo LC-USZ62-92833.)

John Foster Dulles as a special ambassador to negotiate a peace treaty with Japan. Because Dulles' brother Allen was a close friend of Castle's and because he maintained close ties to other key ACJ members, Dulles would serve as a link to the official negotiations for peace.

Before Kern left for Japan, Castle compiled a list of "well-informed" Japanese for Dulles to consult and from whom he could receive valuable information. Indeed, Kern persuaded Dulles to terminate plans for extensive meetings with various groups and instead to attend a private dinner at Compton Pakenham's residence.[34] Such a meeting, Castle and Kern hoped, would serve to bridge the chasm between American peace-treaty objectives, which included the unpopular retention of American bases and Japanese rearmament, and what was politically acceptable to the traditional governing class, which demanded respect for Japanese sovereignty, neutrality, and demilitarization.[35] The guest list Castle had suggested to Kern included Castle's personal friends Yasumasa Matsudaira, who represented the imperial institution, which Castle felt was a key to the treaty; Renzo Sarada, a former vice-minister of foreign affairs who was closely tied to the Mitsubishi *zaibatsu;* Osamu Kaihara, a policy and military expert who was helping to expand the existing "constabulary"; and the ubiquitous financial expert Takeshi Watanabe. Articulated only three days before the Korean War erupted, Dulles' ideas on the necessity of Japanese cooperation against communism in China and the Soviet Union were solidified by the unexpected military onslaught.[36]

With the outbreak of the Korean War in June 1950, Japan's industry was bolstered by United Nations military procurement orders, American technology, and foreign investment. The need to rebuild Japan—an old idea for the ACJ—was now accepted by a majority of Americans. With Japan's industrial leaders partially out of commission as a result of postwar purges, MacArthur's policy of purging such prewar captains of industry would have to be ended and the economic concentration of the old *zaibatsu* restored. More importantly, to secure the vital cooperation of Japan against communist aggression, an early peace along the lines suggested by Castle and the ACJ would have to be reached. The rewards of such a peace were, in the eyes of Castle and other ACJ members, already being anticipated. In addition to economic support for the United States in the war, Castle informed Dulles that Japanese intelligence agents, who formerly had operated in China, could be recruited by the United States.[37]

To ease the acceptance of a treaty with Japan, Castle joined other ACJ leaders in using the anticommunist hysteria of the early 1950s to disarm potential critics of the treaty. In constant contact with his Senate friends such as William Knowland and Alex Smith, Castle urged early acceptance of a treaty that would ensure Japan's connection to the United States. As for the troubling issue of U.S. military bases, Castle told Senator Smith the United States "ought to impress on the Japanese that we were not asking for military bases with any idea of keeping them, that we wanted them only so long as the possession of the bases minimized the danger of an attack by Russia on Japan."[38] Privately, Castle communicated this position to his friends in Japan.

In addition to lobbying influential Senate allies, Castle continued to propound the ACJ view before business forums, the national press, and meetings of the United States Chamber of Commerce. Through this latter organization, he delivered numerous luncheon addresses while reviewing and assisting in the writing of speeches delivered by Harry Kern at such forums as the Bankers Club and the Export Managers Club.[39]

The objective of a successful peace treaty was soon realized. In early 1951, Dulles convinced the Yoshida government to make a deal whereby the Japanese could retain full independence if, in return, they agreed to create a small defense force and sign a ten-year treaty (which could be renewed) guaranteeing U.S. military bases in Japan and Okinawa. The Soviets would be excluded from the treaty as they had been from the occupation. In September of 1951, forty-nine nations formally ratified what Dulles had already achieved with the assistance of the ACJ. Essentially a peace without Asians—China, India, and Russia did not sign—it was a treaty tailored to America's Cold War needs and interests. To weaken China, Yoshida even had to guarantee Japanese recognition of Chiang Kai-shek and agree to forgo trade with mainland China as a condition for Senate ratification.[40]

Within a year or so after the treaty was ratified, the Japanese antimonopoly law was effectively negated, the Mitsubishi combine had essentially been resurrected, and other *zaibatsu* were in the process of reforming. The revival of the Japanese economy was hastened by American investments, and the American market was opened to unlimited exports of Japanese goods. As Castle and the ACJ had predicted, Japan's economic reliance was followed by its political alliance and support of U.S. policy.[41]

Although the objectives of the American Council on Japan had been realized, and it partially disbanded as a formal group in 1952, William R. Castle continued to serve as a link between businessmen and opinion leaders in both countries. Indeed, Yoshida credited Castle with much of the success of the treaty and petitioned Dulles to appoint Castle as ambassador to Japan.[42] Because of his advanced age and precarious health, this was out of the question. Nonetheless, until the late 1950s, Castle was frequently consulted by the Japanese ambassadors to the United States, Prime Minister Yoshida (who called on Castle in person on November 12, 1954), members of the Japanese Diet, foreign ministers, top-level Japanese business leaders, and Crown Prince Akihito and his wife. Castle continued to provide reliable assistance in lobbying Congress on policy related to Japan, in obtaining loans for Japanese industry from wealthy friends, and in introducing young Japanese businessmen to important business leaders in the United States. In his numerous visits, Castle was often given privileged information by Japanese contacts who solicited his opinion about how U.S. policy makers in the Eisenhower administration would react to various diplomatic positions.[43] Indeed, the de facto headquarters of what remained of the ACJ had shifted to Castle's home in Washington. His prewar dream of a Japanese civilian democracy led by civilian conservatives and a demilitarized Japanese economy aligned with U.S. interests was largely realized by 1956. His continuing unofficial service to the ideal of peaceful, economic containment of communism and a revived Japan committed to peace and prosperity would be the last in the life of this active ex-diplomat. In Castle's final meeting with Secretary of State John Foster Dulles in 1956, it surprised no one who knew Castle that Dulles told him that while he was in Japan that year, "the Japanese talked about you [Castle] more than any other American and said you really understood their people and their problems."[44] The "people" Dulles and Castle knew were the elite, conservative, dominant class of Japan who, under a constitutional monarchy, maintained their prewar power and accepted a privileged position in the American-dominated system of global capitalism.[45]

Castle's influence on the changed U.S. policy toward Japan after 1947 was, finally, far from determinative. Although widely respected by conservatives familiar with his quiet power and influence in the 1930s, he was no longer able to move those not already convinced by his view of Japan after the war. His leadership of the ACJ was largely symbolic of the group's continuity with prewar conservative policy.[46] Although Castle's role in effecting change in U.S. policy toward Japan was not a pivotal one, he nonetheless played a quiet, behind-the-scenes role in facilitating, brokering, advising, making key contacts, and drafting speeches. His contacts with top business leaders, quasi-official policy-making bodies, and the highest orders of government aided the ACJ substantially. His views on Japan, though not profiting him personally, did coincide with the interests of American business. In the emerging postwar anticommunist bipartisan consensus, his views blended with those of the more significant players such as Kern, Harriman, Truman, Kennan, Dulles, and Dean Acheson. William R. Castle continued to be respected and consulted by Japanese prime ministers and some Republican leaders alike, and his diplomatic realist dream of a democratic and capitalist Japan, tied to the U.S. economy and a bulwark against communist expansion, seemed realized by the mid-1950s.

11 An Aged Realist Examines Cold War Assumptions

Other than his involvement with the American Council on Japan, W. R. Castle began to spend less time on foreign-policy issues and more time on volunteer and family activities. From 1945 to 1952 he served as president of Garfield Memorial Hospital, president of the Washington Literary Society from 1945 to 1947, and served for some time on the Hospital Council of the National Capitol Area. He continued his philanthropic support of Harvard University, the National Symphony Orchestra, and the Washington Cathedral Choral Society. His home at 2200 S Street, N.W., continued to be the venue of numerous receptions for visiting historians anxious to interview him, dignitaries, politicians, and Episcopal Church leaders.

With his health and strength fading, Castle wrote less for the public and relegated his private observations of foreign policy to his diary. Long out of public service, he discontinued writing in his diary in 1956. His last public honor was to sit behind President Eisenhower at the 1953 inauguration ceremonies. Privately, he was amused that the Republican Party had chosen to honor "a dinosaur" from an earlier era.

Castle's private observations of the Cold War's early years, however, demonstrate the continuing relevance of his diplomatic realism and noninterventionism. His critique, which was largely private and without public impact, resembles the early critique of Walter Lippmann and George F. Kennan. Although out of the mainstream of popular opinion,

Castle's reservations about a militarized economy, the growing security state, and the danger to traditional civil liberties are more favorably received today. A staunch anticommunist all of his life, Castle nonetheless felt that the ends never justified the means and that the United States should not compromise its political values, its traditions, and its collective security to carry on a military containment campaign around the world. Though lacking inside information about security and foreign-policy matters in the late 1940s and the 1950s, he nevertheless suspected that the United States was overextended and occasionally lacked a sound sense of where its real economic and strategic interests lay. At the heart of his critique of the Cold War rhetoric and military buildup was the fear that the imperial presidency and big government would distort the U.S. economy, curtail traditional liberties, and reduce open debate. Political pressures, particularly after the beginning of the Korean War in 1950, to consent to bipartisan acceptance of increased military expenditures and atomic weaponry was, as he saw it, a threat to the free competition of ideas and alternative solutions.

A consistent concern of Castle's was the extent to which even honorable men were seduced into covering up the truth to meet Cold War orthodoxy. Most particularly, Castle objected to Secretary of War Stimson's rationalizations regarding the decision to use the atomic bomb to force Japan's surrender in August of 1945. The centrality of the bomb to Cold War security, the secrecy of its original plan, design, and construction, and the controversy surrounding Truman's decision to drop the bomb agitated Castle for the rest of his life.

Like Hoover, Castle suspected that the bomb was dropped unnecessarily by men, such as Stimson, Truman, and George C. Marshall, who had failed to negotiate flexibly and realistically with Japan. Castle agreed with Hoover and Grew that Japan might have surrendered in the spring or early summer of 1945 had it been allowed to retain its emperor, some territorial concessions in Taiwan or Korea, and control of most of its domestic institutions. Castle privately wondered whether the war with Japan might have been prolonged long enough to test the new atomic weapon against an enemy that most Americans despised.[1] His speculation did not include a specific appraisal of Russian-American tensions, but his theory is compatible with the later revisionist argument that it was important to demonstrate the bomb to Russia.[2]

Moreover, Castle strongly opposed the distortions used by Stimson in his famous article in *Harper's* magazine justifying the use of the bomb.[3] Such post-hoc rationalizations were, for Castle, a sign of the pressure government officials were under to cover up official secrets. The fact that

Stimson, a former secretary of state and secretary of war, would bend the facts boded ill for open dialogue and national debate in the future. Specifically, Stimson had attempted to end the debate over the bomb by giving a seven-thousand-word "official" account of what happened. In the essay, which shaped the terms of the debate for most Americans for decades to come, Stimson argued that he had been central in the decision to drop the bomb and that he had never doubted that only the use of the bomb could end the war and save hundreds of thousands of American lives. Castle, seeing a copy of the article before it was published, fulminated privately that Stimson's official accounts of events often had been incomplete or disingenuous. Stimson, he argued, had suppressed the fact that Russia had informed the United States of Japan's willingness to negotiate peace long before the bomb was dropped. The article, while appearing to be a neutral and objective account of the decision to drop the bomb, was really a selective rendering of the facts meant to defend Stimson and Truman's actual record of callous disregard for the truth. Since Stimson was a primary source of information, the historical record had been compromised by one of government's most credible former leaders and the damage might not be undone.[4]

To check his impressions, Castle met with former State Department Far Eastern expert Eugene Dooman to discuss the *Harper's* essay. Both agreed, with Hoover, that Stimson had clearly distorted the willingness of Japan to end the war peacefully. Stimson's claim that Japan was determined not to surrender was proven false by intercepted messages decoded by the Navy indicating that Japan's economy was wrecked and that peace was at hand when the unnecessary bomb was dropped August 6, 1945. The second bomb, dropped on Nagasaki on August 9th, was even less excusable, but Stimson's article did not meaningfully distinguish between the two. The distortions of the historical record were, for Castle, one of the greatest dangers of the emerging Cold War. He feared correctly that the pressure to present a unified front to the Soviet Union would come before truth.

Although much of Castle's thoughts about the Cold War are no more than the informed opinions of a private citizen, and his diaries from 1951 to 1956 mainly concern family matters, a reading of them gives us a broad sense of continuity with his diplomatic-realist position. In broad outline, Castle questioned the common analogy between Hitler and Stalin and the militarization of the Cold War's economy and foreign policy. Moreover, as the Cold War progressed in the late 1940s and early 1950s, Castle saw a lack of readiness to admit the validity of power realities and aspirations to accept them without rigid moral judgment, and to seek a balance of power in both Europe and Asia.

Although staunchly anticommunist, Castle questioned the Truman administration's analysis of Soviet intentions for expansion. Specifically, Castle charged that the inexperienced Truman had assumed, by 1947, that Stalin was just like Hitler in his desire for military conquest and that U.S. foreign policy had been weakened by the inapt analogy to Munich and the lost opportunities to halt Hitler through greater Euro-American military preparedness in the 1930s. Castle agreed with the architects of Communist containment that Stalin was a dangerous and ruthless totalitarian tyrant whose domestic power depended, in part, on depicting the West as a danger to the Soviet Union's autonomy. He also deplored Stalin's hegemony in Central and Eastern Europe. Clearly, Stalin had avoided any chance for continued good relations with the United States after World War II and intended to subvert France, Italy, Greece, and other rebuilding Western European countries through support of indigenous communist parties. The postwar economic dislocations invited Soviet propaganda and subversion throughout Western Europe. Clearly, the contestation with the Soviets for the European continent and other parts of the world would require patience and a long-term commitment to strengthen Europe economically and politically. Still, Castle saw no evidence that Stalin wanted war. Stalin, though very dangerous, was cautious about all-out war and had substantial challenges in rebuilding his own shattered economy. The last thing Stalin needed or wanted was an all-out war with the United States over Western Europe or Japan.

The second, and related, foreign-policy mistake of the early Cold War years was, as Castle saw it, to guarantee our military and political dominance through dependence on nuclear weapons. The secrecy of the weapon had always bothered Castle, and its mass destruction of Japan, a likely bulwark against communism and a supporter of U.S. policy, at the end of Japan's ill-fated experiment with fascism, was most unfortunate. Moreover, the destructiveness of the atomic bomb made it impossible to discriminate between military and civilian populations, as one could do with traditional weapons. Traditional American war aims had been to gain strategic objectives with the minimum amount of destruction. The atomic bomb challenged this tradition while inviting environmental disaster and the most dangerous arms race the United States had ever participated in. Use of the weapon also promised to undermine traditional claims for U.S. moral exceptionalism in foreign policy. The suicidal weapon was unsuitable for rational military purposes and eliminated reasonable options for flexible, self-interested negotiations with communism in the international arena.

An important correlative to the above was Castle's concern about the seemingly permanent militarization of American life after the late 1940s.

His views were consistent with his earlier and public denunciations of armaments in the 1920s and 1930s. Now, however, the stakes were higher. Internally, the growing militarization of the economy was aiding the centralization of government with attendant higher taxes, waste, secrecy, duplication of effort, and a distorted national economy. Increasing annual military budgets, beginning with the Korean War, committed vast sums of the nation's income to nonproductive use. Budget deficits were not the worst of it. Millions of Americans and tens of thousands of businesses had quickly become used to government contracts. An invidious connection between arms manufacturers and officials in Washington had created the permanent condition for a huge armed military establishment in peace as well as war. The problem was made worse by the dependence of American allies and the growing number of Third World client states were dependent on the United States for arms to oppose communist aggression. Thus, a set of powerful vested interests had developed which went uncontested as long as Soviet behavior could rationalize the expenditures.

The distorted economy also had negative effects for American foreign policy. Specifically, the economic dependence on a militarized economy had fueled a constant justification for the military budget and thus led to overrepresentation of the military potential of the Soviet Union and its allies. This potential to exaggerate the Soviet military threat heightened the suspicion of the adversary and the distorted popular opinion in the country. Most important, a militarized economy for Castle foreclosed political solutions and compromise to complex international problems. For Castle, as for George F. Kennan, containment of the Soviet Union was best guaranteed through economic and political means rather than needless unilateral military means. Military options should be exercised only as a last resort and only when core U.S. interests were at risk. The use of conventional forces was always preferable to the use of nuclear weapons.

Compounding the roiled international environment of the late 1940s and 1950s was the political opportunism of politicians playing to domestic political passions. Castle had long valued the work of disinterested experts working to adjust international differences in unimpassioned fashion. He had always shared the suspicion of Tocqueville that the United States was not well disposed to carry on foreign policy where foreign-policy questions were decided on purely domestic considerations. Now that the United States had become an unrivaled superpower, the tendency of politicians to play to domestic constituencies was more dangerous than ever. These constituencies tended to be aggressive, noisy minorities or lobbies, often arguing selfishly in militaristic or chauvinistic fashion on behalf of a particular nation or ethnic group overseas. Because of their political clout and ability to mask their appeals in the American flag, politicians were tempted to subordinate long-term U.S. interests. In the Cold War era, Castle deplored the rhetorical excesses that involved charges of communist sympathies in the State Department, Army, and in Congress. The bipartisan nature of anticommunism prevented rational assessments of national interests. Castle privately urged friends in the State Department to consider the limitations of the U.S. political system in the field of foreign policy and to bear these limitations in mind before accepting binding obligations that could lead to war. Commitments to NATO, to Japan, and to Germany seemed reasonable and defensible to Castle as they represented a wise means of defending U.S. interests. But the United States, as a new world power, would find it tempting to expand its involvements to please various constituencies and to prove its strength against the communist challenge from the Soviet Union and China.

When selecting new alliances, defense commitments, foreign-aid postures, and the like, Castle continued to feel, up to his serious illness in the late 1950s and early 1960s, that the United States should consider the costs of each new responsibility and to accept the real limitations of the country's capabilities. He also continued to feel that the problems of the Cold War world were so complex that no country—the United States included—could solve them. The depths of these problems meant that the United States would need to forgo involvement in most international problems and have greater faith that solutions could be found without any U.S. participation. He would, at the end of his life, find ample reason to agree with the sentiments of Kennan, who concluded that

> This is not a plea for total isolationism, such as our grandfathers and great-great-grandfathers cultivated. It is only a request, if I may put it that way, for a greater humility in our national outlook, for a more realistic recognition of our limitations as a body politic, and for a greater restraint than we have shown in recent decades in involving ourselves in complex situations far from our shores. And it is a plea that we bear in mind that in the interaction of peoples, just as in the interactions of individuals, the power of example is far greater than the power of precept, and that the example offered to the world at this moment by the United States of America is far from being what it could be and ought to be. Let us present to the world outside our borders the face of a country that has

learned to cope with crime and poverty and corruption, with drugs and pornography. Let us prove ourselves capable of taking the great revolution in electronic communication in which we are all today embraced and turning it to the intellectual and spiritual elevation of our people in place of the enervation and debilitation and abuse of the intellect that the TV set now so often inflicts upon them. Let us do these things, and others like them, and we will not need 27,000 nuclear warheads and a military budget of over $250 billion to make the influence of America felt in the world beyond our borders.[5]

W. R. Castle, Jr., died after a long illness on October 13, 1963. His diary ended in 1956. Clearly his period of public influence had come and gone. Nevertheless, diplomatic realism remains a salient feature of twentieth-century foreign policy, a policy that has had uneven success. Castle was a member of a homogeneous elite that no longer predominates in the foreign-policy establishment. One can look back at the record of men like Castle and find enormous blind spots in their vision of the world. The exclusionary world of U.S. foreign policy up to the 1960s meant that the insights, experiences, and outlooks of women and America's minority populations were left out of the mix. Professional diplomats like Castle were often too sure of their Eurocentric assumptions, too quick to exclude individuals of cultural and economic difference. The absence of women, people of color, and people of lower income prevented the foreign-policy establishment from truly representing America's interests or from drawing on all of its strengths. Castle could, as some of his contemporaries knew, be occasionally insecure, parochial, stubborn, and even unforgiving in his judgment of people and events. His faith in Japan's civilian leadership of the 1920s and early 1930s proved to be poorly placed, while his disdain for the New Deal and its leader tended to be too unbending and tendentious. His faith in Hoover's judgment was not qualified or perhaps nuanced often enough.

One can, upon examination of the record, find many drawbacks in Castle and the foreign-policy establishment of which he is emblematic. The interlocking directorate of graduates of New England and New England-like preparatory schools and Ivy League colleges who moved in and out of government while maintaining a legitimate esprit of public service is hard, now, even to properly imagine. As Mark Falcoff, a resident scholar of the American Enterprise Institute, recently noted,

Time and history have not on the whole dealt kindly with these people. No doubt they suffered from a certain smugness and a provincialism of their own, and may even have occasionally abused class and tribal loyalties. They were not always right on the issues. But how refreshingly idealistic they seem compared to those men and women on the make who have flourished in our most recent anti-elitist age![6]

This book, then, is a small effort to revisit that flawed but honorable record and to learn from it.

Appendix
Selected Radio Speeches to Japan

In the spring of 1942, W. R. Castle, Jr., was asked to write and deliver propaganda speeches for the Office of War Information and its director of overseas operations, Robert E. Sherwood.

The speeches were broadcast to Japan until suddenly discontinued, apparently at the request of Franklin D. Roosevelt, by the early summer of 1942.

The speeches are illuminating for what they tell us of Castle's experiences and perceptions of Japan. They also adumbrate his hope for a friendly postwar Japan once again integrated with the U.S. economy. His diplomatic realist assumptions form the basis for this extended plea for conciliation and a victory without rancor. The following transcripts of the radio speeches, which are held in the Castle Papers at the Herbert Hoover Library, are published here for the first time.

I

If I am to talk with you in Japan from day to day for a time it is important that, before I begin, you should know my attitude and something of the things for which I stand. Some of you may remember that I was Ambassador in Tokyo for a few months, sent there primarily to explain as fully as I could the American stand with regard to the limitation of naval armament. There is no reason why you should have known anything more. You may understand me a little better, however, if I tell you that I was born and brought up in Honolulu, where I never thought of Japan as a strange and distant country, like many Americans, that I went to school with Japanese and knew many more, among whom were some of my good friends. Later on I went to Harvard College and for several years taught there, making always more Japanese friends. Later, as a Harvard Overseer, I was head of the committee on the teaching of Far Eastern affairs and languages. Naturally, during, my many years in the Department of State I was officially in close touch with your part of the world. It is perhaps worth noting, also, that for many years we have been collectors of Japanese art and have a large collection of books on the subject which we have read, not merely looked at. And in connection with our study of your art we read widely in Japanese history so that the names of your great leaders are almost as familiar to us as are the names in English and American history.

With this background you will see that I am not anti-Japanese in the sense that most Americans are who know little of you beyond what has happened in recent months. I had many friends in Japan who, I hope, may still be alive to assist in the sound rebuilding of the country after the war. I hope also that they will still be my friends when we are again able to speak to each other face to face. There is very much in the true character of the Japanese people which appeals to me and to thousands of other Americans who know you. Among these traits are your chivalry, your love of all things beautiful, your splendid scientific attainments, your powers of organization, your ability to adapt to your own uses whatever you see abroad that you think will be useful. This is not imitation; it is rather a wonderful power of adaptation. All these things and many others are on the credit side and for them we respect and admire you. But today they are all obscured in the smoke of battle. Your love of country seems to have turned into a kind of cruel nationalism that lashes out at everyone, no matter how unoffending or how willing to be friendly. Your power to stand up to physical suffering in your own bodies seems to have degenerated into sadistic pleasure in hurting others. Many of you seem to have forgotten the tenets of your religion and the lessons of your fine tradition. That, at least, is the picture of Japan which your militarists are giving to the world. That is the Japan which we are fighting against and must bring to its senses through defeat. That is the Japan which Americans hate. And it is a tragic hatred because it is a hatred of something detestible [*sic*] which I am sure is not the true Japan.

But whatever my feelings may be toward the old Japan of high ideals and unsullied honor I am first of all an American and it would be dishonest for me not to say that I am eager to help defeat the Japan which at present is at war with the civilized world. My friends among you have always been honest with me and I must be equally so with you. I repeat then that I am an American, anxious to win the war, and as quickly as possible. This you can understand because you know the meaning of patriotism and love of country. Indeed I am sure that you would despise me if you thought there was any flaw in my love for my own country. This love, nevertheless, does not mean that I am unable to see good where it exists. Seldom has it been no completely hidden as in the Japan of the moment, but it is there, even if deeply buried, and all your friends hope that as soon as possible the evil that now masquerades under the name of Japan may be destroyed so that we may once more see the good emerge.

In these short talks, then, just as I shall never be anything but a loyal American, I shall also try never to be unfair to the real Japan which is not represented by your militarists but was represented by your statesmen, as fine men as I have ever known anywhere. I shall never mention their names because they might be made to suffer for past associations although I have never heard one of them, here or there, say or suggest anything even remotely disloyal to Japan. I shall always try to speak the truth, whether talking of past, present or future.

II

Even after the adoption of your modern constitution there were always militarists in Japan, people who had no respect for the Constitution, who felt that arms were the only symbols of progress. Until recent years these men did not try to control the country. The great success of the Russo-Japanese War turned their heads a bit but in those days there were superb old men like Togo and Yamamoto who were able to keep them in check. These men knew there was no statesmanship in bullets, that arms might be necessary to repel an enemy but that they never built a permanent state. They knew that military men should be secondary, that they were the bulwark behind which the statesmen maintained the nation. Prince Shotoku, who is one of the most wonderful characters in history, knew this fact well and his life exemplifies the idea.

But in recent years Japanese militarists have become more restless and more conceited. The took over Manchuria. They invented an attack on the South Manchuria Railroad and that served to open excuses for absorbing the entire province. Apparently they cared something for what the world thought about their spoliation as they made one specious excuse after another and promised day by day to go no further. All these excuses and promises were duly repeated to us in Washington by your Ambassador who finally, I am sure, was ashamed to enter the Department of State because he knew that what he said one day would be cynically repudiated the next. He suffered because he was himself an honorable man and he suffered for his Government, which was made up of honorable men, forced day after day into impossible positions. Certainly it was the wanton attack on Manchuria which first turned American opinion sharply against Japan. The new situation was wholly unlike that of the war with Russia. Then American opinion was strongly pro-Japanese because people believed that Japan was the under-dog, a weak nation attacked by a bully. In attacking Manchuria Japan was the bully, so far as America could see, and that attack gave tremendous impetus to the latent pro-Chinese sentiment in the United States. This attack was our first clear proof that you Japanese, in spite of your modern ideas and your ancient culture, were unable to play the game of international relations because you were unable to control that small minority of your people who were willing to cheat to win.

A thing that impressed me at the time as it did a lot of other people was the fact that your militarists so grossly underestimated the intelligence of the rest of the world. Apparently they really thought we would believe their childish tales of aggression. This sillyness became all the more apparent at the time of the trouble at the bridge, which absurd little fracas served, so they seemed to think, as sufficient excuse for a war on China. It was then that American opinion turned definitely against Japan. Then, perhaps, we should have declared war in order to defend the integrity of treaties and to rescue other nations unjustly attacked. Instead there were many of us, hating war, who persisted in trusting the sane elements of Japan to restrain the Army and to bring about some kind of peace. We continued even to sell you what you needed. We were eager to limit the war and we hoped almost against hope that reason would prevail, that in the long run we might be able to help persecuted China more by remaining neutral and exerting whatever influence we had to assist the real Japan to restrain the war mad Japan. We saw almost immediately that this military adventure would disastrously weaken Japan as it might keep on for years if the Chinese resorted to guerilla warfare as they were bound to do in time. We saw that it must destroy your trade and your economy, your plans for a greater prosperity sphere in East Asia and we felt that in time you would come to your senses and repudiate those who had led you astray. You had your successes in China but you did not conquer China and your resources were drained. You were looking for some way out when the world war intervened. And then your militarists, having learned nothing from the fact that when there was real defense and approximately equal forces you were unable to advance, dragged you into the greater conflict and first of all into war with America, the nation which had been honestly your friend and had honestly wished you well.

III

When Japan attacked the United States on the 7th of last December your military men counted on surprise because they thought they knew—and rightly as it turned out—that, a good portion of the world still believed in Japanese promises and in Japanese integrity. We were foolish enough not to have learned that the military had already taken over complete control of the Government. If we had fully understood that we should not have been caught napping because, after all that had happened in China, we realized that your military are not to be trusted, that the ordinary rules of civilized life are not included in their books of conduct. They are perfectly willing to depend on the stab in the back and fail to see that this form of conflict stains the honor of their country, of the Imperial Family of which they pretend to be the guardians, of the great and honorable warlike traditions of the nation, The world, alas, is beginning to understand, in spite of this, that your officers depend on this stab in the back for success, that they cannot win in fair fight unless they have overwhelming superiority in numbers. I have often pictured to myself the sufferings of the spirits of the ancestors of these men when they see their sons disgracing the family name and still more the name of the nation.

In this war the stab in the back worked once because it was wholly a surprise. It will not work again because now we know what to expect. It was at first successful to such an extent that it will hasten the defeat of Japan. When your officers led their men through countries which had little or no power of resistance they were so intoxicated with their military genius that they went on and on, boasted over conquering islands that made not the slightest attempt to defend themselves. And all the time your lines, as they stretched out, became thinner and thinner. The strain on the manpower of Japan grew always more intense. Your troops were where they should never have been from the strategic point of view and they were afraid to retreat because this would have been an admission on the part of the military that they had made a mistake.

We Americans can understand, without sympathizing, the ambition of certain men among you to unite in one great group under the leadership of Japan all the nations of East Asia which have blood similar to yours. Scientifically these are called the yellow races. We cannot at all understand the desire on the part of anyone to include totally different races in this group. We know that even a large grouping of the yellow races would fall apart just as all the attempts throughout history to found empires against the will of the people have led to disaster. But we know even more certainly that if in this attempted grouping were included units of Caucasian descent the disintegration would become an explosion. Yet beyond the East Indies your generals have led their troops southward through groups of unresisting islands. Why? Because they thought it would be a great thing to conquer the continent of Australia. I wonder whether any thinking Japanese have any idea that they could rule a continent inhabited by a white, English speaking race. The idea is so silly it will not bear discussion yet some of your officers must have thought this since there can be no other explanation for your dangerous spread to the south. You have weakened your lines and have suffered terrible loss of life. We all know that loss of life is necessary in war if something is to be gained thereby but your loss of life in the islands of the South Pacific is a waste.

It speeds your defeat because you are numerically not strong enough to throw away your men. Do you remember the story of the Chinese in America who was asked how the war between Japan and China was going. "Very well," he answered. "Papers say that in fighting yesterday ten thousand Chinese killed and one thousand Japanese. Soon China win because no Japanese left to fight." Much the same thing is true today when you are fighting the associated nations. Japan ought to consider all these matters, thoughtfully and without emotion, because disaster stalks always nearer. It was a black day when Matsuoka signed the Axis pact and I am sure it will be in the future a day of national mourning.

IV

I am going to say today a little more on the subject I discussed yesterday, but this time applied to a specific situation.

The fighting in the Solomon Islands has cost thousands of lives, much materiel and millions in money. None of us, Americans or Japanese[,] yet know the details of this fighting because details cannot be told one side or the other until much later. This is, of course, for the reason that messages carried by radio waves can be read by all. Because of this very thing it seems to me that we should be utterly accurate in what we put on the air, since lies will always come back to plague us, and that naturally we must be careful to say nothing that might help the enemy. We are not worried about the morale of people in the United States but it may be that you in Tokyo are tremendously worried and that this accounts for the fact that your radio tells of great Japanese victories in the Solomons and at Midway, for example, victories which never occurred. All that you or we know certainly of the Solomons is that your militarists occupied the islands in force, presumably to cut the line of supplies from America to Australia. This you did not succeed in doing but as the occupation was obviously a danger American marines landed on the islands and destroyed or took prisoner the Japanese occupying forces. A few days later certain units of the Japanese fleet returned, probably with the purpose of driving out the marines, but were unsuccessful. A number of aeroplanes on both sides were destroyed and a good many Japanese ships were injured if not also destroyed. These first fights, which the Tokyo radio described as great Japanese victories[,] were actually minor American and Australian successes. They might be called major successes in the light of the story I told you last time about China, the story being applied now to planes instead of human beings. Although actually more Japanese than American planes were destroyed, it would have been to the advantage of America if the toll had been equal or even if we had lost twice the number. I think that even the most obstinate of your military men would have a sinking of the heart if they could see the mighty American aircraft factories scattered over the country, turning out planes, both bombers and fighters[,] at a speed which you can never hope to attain. In saying that I am not denying Japanese inventive genius or ability to work effectively and at high speed. American flyers are loud in their praise of your Zero planes but are not worried because they know that American factories are tuning out better planes in huge quantities. We are surpassing you because we have infinitely greater capacity, infinitely larger sources of raw materials, a working force of men which, in numbers, you cannot possibly equal. This means that, work as you may, we shall always be able to work more successfully, that large as your air force may be today, the American air force will be in the course of time ten times greater.

Nobody can deny these facts and they make such engagements as that in the Solomons all the more gloomy for your future. I said the islands were useless to you except to enable you to interfere with our supplies to Australia. But why should you care about this since Australia, even if you could capture it, which you cannot, would be only a millstone around your neck? Why risk your precious aeroplanes and the lives of your diminishing number of soldiers on something, which would be worthless to you if you had it? This whole episode is typical of the stupidity of the Japanese military mind. Your soldiers do not think of the future; they do not stop to ask whether the next move will be good or bad for the fatherland. Just because they have reached one objective they move on toward the next because it is there in sight and because its capture may bring them a little cheap glory. It is true that we shall have to lose men and materiel to retake these various islands but your losses will be as great as ours—greater in comparison—and as these useless advance posts begin to fall, as your men are captured and held as prisoners, as your Army begins to retreat and both the Army and the nation find that it is not invincible your morale will begin to break and what began as an orderly retreat may become a rout. All these things, which result from the arrogance of the military mind, work to the advantage of your opponents. I am sure that your probably admirable strategical plans never included a battle in the Solomon Islands. Brilliant initial strategy has been followed by blunders and with these blunders begins the end of Japanese successes.

V

During the last world war, when you in Japan were fighting on the right side, I took up with President Wilson the question of permitting restricted communication between prisoners held in enemy countries and their families at home. There was, of course, sharp opposition from some of the military people on the ground that somehow news of military value might be transmitted, that spies could use the service to receive and distribute as well as to receive information. But President Wilson, a wise and far seeing man, insisted that the plan be given a trial at least. He knew that the dangers would almost surely be outweighed by the benefits, especially to morale, and he wanted to create a precedent for future wars. The Germans kept us currently supplied with lists of American prisoners, and we, of course, sent them lists of German prisoners. Through the International Red Cross we transmitted carefully censored letters to these prisoners and received letters from them. Some letters were undoubtedly confiscated by the German authorities and some undoubtedly by our own censorship authorities, but on the whole the system worked admirably and I never heard of any leak of military information. The system worked wonders in the comfort it brought to tragically worried families and equally unhappy men in the camps. Food packages were sent in immense quantities and they helped physically as the letters helped morally. Until the Japanese ruling I had supposed that this amelioration of the horrors of war was permanent.

Unless the questions being asked today must have the dreadful answers which so many take for granted cannot this cruel ruling be changed? Is there not in Japan a single great man of the calibre of President Wilson who will insist on re-examination of the subject and will change a ruling which now and in the future must be so disastrous to world opinion of Japan. Germany and Italy accept the Red Cross convention as, of course, do the United States and England. I do not want people to be able to say, as they are beginning to say, that Japan is the least civilized of the Axis partners, that only Japan is turning back the hands of progress, only Japan is brutally treating its prisoners. I don not ask any special favors, only that Japan shall be willing to treat our nationals as well as we treat Japanese nationals captured in battle. Anything less than this is barbarity.

VI

The cruelty involved in your refusal to permit the International Red Cross to send supplies to prisoners is unfortunately of the wholly unexpected and to me inexplicable conduct of certain Japanese today. When the time came for fighting we expected you to fight bravely and furiously. We also expected you to behave with decency to civilian and military prisoners in your hands. We expected you to repeat the splendid record in such matters that you had in the war with Russia. I myself have always doubted stories of rape and murder, the slaughter of children in cold blood and the calculated maltreatment of prisoners. I was pleased a few months ago but not surprised, therefore, when an American officer told me that the information they had from the Philippines indicated that you were treating your American prisoners well, were feeding as you fed your own troops. This officer said with some amusement that you gave American officer prisoners only one meal a day because that was all that Japanese officers had and that some of our men were asking to be allowed to work as though they were privates so that they could have three meals. There was nothing in all this to blame the Japanese for. It was just that in this case American stomachs did not agree with the international regulations to which you lived up.

Since the Gripsholm brought back its quota of diplomats and other repatriated Americans, however, the stories many have told of their own, personal mistreatment in prison camps must make me doubt whether foreign military prisoners are faring any better, whether they are receiving the treatment which is their due under the rules of international law and custom. When an unoffending missionary seventy years old is hung by the feet and given the water treatment, when others, newspaper reporters and teachers and business men are beaten and starved, one wonders whether the dark ages have returned. I cannot disbelieve stories of torture and beastliness when I have them from the actual sufferers, people whose broken bodies support the testimony of their lips. I am sure that knowledge of this sort of cruelty must come as a shock to those fine citizens of Japan who are just as cultivated and as honorable as any citizens of western lands. These fine Japanese, moreover, know that such actions on the part of a bloodthirsty military caste bring deep disgrace on Japan as a whole, will make it almost impossible for the world to forgive when the war is over.

There have been many Americans who have given their lives to Japan. I wonder, for example, whether Dr. Teusler, who built St. Luke's Hospital with money collected here, who saved the lives of countless Japanese, who labored and died for you—I wonder whether he would have fared any better if he had been alive or whether he too would have been hung by his feet and asked to confess something he never did. Probably the officers and non-commissioned officers who were responsible for the maltreatment of these people who have just reached home would say they suspected them of spying. That is a flimsey and dishonest excuse that would have been used against Dr. Teusler also. Even when I was in Tokyo some stupid and reactionary journals were saying the hospital was being built high in order that the doctors might spy from the upper windows. Spy at what? At the merchant ships discharging their cargoes or at the harmless men and women shopping along the streets of Tsukigi? Sane Japanese knew that the hospital was built high because it could not spread out and because Dr. Teusler wanted as many wards as possible to serve the largest possible number of sufferers.

It is not a pleasant contrast to put before the people of America, this picture of devoted Americans laboring in Japan to educate and to heal, helping the Japanese in every way they could; and over against it the picture of savage, sneering militarists, repaying them with torture and sometimes with death. Have you heard stories from your own people who have returned from the United States of any similar acts perpetrated by Americans? I know you have not because if anything of the sort happened here it would be punished as a crime. You do not win wars through unnecessary cruelty. All you do is to create a pool of world hatred which will not dry up for generations, and, what is important for you, bring about the debasement of your own people. To fight against an armed man is one thing; to torture a man who is defenseless is to put on the character of the cowardly beasts of the jungle. Torture may break the body of the man attacked; it destroys the soul of the attacker and through the contagion of his degeneration poisons his nation.

VII

Mr. Grew, who has recently landed in America after ten years in Tokyo publicly confirmed all that I have been saying about the infamous conduct of the Japanese military. I was glad, moreover, that he agreed with me in placing all the blame for the dreadful things that have happened on that one class, that group of fanatical militarists which seems to have lost all sense of decency and is degrading the reputation of their country. He appreciates just as I do the admirable people of Japan whose advice is not now listened to. He said in his speech, "I have had many friends in Japan, some of whom I admired, respected and loved. They are not the people who brought on this war. As patriots they will fight for their Emperor and country, to the last ditch if necessary, but they did not want this war and it was not they who began it."

In this part of his description of Japan Mr. Grew was unconsciously describing his own country as well. He said that Japan counted on the divisions of opinion in America to prevent us from vigorously prosecuting the war when war should come. You in Japan should have looked at yourselves and have realized that we, who are patriotic as you are would react to war as you have done. You knew that many of your best people were opposed to war with the United States but you counted rightly on their patriotism to rise to the defense of Japan and work for the greater glory of Japan if war became a reality. In exactly the same way the entire American people has risen to the defense of America and are working for its greater glory. It is quite true that we had our disagreements before the attack on Pearl Harbor. There were groups who wanted to go to war long ago, to protect China, to help England or France or Greece. There were other groups who felt with the President that America was "isolationist only in wanting as long as possible to be isolated from war." This part of America wanted to postpone the conflict if possible until the country was better prepared. Your attack united the nation as it has seldom if ever been united before. I do not know a single individual who was opposed to war before war began who is not now determined to carry it through to a successful conclusion and is doing whatever lies within his capacity to help the war effort. Thanks to you we Americans are standing shoulder to shoulder.

In one way, at least, we are far more fortunate than you. Like you we realize that war is the one business of the nation, but unlike you we have refused to surrender to the military. All classes are working harmoniously together because all have the same aim, not at all because one class coerces the others as in Japan. In this country it is the business of the military to lead troops, to deploy ships where they will be most effective, to see that the increasing thousands of pilots are properly trained to give maximum support in the air to our men and ships, to make the strategical plans which will eventually win the war. The civilian population, on the other hand, are engaged in the production of war materials, not under the lash of the soldier but under their own leaders, who are as eager to carry through successfully as are the soldiers themselves. Men are fitted in wherever they will be most useful in accord with their age, ability and former training. Teachers are enrolled to teach recruits the things of the mind which will make them more effective fighters. I know of one man who spends his time travelling from college to college to teach to airmen and sailors the geography of the South Pacific so that they may finally fly or said [*sic*] with confidence from island to island for the great assault on Japan. As usual civilian courts are functioning and the civilian spirit of impartial justice is carried into the military tribunals by the thousands of lawyers and judges who are in the Army and Navy. This means that such brutality as has been indulged in by your troops and police, often under the guidance of their officers, would here receive instant and severe punishment. It is not necessary to be a brute to be a good soldier. It is no proof of courage to disgrace one's country by torture of defenceless prisoners as has been done again and again in Japan, and I greatly fear with your armies in the field. As I have said and shall always say this will mean hatred of Japan for generations to come unless it stops now. And what is even worse for you, it is bound to lower the standards of your people and pull you down, perhaps for centuries, from your once proud place among civilized nations.

VIII

We talk a great deal about the differences between races and say, for example, that Japanese and Americans have very little in common and can never understand each other. It is true that in war time differences show up tremendously, but when we are not fighting each other it is my opinion that we are really very much alike and that each can pretty well adapt himself to the manners and customs of the other—at least up to a certain point. If I had been born in Japan and had been brought up by Japanese speaking their language, I should probably have felt myself thoroughly Japanese. Any number of Japanese born in the United States have grown up to be thoroughly American and feel so even now, when a war is going on. Yet there would always be some traits and some inhibitions due to blood. No man of American blood, even if brought up by Japanese[,] could possibly bring himself to torture old and defenseless people as many of your officers and soldiers do. Yet perhaps these same people would do the same things under the provocation of war because their blood would permit it even if they had been brought up here in the best of American surroundings. So some of your best traits seem also to be of the blood.

The love and reverence which a Japanese has for his family is a splendid trait, one admired by everyone and one which would never be blotted out of the blood. If he were cared for and educated by a good American family he would retain for them the same loyalty he would have had for his family at home. This is not environment but blood.

Usually, however, we all take on the character of our surroundings. That is why the Japanese of American birth, all of them American citizens by right of birth, have almost always been splendidly loyal and so are eager to fight. They have learned that loyalty is bigger and more widely extended than loyalty to family or tribe or even to the land of their ancestors, which is the definition of loyalty given by your reactionaries. They have learned that the supreme loyalty is to principles and ideals and because they believe in the principles and ideals of America they are loyal to America. Your reactionaries teach that only the ties of blood are important, that because of his blood a Japanese in a foreign country has the right to be treacherous to his friends in that country. This war has proved such a theory all wrong, or at least has proved that Japanese abroad do not react as your militarists wanted them to. I have friends of Japanese blood here who are as eagerly loyal to the country of their adoption as their relations in Japan are undoubtedly loyal to their fatherland. A man said to me in Tokyo a long time ago that Japanese born abroad would always be Japanese first of all. I answered that Japanese born in a foreign country should devote themselves to that country or return to Japan. His statement was disproved to me a few days later when a couple of young Japanese-Americans came to see me at the Embassy. "We are eager to go home," they said. "We came here to teach for a year in order to know the country of our ancestors. But we are homesick. We are Americans and think as Americans. This is the land of our ancestors but America is the land of opportunity."

So, since this war began, the Japanese on the mainland and in Hawaii have behaved like all other good Americans. Most of them think with deep sympathy of Japan, the land of their ancestors, and many of them wonder how it can have fallen so low. But the fact remains that they are Americans and rise to the defense of their country just as they would have risen to the defense of Japan had they been born and raised there.

It is sad, of course, that among them must be some few who would be disloyal to the United States, people who have not yet wholly learned what it means to be an American. It was the presence of those few which made it necessary to move all Japanese away from the Pacific coast where the disloyal few might have acted as enemy agents. As I said before in another connection, the innocent have to suffer with the guilty. But in Amer-

179

ica we try to separate the innocent from the guilty as far as it is possible. Always on the outlook for traitors, as we must be, we go on as usual with our Japanese-Americans in parts of the country other than the Pacific coast. Japanese teachers in the universities are still teaching; the Japanese language is still being studied. Certain universities are collecting great sums of money for scholarships for young Japanese who have had to leave their homes on the coast. All this is very different to the treatment meted out to the few Americans—thank heaven there were not more— who were in Japan when war broke out. The Japanese here know it and the contrast makes them all the more loyal citizens of America, their land of opportunity.

IX

Your military people seem to think that because they struck unexpectedly at the United States when our two countries were at peace and gained much through their treachery, they can keep right on surprising us, whatever they do. We shall not be surprised again and there will always be planes in the air to meet you unless we have kept them out of the air to surprise you and lead you on. That is exactly what happened at Milne Bay in New Guinea. Our officers did far better thinking than yours. It was a natural place for you to land troops because it was fairly near Australia and because it seemed to be an excellent base from which to get rid of Australian stations in other parts of the island.

I have in my mind a clear picture of that Japanese occupation, the long, narrow bay, with mountains coming down nearly to the water, your troop-laden convoy stealing in, probably under cover of fog. "Those fool Americans and Australians," your officers probably said to each other, "without sense enough even to defend a fine haven like this." They were already gloating over the decorations they would receive for their great achievement. There was evidently nobody to fight, unless perhaps a few natives who could be slaughtered in order to make the rest of the natives throughout the island all the more eager, some fine day, to receive the permanent troops of occupation. Guns and bayonets are the only things, your officers believe, to make a population contented and loyal. Then I can see the fog lifting and the already landed troops watching for possible enemies on shore or invading forces coming over the sea. But there was nothing and so, of course, the ships sailed away, leaving a new outpost of Japan almost off the shores of Australia. It was naturally heralded in Japan as one more successful attack by your glorious Army and Navy.

The reason it happened this way was, however, merely because our strategists thought a lot more clearly than yours. If you are planning to extend your occupation in New Guinea it stood to reason that Milne Bay was the next place to get hold of. It is deep, protected from storms, gives easy access by water to other parts of the island. So American and Australian officers decided it must surely be your next objective. It was and your officers went right ahead with their plans. We were so sure you would go there that we could easily have had ships and planes on hand to give you a warm greeting. But you found the place deserted. Now if your troops had landed in a place where there was no reason whatever to expect them to go it might not have been surprising to find an empty and unprotected harbor. But at Milne Bay, which was so obviously your next move, your officers would instantly have suspected the calm and solitude of the place if they had been only half as clever as they think themselves to be. They did not think at all but did just exactly what we had planned that they should do. They landed a large number of troops and the ships sailed away to be sunk at a later date. The troops ashore were completely trapped. There were plenty of Allied soldiers at the end of the bay and plenty of ships ready to sail in at short notice to help in whatever fighting there might be and to evacuate prisoners to Australia.

Japanese officers who not only believe that they can carry on a great war to a successful conclusion but also have the ridiculous obsession that they know how to govern Japan and that they can somehow organize a Japanese world—or at least as much of a world as Hitler may be generous enough to let them have. Nobody can govern unless he is able to judge what the other man is likely to do and this little incident at Milne Bay shows that you cannot win a war unless you are clever enough to take for granted that the enemy is intelligent. Your militarists seem to think that the gods have given them all the intelligence there is in the world, and they forget that the gods get men to think just this when they are getting ready to destroy them. Japan is going down hill and further down hill until the happy time comes when the military is once more dominated by wise civilians who know how to govern because they know how to think. When that time comes perhaps we shall be approaching the end of the war.

X

The resignation of Mr. Togo from the Japanese war cabinet made little impression in the United States except that people reading the news shrugged their shoulders and said, "That means a complete sell out to the military." Not that anyone thought Mr. Togo had played a strong civilian role. When he spoke at all he seemed to speak the lines which had been dictated to him, but nevertheless he was the one civilian in the

181

cabinet and therefore seemed to be a possible nucleus of a new group who might eventually do a little constructive thinking for themselves, to the everlasting benefit of Japan. Perhaps, however, it was personally wise for Mr. Togo to resign when he did. He may have dared to make a few suggestions and to tell a few truths and if he did that he was probably in danger of being murdered as so many splendid people have been murdered during the last few years when they seemed to stand in the way of the military. When I think of a great finance minister like Mr. Inouye, or of such a wise and inspiring leader as Admiral Saito, of a man like Baron Dan, not in the Government but a man who would gladly have lent his great knowledge of affairs to pull Japan through difficult times—when I think of men like these and the many others whose names and characters you remember far better than I, murdered in cold blood because they might have opposed some of the crazy schemes of the reactionary militarists, it makes me despair for the after-war future of Japan. It was an easy thing for these murderers to say that they acted in behalf of the Emperor, to shield him from bad advisers. But that was not the truth. They acted in the interest of their own savage ambitions, as you thinking Japanese very well know. They acted because they were jealous of the superior abilities and the higher patriotism of the men they killed. And they were cowardly enough to hide behind the sacred name of the emperor as they stabbed Japan in the back.

We should have taken notice of what was happening to Japan right then, at the time of the murders because it would have put us on guard for our own future. We ought to have known that when men would murder the best among their fellow citizens, thus making themselves traitors to the best interests of their own country, they would not hesitate to be traitors to the truth and to the pledged word of their Government, that they would stab in the back another nation with as little compunction as they stabbed the leaders of Japan. I think I can understand your reverence for the Imperial family, that deep respect and affection for one of the oldest and most distinguished families in the world. What I cannot understand is the base use of that noble sentiment as an excuse and a shield for actions motivated only by personal ambition. At the time of the famous purge in Tokyo a few years ago, you permitted a minority group to destroy some of the finest among you and were afraid to punish them although you knew their motives quite well. Now you are permitting these same fanatics to run your country. When you stop to consider, however, I am sure that you realize that these men are essentially destroyers, not builders. They are popular at the moment because they have carried the power of Japan overseas, but do you think for a moment that the empire they appear to be building is based on anything permanent? These men have no conception of the fact that a house cannot long stand without foundations, yet that is how they are trying to build an empire. It is only a facade that will crumble with the first adverse winds.

Mr. Togo, not being a militarist himself even if he was dominated by militarists, must have known this. Perhaps you put him out because he had the courage to warn you. Perhaps he told you that it was time to consolidate what you have gained—if you could—and not to start out on new adventures. Perhaps he said that you already have enemies enough. We don't know anything about this but we can guess and our guesses are based on the fact that you have disposed of the last civilian in the cabinet.

XI

There were reports—and the numbers are probably much larger now—that one hundred and twenty two Japanese planes were lost during the first four weeks of the fighting in the Solomon Islands. I wonder how difficult it will be for you to replace those planes and their pilots and their radio men and gunners and crews lost with them. It does not amount to much, this battle of the Solomon Islands, as I have said before, except that it proves that your troops are powerless unless they greatly outnumber their enemies and except that it seriously weakens you when you are needing fresh troops and fleets of planes to fight in a dozen other places, And then you keep on trying, and sometimes succeeding, to land other troops on the islands. I wonder why. There can be no sound military reason. The troops can be of no use. They will be wiped out in time. The task of doing this will mean the death of many American soldiers but it will cost the lives of far more Japanese soldiers and you have no such reservoir on which to draw as we have.

This month old battle of the Solomon Islands has taught us a great deal, some of it pleasant to know and some of it dreadfully unpleasant. I wonder whether it has taught you in Japan anything at all. The official reports given out in the United States do not tell very much because we do not want you to know until the knowledge would be of no value to you; but as far as they tell anything they are truthful, which is more than can be said for Japanese reports. Our reports do not say, for example, that this or that ship is destroyed until we are entirely sure that you know it already, but they do say such things as that "American losses were necessarily heavy." This they do because they know that the American people can stand bad news without cracking and that they are always more courageous if they know they are being told the truth as far as it can be told. That is not done in Japan. According to your radio and your press everything is always going beautifully. The result of that will be that when the time comes that your people must know the truth, even about such minor engagements as that in the Solomon Islands[,] the crash in morale will be very bad. You cannot lick people into smiling and a people that is discouraged does not fight well. Personally I think the Japanese could take the truth just as we take it here, that it would be better for them, and that your militarists withhold it from them just because they are afraid of losing face by admitting that anything under their inspired guidance has gone wrong.

With regard to this particular battle have the facts ever been published that you have been driven from some of your best positions, that you have lost the best air field in the Islands and that we are making a first class field out of it, that your troops have been driven into the jungles, where they lead the lives—such of them as are left—of any jungle beasts? Have your people been told anything about the fighting qualities of the American marines, as fearless as any Japanese, as willing to sacrifice life when necessary, but twice as strong and twice as wily! Have they been told that Japanese have surrendered and then shot their captors in the back? I should like to know whether your soldiers have been taught that no rules of decency hold any more, that treachery is justifiable always if it pays, and that the treacherous shooting of an American soldier always pays if it involves only the death of a single Japanese who has done the shooting. This, it seems to me, is making your rather splendid contempt of death a thing of cheap dramatics. It is just showing off to the detriment of Japan because everyone who thinks and reads knows that the Allied nations can far better afford to lose men than you can. It is a kind of showing off, moreover, which does nothing to forward your war aims and must eventually lead to retaliation and to a more cruel and ruthless style of fighting. Even if American and Australian troops cannot be taught to shoot their captors in the back after they have surrendered; even if they cannot be taught that the best way to get ahead is through treachery; even if they cannot be taught to torture defenceless men, women and children; they can and will learn from you that these are your principles and that you must be treated with that knowledge in mind, that a prisoner is a snake that must be prevented from striking, and that all the much talked of chivalry of Japan is an idle tale drawn out of a mythical past. So our marines are learning in the Solomon Islands to beware of many traits in the character of your soldiers, and they are also learning the welcome fact that your troops have no superior cunning in fighting, that although they may be more reckless they are no braver than

American soldiers, and that when the odds are equal in numbers and equipment the Americans have all the advantage.

XII

It is said that America is not yet fully awake to the fact of war but I wish you could travel through the country and listen to what people say and read the little country newspapers that have discovered the outside world and are trying to think out what this war means. Here, for example, is a part of today's editorial in a small paper in the town of Covington, Virginia. It says this: "Japan and Germany are strangely alike. Both are militaristic and predatory, inclined to war and eager to flourish at the expense of other nations. The love of peace, normal to Britain and America and other modern, enlightened nations, is not in them.—They represent organized banditry against constructive progress. Of these two nations the Germans are obviously the more civilized. These two national villains," the editorial goes on to say, "are bound to come into collision sooner or later because the world is not wide enough for both. But in the mean time they make common war upon the constructive, progressive nations, to destroy the civilization made by peaceful men. It is well to keep these facts clearly in mind, in order to understand the present war and the overwhelming importance of victory for the live-and-let-live Allied nations over the destroyers."

I have quoted this typical editorial which is, as I say, from a little country newspaper, to show you that, contrary to much propaganda, the people of the United States are not only vitally interested in the war and determined to win at whatever cost, but that they also pretty well understand what it is all about. They know that the world is a normally peaceful place and that the majority want to keep it peaceful but that these two militaristic and predatory nations are determined to go out to sieze [sic] the property of others and to enslave them. They know that love of peace is characteristic of the more enlightened and civilized nations and that the time has come when these more advanced nations have the unwelcome task of crushing the backward nations which, as the editorial says, "represent banditry against constructive progress."

These people in the country districts naturally think of Germany as the more civilized of the bandit nations because they have known many people of German descent and because they have listened to much beautiful German music. I think they are wrong in their conclusion. They do not know and have never had a chance to know anything of the culture of Japan. What they have seen of Japanese art has struck them as strange;

the Japanese they have met have had curious manners and have seldom spoken good English. Above all, in the weeks since they have been hearing much about Japan your militarists have succeeded in completely hiding the good qualities of the nation and have made Americans think of the Japanese merely as a cruel and treacherous race. It seems to me, in spite of your militarists, however, that Germany stands on a lower plane than Japan because it has been so much longer in close contact with the peace loving and therefore most civilized nations that it has less excuse for war madness and for releasing all the vilest instincts of its still only half civilized people. Japanese civilization was utterly different from that of the west but I am sure that in your great days you reached a higher plane than Germany has ever reached. However, these little country papers which mould public opinion see only the present and it is not strange that they see Japan as less civilized.

And lastly, one of the most interesting bits of this editorial seems to me to be the foresight on the part of the editor as shown by his knowledge that Germany and Japan are bound eventually to come into conflict with each other. This, of course, only if the Axis should win the war, and that cannot happen. But granted, just for the sake of argument that it might. Germany would take over Italy and whip it into good behaviour. Germany would demand of Japan the most important of its conquests in East Asia. Japan would refuse and then there would be another war. You know as well as I that really the Japanese detest the Germans and that the Germans despise the Japanese even now, and you may be sure that these feelings would flame into bitter conflict the moment the two nations were not fighting some other nation. If the editors of the little papers of America see these things and tell them to their millions of readers the American answer will be to fight always harder in order to end the war successfully before civilization dies.

XIII

You in Japan are said to be celebrating this month the tenth anniversary of the founding of Manchukuo. You are thus celebrating also the beginning of your break with the civilized world because it was the wanton attack on Manchuria which first turned civilized nations against you. In addition to this you are celebrating the surrender of the Japanese Government to the military, since, up to the time of the attack on Manchuria the military were not arrogant enough to pretend to run the civil government. It would hardly seem that these are causes for celebration but your ideas are evidently different from ours.

Today I want to consider just the first of these so-called celebrations, that over Manchukuo itself. As it stands now it is a fraud because you pretend that it is an independent nation. If you would just frankly admit that it is one of the provinces of Japan—at least for the time being—you would be honest about it. The real tragedy of Manchukuo is the tragedy and disillusionment that it has been for Japan. I used to read the accounts in your press and the propapanda sent out by the South Manchurian Railway and other corporations in the territory and they all glowed with rosy promises of what the conquest would mean to Japan. They pointed out the endless riches of Manchuria and of course all the home propaganda spoke as though these riches were the exclusive property of Japan. The talk about the full independence of Manchukuo was reserved for broadcast to the rest of the world. Then these benefits were detailed. There was, of course, the inexhaustible granary, which would mean that famine could never again strike the islands of Japan; there was this fertile land of limitless area open to Japanese colonization; there were minerals of all kinds waiting to be dug from the ground; in general the exploitation of Manchuria was going to destroy poverty forever in Japan and pour riches into the lap of every Japanese. So far as I know the only promise made by the conquerors of Manchuria which has been even partly fulfilled was that to eliminate bandits. People who have been lately in Manchuria have said that today one's chances of surviving a trip through the country are distinctly better than they were in the days of Chang H'sui Liang. In other words the Army has kept part of its promise by doing away with some of the bandits. As to the promise to bring riches to Japan I have no doubt that the exploitation of Manchuria has brought more wealth to many who were already rich. I am equally certain that the lot of the people of Japan has not been improved.

Quite the contrary is true because, to enable the profiteers to carry on their operations without interference, the Japanese Government, through heavy taxes drawn from the people in general, has paid and paid and paid. If Manchuria had been honestly administered it might have proved a profitable national investment. Instead its cost has been a drain on the nation since whatever profits there were went into the hands of the land speculators and the tax gatherers and the sellers of opium.

Here in Manchuria, even though the annexation was a shameful performance, you in Japan had a golden opportunity to build up a happy, honest, prosperous state, devoted to Japan because of all that had been done to bring security and prosperity. Instead the Japanese administrators have winked at dishonesty in the government so that in many ways conditions are no better than in the old days of war lord rule. They have

187

exploited the inhabitants of the territory to the advantage of a few favored Japanese. The result is unhappiness, unrest, a falling off in income which might be helping Japan. The result is that the Japanese are now in Manchukuo only on sufferance because there seems no way to throw them out. There is little or no Japanese colonization because the Japanese do not like the climate and because, even if they go to Manchuria they have no more chance to get ahead than do the original inhabitants of the region. So far as advantage to Japan is concerned the whole Manchurian affair has proved a failure and it is hard for us in America to think of you as celebrating a ten year failure with any great enthusiasm. And it might so easily have been a great success if only the wise statesmen of Japan had been permitted to do the job in the same intelligent and honorable manner that they used to work before the military took over.

XIV

In celebrating the tenth anniversary of the founding of Manchukuo I said that you must also be celebrating the initial step in your break with the civilized world. It was a rupture brought about largely by the absurd dishonesty of the Japanese Army. When the trouble began you sent word, at the behest of the Army authorities, to the various foreign capitals to assure all governments that nothing was going to happen beyond the punishment of those mythical people who were alleged to have attempted to destroy a bit of the South Manchurian Railroad. The Japanese Government was loud in its insistance [sic] that it was not offending against any of the treaties with China, and the other powers of the Washington Conference. Then immediately began that tragi-comic series of explanations as to why, day after day, it had become necessary to contradict the assertions of yesterday, when, day after day, your military people in Manchuria had to make up always more fantastic stories so there could be something to be contradicted later. In Washington we said that we could predict the progress of the Japanese Army by the places which they said they had no intention of taking. According to the stories retailed to us and to other foreign offices the ragged bandits of the territory must have compared favorably in fighting power to the German Army of the present day. At any rate the dauntless Japanese Army kept creeping forward, scattering the poorly armed and undisciplined bandits to right and left. When there was a town ahead your army promised not to take it under any circumstances and as soon as it was taken promised not to take the next town. It promised with special solemnity not to go beyond the great wall of China and of course promptly did so, probably still in pursuit of the elusive bandits. It promised not under any circumstances to enter Jehol, and, as we all expected, immediately invaded the territory, this time, however, only to be turned back by the Russians who considered the Japanese as trespassers. The situation was only stabilized when your Army met real resistance. Then it set up a puppet government which the Tokyo Government recognized as independent in all solemn ceremonies and tried to introduce to the rest of the world. The rest of the world was not interested and it was thoroughly bored with all the lies and the pretenses of legality. The world was not ready, however, to restore Manchuria to China by going to war about it, especially as this would also mean the restoration of a troublesome war lord to power and the territory to the bandits. So it pretended to believe Japanese protestations of virtue. It would probably have taken a stronger stand if it had recognized this move to be what it was, the first in a series of predatory attacks.

That was the story of the conquest so far as it could be read through the cloud of lies and excuses poured out like a smoke screen. It completely shattered foreign confidence in the good faith of Japan. It made all the more acute the misunderstandings between Russia and Japan, added greatly to the difficulties in the negotiations over the fisheries and the general question of Sakhalien. Russia had seen your attempt to penetrate Mongolia contrary to your promises. It had fought your troops and this time had found them not so good. It looked on the Japanese army in Manchuria as a potential threat to Siberia and consequently built up its own far eastern army but became more and more determined against any further concessions. It was only the intervention of the powers which saved you from war and in the light of what has happened since I doubt whether the powers would have thought it worth while to take a hand. Germany looked on cynically, ready as usual to help whatever side was likely to win. As showing its inclination, however, it began to send large numbers of officers to train Chinese troops which could not possibly fight anybody except Japan. Britain saw the uselessness of trying to work in sympathy with Japan because it saw that, as the appetite of the Japanese Army increased with its initial success no territories of the Orient would be safe from aggression. The United States was bitterly disappointed with this ancient and yet new nation which it had presented to the rest of the world. We here had been thrilled with your ability to meet modern conditions and to build a great place for your nation. We realized then that the appearance of civilization was outward appearance without inner reality. Then, naturally we turned to China as our friend in the Far East.

Is this ten year old break with the civilized world a reason for celebrations?

XV

Perhaps there is one class in Japan, the military, which can celebrate with enthusiasm the tenth anniversary of the founding of Manchukuo because, as I said, the successful attack on Manchuria marked the beginning of the assumption of all power by that class. The militarists are more or less intoxicated with their power, and glory in it, not because their country benefits from it but because they, personally, can strut before the people and exhibit their power. But Japan as a whole cannot celebrate the event. Of course the people will cry "Banzai" when their rulers march past but it will be because they dare not do otherwise. They will celebrate within the shadow of prison or at the point of a gun. It is as though the military said to them, "Rejoice openly in our greatness or you shall rot in prison. Smile to show how happy you are or you will be put against a wall and shot." That is the kind of celebration being held in Japan in honor of the founding of Manchukuo and all that went with it.

I wonder what those of you who were trained along other lines than those of arms think about it, whether you like being put in the discard. All you fine men of the Gaimusho, for example, who have devoted your lives to the study of foreign affairs and the best methods to maintain the prestige and influence of Japan among the nations, what do you think of the new kind of diplomacy which has discarded the pen for the sword and has taken away your own usefulness to your country? Do you think there is anything permanent in this military diplomacy? And all you, who are officials of the Imperial Court, who come of long lines of the nobility who have devoted themselves for centuries to the care of the Emperor, to enable him to carry on his work of ruling Japan with justice and mercy, what do you think of the necessity of turning over your responsibilities to the soldiery? You have read Japanese history and know what the results have been in the past. You of the Treasury and of the various ministries, who have carried on so efficiently the government of a great country, what do you think of resigning your positions into the untrained and bungling hands of a military dictatorship? What do the able and forward looking newspaper editors and publishers think of having to restrict what they say to the most avid newsreading public in the world, to the half-baked and often obviously false stories handed out to them by the authorities? And what do thoughtful readers think who no longer find anything in their papers which they can honestly believe and trust? And the farmers, who watch their sons carried away to war, leaving them with no hands to till the soil? And the industrialists, who see their factories and their laboratories controled by the Government, run only for maximum production, without thought of repair or replacements? Are these reasons why you should enthusiastically celebrate the founding of Manchukuo? For all classes except one it will be celebration at the point of a gun.

I know that your propagandists will say that every class is willing to make every sacrifice for the fatherland. And I also know that this is a very nearly true statement. But it is also true that all classes are capable of thinking and that many of you realize that the military are not trained for the duties they are carrying on and that therefore your sacrifices may not, after all, be for the ultimate good of Japan. You of the Gaimusho understand that the foreign policy of the sword cannot be permanent and cannot lead to the permanent good of your country internationally. You want to build up trade and you know that trade is an uncertain matter without good will. You want to send to foreign countries men who will make a good impression through courtesy and truth and intelligent grasp of great problems, and of all these matters you know that your military class has little knowledge. You of the Imperial Household know that, with all their protestations of loyalty to the throne, the kind of militarists now in control, the kind who murdered Admiral Saito and would have liked to kill Prince Saionji, would make the Emperor of Japan as much a puppet ruler as they have made the Emperor of Manchukuo.

No. I am sure that with the failure to make Manchukuo the support to Japan that was promised; that with the break with the civilized world resulting from the attack in Manchuria; that with the rise of the military to supreme power which followed, such celebration as may be held in Japan will be anything but spontaneous, will be hollow because forced.

XVI

When I went to Japan as American Ambassador I went as a friend. When I left there I left as a friend, more than ever determined that much of my future work must be to help maintain and promote the good relations between our two countries, which were so valuable to us both. In Japan there were many Japanese as eager as I was to continue this work because they were just as conscious of the value of co-operation as I was. But the first shot at Pearl Harbor destroyed my hopes and wrecked that structure of understanding which so many of us, in both countries, had labored to build.

Twelve years ago I saw Japan as I believe it still is, at heart at least, today; its people friendly and hard working, its statesmen, pushed into retirement for the time being, wise and far seeing just as they were a few years back. There was already when I was there a little group of militarists who thirsted for adventure and were already making trouble because they cared nothing for the rights of others and were pushing their own fortunes under the false name of patriotism. Foolishly I believed that this minority, potentially so dangerous to Japan, could be controled. I believed that Japan, through its superb organizing genius, was on its way to being the leading nation of the orient. I saw it growing rich and powerful through cooperation and friendly dealings with its neighbors, gaining the respect and admiration of the world because it was reaching a position of eminence through honorable and praiseworthy methods. That would have been a Japan sure of itself and universally respected, a Japan well governed by men of high intelligence and high ideals, a country where there was a chance for all to rise, where poverty would be almost unknown, because the immense returns of peaceful trade would reach all classes. This glowing future was in the hands of the leaders but, alas, their power was siezed [*sic*] by ambitious and ruthless militarists who shattered the dream that was so near realization.

You Japanese have had great military leaders in the past but they have been men, like Hideyoshi, who remembered that they were something more than men at arms, that they were truly leaders of the people, must be their leaders in thought and in behavior, who fostered art, who preserved everything that was beautiful. Sometimes they seemed cruel but they conformed to the standards of their times and never hurt for the sake of hurting. We all thought, Japanese as well as others, that the world had progressed, and that modern military leaders in Japan as well as in America would live up to the more humane standards of modern times. We believed that Japanese military leaders would at least be patriotic enough to avoid dragging the fair name of their fatherland in the dust. But we were all desperately wrong. Japanese generals today seem to have forgotten what bushido means. Their cruelties have disgraced their country and have turned the civilized world against it. We outsiders are compelled, today, to judge Japan not by its art and its philosophy and its love of beauty, its theatres and its wonderful forward march as a great modern economic power. No, we are compelled to see Japan as its militarists have given the picture to the world when they drenched their flag in the blood of Nanking and Hongkong. Instead of a nation respected and admired everywhere Japan is now a nation everywhere hated. And this hatred, in spite of temporary military successes, means that in the years to come, instead of being a rich and prosperous nation, the economic and intellectual leader of the Orient, with plenty for all at home and showing

Asia how to live well and happily, Japan must struggle with dire poverty, must be loaded with debt, must be surrounded with peoples who hate her because she betrayed and attacked them, people who could have been her friends and helped to make her prosperous. To satisfy the ambitions of a minority of proud and evil men Japan has thrown away a great destiny.

Your military leaders forced the Government to join the Axis because they believed that Germany would win the war. They guessed wrong, but even if they had been right what would Japan's future have been in a German-dominated world? Some of you who are older will remember when Germany had a foothold in China and what trouble that meant in East Asia, including Japan. One reason you went into the last war was to drive the Germans from their last foothold in Asia and you succeeded. But if the Axis should win this war you may be sure that Germany will again be in possession of parts of the China coast facing you across narrow seas. Many of you must realize that this would mean another war unless Japan was willing to be completely subservient to its rapacious ally. Do even your militarists have the delusion that Germany would permit you to hold the East Indies in case of an Axis victory? Germany wants to control oil and rubber producing regions: it has its heavy heel on Holland, that splendid and courageous little country which had grown rich and contented because it had learned to mind its own business. Since Germany is crushing the mother country it intends to take the colonies as well. Germany wanted Japan in the Axis to use for its own purposes. There was no friendliness in the Nazi bid for Japanese support. Your militarists were so stupid as to believe German promises and in consequence of their arrogant stupidity Japan, in spite of its easy initial victories, faces ruin. It faces complete degradation if Germany wins; it faces well merited punishment if the associated nations win but in that case it also has a chance to become once more a great power if it proves itself willing to grow through honorable and peaceful means.

In all human history there was never a nation which thrived for a long period on the hatred of its fellow nations. Yet that is what your military men pretend to believe that Japan can do. You have conquered, for the time being, neighboring territories, and your armies have cruelly maltreated the people of those territories. Your Army men know nothing but force and therefore they leave hatred and the determination once more to be free in every territory through which they pass. They miss every opportunity to build for Japan. Your beautiful islands are therefore almost surrounded by people who hate you and can hardly wait for allied armies to appear so that they can help to drive you into the sea. This is only because your militarists listened to the flattery of Germany and went mad.

And since the lands you have conquered hate you they could be held only at the expense of gradually draining away the life blood of Japan itself. Your men would always be in other countries, struggling to hold in check the people you have conquered. At home your fields would be untilled because there would be none to cultivate them. Your beautiful terraced rice fields would dry up and their walls break down because there would be no one to give them the constant care they must have. Your boys would be raised only to fight, not to rebuild the fatherland. Your greatness in the arts and in the advancement of human thought would vanish because those who might have been artists and philosophers would be dead or doing useless sentry duty in hostile countries. And all this misery for Japan because a small minority of your men, imagining themselves great, longing to rule over other men, have siezed [sic] the power and dragged your once great nation far from the road which leads to peace and the opportunity to be really a leader among nations. The fruit of what you have gained looks big now but already your armies are beginning to be driven back and one by one the conquered lands will regain their independence from the hated Japanese domination.

The Axis is not going to win this war and all Japan must pay the penalty for the misdeeds and the miscalculations of the minority of militarists. Your cities will be destroyed and thus will perish the artistic and beautiful records of your past great history, for the fires that follow bombardments have no power to spare those things which ought to be eternal. I grieve for the tragedy which faces the innocent, that they must pay for the sins of others. But that is the law of life. When this frightful war is over, and the Axis menace is crushed, Japan can have hope in the future, can know that when it is willing to take its honorable place in a society of free nations it can also regain its place as a leader of oriental thought and an organizer of world trade. As a nation at peace it can support a diligent and contented population and it can regain world friendship in place of the well merited hatred that now beats against it from all sides. The goal can be reached sooner if the real leaders of Japan[,] backed by the people of Japan, can once again get control of the militarists and thus gain the mastery of their own future.

Notes

Preface

1. William R. Castle, Jr., "Hawaii—Equal or Outcast?" *New York Herald Tribune,* July 22, 1934. Castle Papers, Herbert Hoover Library, West Branch, Iowa. See also W. R. Castle, Jr., "Shall Hawaii Go East or West?" *World Outlook* 6 (May 1920): 16–30.

2. See Castle's autobiographical sketch for the *Twenty-fifth Anniversary Report, Harvard College–Class of 1900,* 113, and his updated autobiography in the *Fiftieth Anniversary Report, Harvard College–Class of 1900.* Copies of these alumni reports are available through the Harvard Alumni Association Library and Archives.

1. A Moral Endowment for Public Service

1. W. R. Castle, Jr., "What it Means to be an Hawaiian," address delivered at Kawaiahao Church, Honolulu, August 31, 1933. Castle Papers, Herbert Hoover Library.

2. W. R. Castle, Jr., *Life of Samuel N. Castle* (Honolulu: Hawaiian Historical Society, 1960), 108–109.

3. W. R. Castle, Jr., "Autobiographical Sketch," in *Fiftieth*

Anniversary Report, Harvard College—Class of 1900 (Harvard Archives–Pusey Library), 119–120.

4. W. R. Castle, Jr., "Propaganda," address delivered to the Episcopal Club of Massachusetts, April 21, 1926. Castle Papers.

5. Castle, "Propaganda."

6. W. R. Castle, Jr., "General Peace Conference of 1932: Disarmament and World Peace," unpublished manuscript, Box 33, Castle Papers.

7. For a complete discussion of the theology of the Hawaiian missionaries, see Sandra E. Wagner, "Mission and Motivation: The Theology of the Early American Mission in Hawaii," *Hawaiian Journal of History* 19 (1985): 62–70.

8. Mary Tenney to S. N. Castle, May 27, 1842, Castle Collection, Hawaiian Mission Children's Society (HMCS) Library.

9. T. Coan to F. Coan, June 3, 1851, and M. Smith to L. Smith, March 5, 1838, Castle Collecton, HMCS Library; George Nellist, *Women of Hawaii* (Honolulu: Paradise of the Pacific Press, 1929), 61.

10. *Reminiscences of William Richards Castle* (Honolulu: privately printed, 1960), 28–29.

11. W. R. Castle, Sr., "Mary Tenney Castle," *The Friend* (April 11, 1907).

12. W. R. Castle, Jr., address given to the Washington Chapter of American Church Union at St. Paul's Church, Washington, D.C., February 7, 1943, Castle Papers.

13. W. R. Castle, Jr., "Our Foreign Relations," *The Massachusetts Elephant* (June 1928): 3.

14. Castle, speech to the Church Society for College Work, Washington, D.C., April 21,1941, 5. Castle Papers.

15. W. R. Castle, Jr., "Evaluating the League of Nations," *The Rotarian* (September 1934): 54.

2. The Beginning of Public Service: The American Red Cross Bureau of Communications

1. William R. Castle, Jr., *Wake Up, America: A Plea for the Recognition of Our Individual and National Responsibilities* (New York: Dodd, Mead, 1916), 110–111.

2. William R. Castle, Jr., "Report on Organization and Operations, Bureau of Communications of the Department of Law

and International Relations," February 15, 1919, 1. Archival and Personnel Records, Red Cross National Headquarters, Washington, D.C.

3. William R. Castle, Jr., Autobiography in *Twenty-fifth Anniversary Report,* Harvard College–Class of 1900, 133. Harvard University Alumni Association.

4. Castle, Autobiography.

5. Castle, Autobiography, 2.

6. The reputation of the American Red Cross for loyalty and integrity made it ideal to fulfill this sensitive mission. Supervised by Louise Thoran, the new Civilian Communications Section of the American Red Cross handled all mail inquiries about soldiers in Germany, Austria, Hungary, Turkey, Russia, Balkans, Belgium, occupied portions of France and Italy, Syria, Palestine, and Mesopotamia.

7. Castle, "Report on Organization and Operations."

8. Castle, "Report on Organization and Operations," 23–24.

9. Charles M. Blakewell, *The Story of the American Red Cross in Italy* (New York: Macmillan, 1920), 157, 160–164.

10. John van Schaick, Jr., *The Little Corner Never Conquered: The Story of the American Red Cross Work in Belgium* (New York: Macmillan, 1922), 241–245.

11. Edward Huyerford, *With the Doughboys in France: A Few Chapters of an American Effort* (New York: Macmillan, 1920), 238–245.

12. Castle, "Report on Organization and Operations," 9–10.

13. Henry Cabot Lodge, "Our New Envoy to Japan," *New York Herald Tribune,* January 19, 1930.

14. See the various entries for the year 1918 in the Castle Diary, Harvard University. Castle's private assessments of many civilian leaders, in both the United States and Europe, which often stress the difference between public rhetoric and private actions, would be basic themes of his written observations.

3. The Corporate State in the 1920s

1. The best discussions of the corporate state are found in: Michael J. Hogan, "Corporatism: A Positive Appraisal," *Diplomatic History* 10, no. 4 (1986): 363–372; Thomas J. Mc-

Cormick, "Draft or Mastery: A Corporatist Synthesis for American Diplomatic History," *Reviews in American History* 10 (December 1982); Robert Wiebe, *The Search for Order, 1877–1920* (New York: Hill and Wang, 1968); Ellis Hawley, "The Discovery and Study of a 'Corporate Liberalism,'" *Business History Review* 52 (fall 1978); Carl P. Parrini, *Heir to Empire: U.S. Economic Diplomacy, 1916–1923* (Pittsburgh: University of Pittsburgh Press, 1969); Michael J. Hogan, *Informal Entente: The Private Structure of Cooperation in Anglo-American Economic Diplomacy, 1918–1928* (Columbia: University of Missouri Press, 1971); Melvyn P. Leffler, *The Elusive Quest: America's Pursuit of European Stability and French Security, 1919–1933* (Chapel Hill: University of North Carolina Press, 1979); and Ellis Hawley, *The Great War and the Search for a Modern Order: A History of the American People and Their Institutions, 1917–1933* (New York: St. Martin's Press, 1979).

2. For critical accounts of the cooperative state of the 1920s, see general works for the 1920s: Joan Hoff Wilson, *Herbert Hoover, Forgotten Progressive* (Boston: Little, Brown, 1975); Warren I. Cohen, *Empire Without Tears: America's Foreign Relations, 1921–1933* (Philadelphia: Temple University Press, 1987); Charles E. Neu, *The Troubled Encounter: The United States and Japan* (New York: Wiley, 1975); Thomas H. Buckley, *The United States and the Washington Conference, 1921–1922* (Knoxville: University of Tennessee, 1970); David F. Schmitz, *The United States and Facist Italy, 1922–1940* (Chapel Hill: University of North Carolina Press, 1988); John P. Diggins, *Mussolini and Facism: The View from America* (Princeton, N.J.: Princeton University Press, 1972); Herbert Feis, *The Diplomacy of the Dollar, First Era, 1919–1923* (Baltimore: Johns Hopkins Press, 1951); William A. Williams, *American-Russian Relations, 1781–1947* (New York: Rinehart, 1952); Manfred Jonas, *The United States and Germany: A Diplomatic History* (Ithaca, N.Y.: Cornell University Press, 1984); Arthur M. Schlesinger, Jr., *The Crisis of the Old Order, 1919–1933* (Boston: Houghton Mifflin, 1957); Joan Hoff Wilson, *American Business and Foreign Policy, 1920–1933* (Lexington: University of Kentucky Press, 1971); Frank Costigliola "The U.S. and the Reconstruction of Germany in the 1920s," *Business History Review* 50 (winter 1976); Betty Glad, "Charles Evans Hughes, Rationalism, and Foreign Af-

fairs," in *Traditional Values: American Diplomacy, 1865–1945,* ed. Norman Graebner (1982).

3. W. R. Castle, Jr., "Germany As She Is Today," *New York Evening Post,* November 26, 1920.

4. W. R. Castle, Jr., "The Leopard's Spots," *The Russian Review* 1 (August 19, 1919): 295–297.

5. W. R. Castle, Jr., "The Outlook in Germany," *The Review* 2 (April 10, 1920): 356–358.

6. W. R. Castle, Jr., Diary, September 14, 1920. Houghton Library, Harvard University.

7. Castle, "Germany As She Is Today."

8. W. R. Castle, Jr., "Moscow's Campaign of Poison," *The Review* 2 (January 24, 1920): 77–80.

9. W. R. Castle, Jr., "The Hungarian Tangle," *The Review* 1 (November 1, 1919): 535–537.

10. W. R. Castle, Jr., "The Austrian Collapse," *The Weekly Review* 4 (January 26, 1921): 73–75.

11. W. R. Castle, Jr., "Our Diplomatic Service," *The Weekly Review* 3 (December 15, 1929): 579–580.

12. Other major instructors included Allen Dulles, Ellery C. Stowell, Tracy Lay, Bernadotte E. Schmitt, Dana Murro, Stokely Morga, Leland Harrison, Paul Hulbertson, and Alanson Houghton.

13. W. R. Castle, Jr., "New States of Europe," lecture to Foreign Service School, August 10, 1925. Castle Papers, Herbert Hoover Library.

14. Castle, "New States of Europe."

15. Robert D. Schulzinger, "The Making of the Diplomatic Mind: The Training. Outlook. and Style of United States Foreign Service Officers, 1906–1928" (Ph.D. diss., Yale University, 1971), 206–208.

16. W. R. Castle, Jr., lecture to Foreign Service School, March 20, 1926. Castle Papers.

17. W. R. Castle, Jr., letters to Hughes, June 22, 1922, and June 27, 1922. Castle Papers.

18. W. R. Castle, Jr., letter to Hughes, March 20, 1924. Castle Papers.

19. W. R. Castle, Jr., Memorandum of a conversation with the German Ambassador, February 15, 1926. Castle Papers.

20. Will H. Hays, letter to Castle, December 10, 1924. Castle Papers.

21. Castle to Coffin, November 2, 1926. Castle Papers.

22. Castle to Grew, October 2, 1926. Castle Papers.

23. Joseph C. Grew, *Turbulent Era: A Diplomatic Record of Forty Years, 1904–1945* (Boston: Houghton Mifflin, 1952), 1: 471–472.

24. Dexter Perkins, "The Department of State and American Public Opinion," in *The Diplomats 1919–1939,* ed. Gordon A. Craig and Felix Gilbert (Princeton: Princeton University Press, 1953), 305.

25. Castle Diary, October 20, 1922.

26. W R. Castle, Jr., to Hughes, October 24, 1922. Castle Papers.

27. W R. Castle, Jr., to Hughes, December 1, 1922; Castle to Hughes, December 13, 1922. Castle Papers.

28. W. R. Castle, Jr., to Hughes, December 12, 1922. Castle Papers.

29. Castle Diary, March 16, 1923.

30. L. Ethan Ellis, *Republican Foreign Policy, 1921–1933* (New Brunswick, N.J.: Rutgers University Press, 1968), 154.

31. W. R. Castle, Jr., Subject File France, 1928–1929. Castle Papers.

32. Ellis, *Republican Foreign Policy,* 218. See also Robert Ferrell, *American Diplomacy* (New York: W. W. Norton, 1975), 515–516, and Castle Diary, May 11, 1927, and December 3, 1927.

33. Castle Diary, January 1, 1928.

34. Memorandum of a conversation between W. R. Castle, Jr., and the Japanese ambassador, July 23, 1927. Castle Papers.

4. The London Naval Conference

1. *New York Herald Tribune,* December 22, 1930.

2. Castle to Hugh Wilson, December 11, 1929. Castle Papers, Herbert Hoover Library.

3. Castle to Hoover, March 25, 1930. Castle Papers.

4. Tatsuji Takeuchi, *War and Diplomacy in the Japanese Empire* (Chicago: University of Chicago Press, 1935), 283–284.

5. Robert H. Ferrell, *Frank B. Kellogg and Henry L. Stimson.* Volume 2 in *The American Secretaries of State and Their Diplomacy,* ed. Samuel Flagg Bemis and Robert Ferrell. (New York: Cooper Square Publishers, 1963), 180–183.

6. James B. Crowley, *Japan's Quest for Autonomy: National*

Security and Foreign Policy, 1930–1938 (Princeton, N.J.: Princeton University Press. 1966), 44.

7. Castle to Wilson, January 29, 1930. Castle Papers.

8. Castle to Cotton, January 25, 1930. Hoover Presidential Papers, Cabinet Offices. Herbert Hoover Library.

9. Castle to Hoover, January 27, 1930. Hoover Presidential Papers, Cabinet Offices.

10. W. R. Castle, Jr., address to the Japan Society of Boston, December 9, 1930. Castle Papers.

11. Castle to David A. Reed, January 27, 1930. Castle Papers.

12. W. R. Castle, Jr., speech at the Indiana World Peace Committee, Indianapolis, April 22, 1931. Castle Papers.

13. W. R. Castle, Jr., address before the Advertising Club of Boston, September 22, 1931. Castle Papers.

14. Cotton to Castle, February 1, 1930. Hoover Presidential Papers, Cabinet Offices.

15. *New York Times,* February 7, 1930.

16. *Congressional Record,* vol. 73 (1930), 229.

17. Tokyo Castle Cable no. 27, February 14, 1930, London Naval Conference 500 A15/A3 1 689. RG 43 (Records of International Conferences, Commissions, and Expositions), National Archives.

18. Untitled manuscript, Castle Papers.

19. Castle to Stimson, February 24, 1930. Hoover Presidential Papers, Cabinet Offices.

20. Cotton to Stimson, cable no. 181, March 6, 1930, London Naval Conference 500 A15 A31741a. RG 43, National Archives.

21. Henry L. Stimson, Diary, March 12, 1930. Stimson Papers, Herbert Hoover Library.

22. Baron Wakatsuki, "The Aims of Japan," *Foreign Affairs* 13 (1935): 591.

23. Cable, Castle to Cotton, March 20, 1930. Hoover Presidential Papers, Cabinet Offices.

24. Castle report no. 144, May 26, 1930, London Naval Conference A15 A31669. RG 43, National Archives. See also *New York Times,* April 2, 1930, 1.

25. Cable, Castle to Cotton, March 23, 1930, and April 1, 1930, Doc. File 500. A15a/774 and 1809. RG 59 (General Records of the Department of State), National Archives.

26. Letter, Castle to Hoover, March 25, 1930. Hoover Presidential Papers, Foreign Affairs.

27. Crowley, *Japan's Quest for Autonomy*, 67.

28. Tokyo (Castle) Report, May 5, 1930, London Naval Conference 500 A15 A31909. RG 43, National Archives.

29. Castle viewed the assassination as the "lone act of a madman" and not necessarily a symbol of a deteriorating democracy. See speech to Japan Society of Boston, December 9, 1930.

30. Stimson had always felt that the chief U.S. hold over Japan during the conference was the threat of an Anglo-American accord.

5. The Hoover Moratorium

1. Stimson to Atherton, June 15, 1931, U.S. Department of State, *Foreign Relations of the United States,* 1931, 1, 18 (hereafter FRUS).

2. Henry L. Stimson, Diary, June 5–16, 1931. Yale University.

3. Lamont to Hoover, June 5, 1931, Hoover Presidential Papers, Box 871, Herbert Hoover Library.

4. Leffler, *The Elusive Quest,* 236. See also Herbert Feis to Felix Frankfurter, June 27, 1931, Feis Papers, Box 16, Library of Congress.

5. Henry L. Stimson and McGeorge Bundy, *On Active Service in Peace and War* (New York: Harper, 1948), 202–213.

6. William S. Myers and Walter H. Newton, *The Hoover Administration: A Documented Narrative* (New York: Charles Scribner and Sons, 1936).

7. Leffler, *The Elusive Quest,* 237. See also Governor Harrison, "Conversations Relative to Debt Settlements," Federal Reserve Bank of New York, June 11, 1931. Folder File, Ogden Mills, Box 2, Herbert Hoover Library.

8. Stimson Diary, June 14–18. 1931.

9. W. R. Castle, Jr., Diary, June 16, 1931. Herbert Hoover Library. See also Walter Edge to Hoover, June 9, 1931. Castle Papers, Herbert Hoover Library.

10. In that conference, Castle implied that the Hoover administration might change its policy to collect war debts if an international emergency required it. Stimson would later find this unauthorized statement an additional reason for regret-

ting Castle's appointment as under secretary of state in March 1931. See Stimson and Bundy, *On Active Service,* 192.

11. *London Daily Express,* June 14, 1931, and *New York Times,* June 14, 1931.

12. See Castle Diary, June 19, 1931. Later, Castle would defend Hoover's actions by saying there was not enough time to do so in the midst of economic chaos and pending disaster. W. R. Castle, Jr., "Intergovernmental Debts" (unpublished manuscript, 1934), 258. Castle Papers.

13. Stimson, Diary, June 19–20. 1931.

14. Herbert Hoover, *The State Papers and Other Public Writings of Herbert Hoover,* ed. William S. Myers (Garden City, N.Y.: Doubleday, Doran, 1934), 1:574, 593.

15. Von Hindenburg to Hoover, quoted in Theodore G. Joslin, *Hoover off the Record* (New York: Doubleday and Doran, 1934), 99–100.

16. Charles P. Kindleberger, *The World in Depression* (Berkeley: University of California Press, 1980), 150. See also Castle Diary, June 21, 1931, and Herbert C. Hoover, *Memoirs* (New York: Macmillan, 1951–1952), 2: 64–65.

17. Leffler, *The Elusive Quest,* 240, and Charles G. Dawes, *Journal as Ambassador to Great Britain* (New York: Macmillan, 1939), 359.

18. Wilson, *Herbert Hoover,* 185–186.

19. Michael J. Sullivan, "Franco-American Relations in the Financial Crisis of 1931" (M.A. thesis, Drake University, 1975), 39–54.

20. Walter E. Edge, *A Jerseyman's Journal: Fifty Years of American Business and Politics* (Princeton, N.J.: Princeton University Press, 1948), 193–194.

21. Geoffrey Warner, *Pierre Laval and the Eclipse of France* (New York: Macmillan, 1968), 31–33. See also Castle, "Intergovernmental Debts."

22. Leffler, *The Elusive Quest,* 242.

23. Walter Fallow, Jr., *President Hoover and Secretary of State Stimson: A Study in International Relations* (Durham, N.C.: Duke University Press, 1957), 30.

24. Stimson Diary, June 25–27, 1931. Although Stimson offered to stay and lead the negotiations, Hoover urged him to go. Nonetheless, Stimson planned to visit Paris after stops in Italy.

25. Drew Pearson claimed that Castle's selection as under

secretary was forced on Stimson by Hoover and powerful Republican Sen. David Reed. The increasing closeness of Castle and Hoover undercut Stimson on more than one occasion before Hoover left office in March 1933. See Drew Pearson and Robert Allen, *Washington Merry Go Round* (New York: Horace Liveright, 1931), 152–154. Hoover, for example, clearly felt he had reason to distrust Stimson. As Hoover told Castle privately, "Stimson wants to run things himself and if he is allowed to run things himself they will come out very differently from the way we want them to work out." Castle Diary, July 19, 1931.

26. Stimson admitted that he had virtually no role in the Franco-American negotiations after his departure but was kept informed by Castle on a daily basis. Stimson, Diary, June 27–July 6.

27. See Castle Diary, September 29, 1927; April 3, July 11, August 16–17, October 3, and November 6, 1923.

28. Barney J. Rickman III, "Ideology and Influence: William R. Castle, Jr. and the Manchurian Crisis, 1931–33" (paper presented at the Conference of the Society for Historians of American Foreign Relations, August 1–4, 1990, University of Maryland).

29. For a summary of Republican views of internal order, see Walter LaFeber, *The American Age* (New York: W. W. Norton, 1989), 316–344. LaFeber's analysis seems, on the whole, correct although he overestimates the importance of foreign trade to American business. See John Braeman, "The New Left and American Foreign Policy During the Age of Normalcy: A Re-Examination," *Business History Review* 57, no. 1 (1993): 73–104.

30. See Alfred L. Castle, "William R. Castle and Opposition to U.S. Involvement in an Asian War, 1939–1941," *Pacific Historical Review* 54 (1985): 337–351, and Ferrell, *Frank Kellogg and Henry L. Stimson,* 7–16.

31. Wilson, *Herbert Hoover,* 168.

32. For a complete description, see Williams, *American-Russian Relations,* and Wilson, *American Business and Foreign Policy.*

33. Robert H. Ferrell, *American Diplomacy in the Great Depression* (New Haven: Yale University Press, 1957), 37–39. See also Robert F. Smith, "Republican Policy at the Pax Ameri-

cana, 1921–1932," in *From Colony to Empire: Essays in the History of American Foreign Relations,* ed. William A. Williams (New York: Wiley Press, 1972), 253–292.

34. Edward W. Bennett, *Germany and the Diplomacy of the Financial Crisis, 1931* (Cambridge, Mass.: Harvard University Press, 1962), 178. See also Jonas, *The United States and Germany,* 198–199.

35. The best example of this was the failure of France to obtain a mutual defense pact with the United States in 1927. See Robert H. Ferrell, *Peace in Their Time* (New Haven: Yale University Press, 1952).

36. Joseph S. Davis, *The World Between the Wars, 1919–1939: An Economist's View* (Baltimore: Johns Hopkins University Press, 1975), 273.

37. Leffler, *The Elusive Quest,* 242. Castle felt the French "were fighting for purely academic points while the world went to smash." See also Castle, "Intergovernmental Debts," 259.

38. Hoover, *Memoirs,* 2:72; Stimson Diary, June 22–25, 1931; Castle Diary, June 28, 1931.

39. Although Castle kept Stimson closely advised, he secretly resented the secretary's occasional cables, which were out of touch with the president's position. As Castle noted in his private diary, "If he wanted to negotiate he should have stayed here—as people in general think he should have done. He cannot play both ends at the middle. He cannot be Secretary of State in the Middle of the Atlantic." Castle Diary, July 2, 1931.

40. Castle to Sackett, Cable 94, June 27, 1931. Hoover State Department papers, Herbert Hoover Library.

41. Henderson to Lindsay, London, June 26, 1931, DBFP 11, 104; Castle to Sackett, Cable 94.

42. Castle to Edge and Mellon, Cable 298; Castle to Edge, Cable 305. Hoover Library.

43. Castle Diary, June 28, 1931. Castle to Edge and Mellon, Cable 295, Hoover Library. Castle cautioned Edge that Hoover's impatience and insistence that the French "take it or leave it" should be communicated with great tact. Under no circumstance must the French feel threatened and backed into a corner. See Castle to Edge, Cable 298.

44. Edge to Castle, Cable 371. Castle Papers, Herbert Hoover Library.

45. Castle Diary, July 1, 1931.

46. Sackett to Castle, July 2, 1931, and Castle Memorandum, June 29, 1931. Castle Papers.

47. Stimson agreed with Castle's use of pressure on Germany and shared his frustration that the Germans were slow to respond with concrete concessions. Stimson to Castle, Telegram No. 2. Castle Papers.

48. Castle to Sackett, June 30, 1931. See also Edge to Castle, Cable 379, June 30, 1931; Sackett to Castle, Cable 106, June 30, 1931. Hoover Library.

49. Castle memorandum, July 1, 1931. Castle Papers.

50. Castle Diary, July 1, 1931.

51. Sackett to Castle, July 2, 1931. Hoover Library.

52. Sackett to Castle, Cable 107, July 1, 1931. Hoover Library.

53. Castle to Sackett, Cables 101 and 104, July 1, 1931. Hoover Library.

54. Castle to Sackett, Cable 106, July 1, 1931. Castle Papers.

55. Castle to Sackett, Cable 108, Midnight, July 2, 1931. Hoover Library.

56. Sackett to Castle, Cable 109, 1931. Hoover Library.

57. Castle to Sackett, Cable 110, July 4, 1931. Hoover Library.

58. Bernard V. Burke, "American Diplomats and Hitler's Rise to Power, 1930–1933: The Mission of Ambassador Sackett" (Ph.D. diss., University of Washington, 1966), 228–229.

59. Castle Diary, July 3, 1931.

60. Edge to Castle, Cable 390, July 1, 1931. Hoover Library.

61. Castle to Mellon, Cable 322, July 2, 1931. See also Edge to Castle, Cable 396, July 2, 1931. Hoover Library.

62. Ray Atherton to Castle, Cable 225, July 4, 1931. Hoover Library.

63. Castle Diary, July 4, 1931.

64. Castle Diary, July 5, 1931.

65. Castle to American Embassy, Paris, Cables 328 and 329, July 4, 1931. Castle Papers.

66. Castle to American Embassy, Paris, Cable 330, June 4, 1931. Castle Papers.

67. Edge to Castle, Cable 404, July 4, 1931. Hoover Library.

68. Castle Diary, July 5, 1931.

69. Jay Pierrepont Moffat, Diary, July 1–6, 1931. Moffat Papers, Harvard University.

70. Transcript of telephone conversation with Andrew Mellon in Paris, 11:25 A.M. EST, July 6, 1931. Hoover Library.

71. Transcript of conversation of Mellon and Hoover, 12:50 P.M., July 31, 1931. Hoover Library.

72. Transcript of telephone conversation with Andrew Mellon in Paris, 2:50 P.M., June 31, 1931. Hoover Library.

73. Transcript of telephone conversation between Castle and Sackett. 4:05 P.M., July 6, 1931. Hoover Library.

74. Castle Diary, July 7, 1931.

75. Castle Diary, July 7, 1931. More appreciated was Henry Cabot Lodge's claim that Castle's efforts had done more for Hoover's image and reputation than those of any other administration official. Castle Diary, July 20. 1931.

76. See Smith, "Republican Policy and the Pax Americana," 253–292.

77. Castle, "Intergovernmental Debts," 258.

78. Ellis, *Republican Foreign Policy,* 207.

79. Memorandum of W. R. Castle, Jr.'s, Press Conference, July 13, 1931. Castle Papers.

80. Michael J. Hogan, "Partisan Politics in the Cold War," in *The End of the Cold War: Its Meaning and Implications,* ed. Michael J. Hogan (New York: Cambridge University Press, 1992), 235–236.

81. *The New York Times,* October 14, 1963.

6. The Manchurian Incident: A Study in Applied Diplomatic Realism

1. W. R. Castle's Anglican-Orthodox view of original sin and its implications for evaluating political institutions is summarized well by Gilbert Chesterton's *Orthodoxy: The Romance of Faith* (New York: Dodd and Mead, 1908).

2. See Archibald Coolidge, *The United States as World Power* (New York: Macmillan, 1910). Castle's classmates included Joseph Grew, William Phillips, and Robert Woods Bliss.

3. See Lewis Einstein, *American Foreign Policy by a Diplomatist* (New York: Houghton Mifflin, 1909) and *A Prophecy of the War* (New York: Columbia University Press, 1917); Paul S. Reinsch, *World Politics at the End of the 19th Century* (New York: Macmillan, 1922) and *Secret Diplomacy: How Can It Be Eliminated?* (New York: Harcourt Brace, 1922); *American*

Legislatures and Legislative Methods (New York: Century, 1907).

4. Schulzinger, "The Making of the Diplomatic Mind," 9–16.

5. Castle was, for example, no anticommunist ideologue. By 1934 he supported the recognition of the Soviet Union and praised some of the social reforms accomplished since 1917. De facto recognition was merely a convenience "implying neither approval nor disapproval of the regime recognized." W. R. Castle, "Russia: Conclusions of a Statesman," *Annals of the American Academy of Political and Social Science* 174 (July 1934).

6. George F. Kennan, "The National Interest of the United States," *Illinois Law Review* 45 (January-February 1951): 736–738.

7. W. R. Castle, Jr., speech at the farewell dinner held at the Peers' Club, Tokyo, May 23, 1930, published in *The American-Japan Special Bulletin* 11 (May 1931).

8. Raymond G. O'Connor, *Perilous Equilibrium: The United States and the London Disarmament Conference of 1930* (Lawrence: University of Kansas Press 1969), 160. For a good general view of the history of China in the post–World War I era, see John K. Fairbank, *The Great Chinese Revolution, 1800–1985* (New York: Harper and Row, 1986), and Foster R. Dulles, *China and America: The Story of Their Relations Since* 1784 (Princeton, N.J.: Princeton University Press, 1946).

9. W. R. Castle, memorandum of conversation with Ambassador Lindsay, August 5, 1930, Doc. File FW893.00111067, RG 59 (General Records of the Department of State), National Archives.

10. C. F. Remer, *Foreign Investments in China* (New York: Macmillan, 1933), 74–80.

11. W. R. Castle, Jr., Diary, February 24, 1931. Herbert Hoover Library.

12. W. R. Castle, "Recent American Policy in the Far East," *The Annals of the American Academy of Political and Social Science* 168 (July 1933): 51–53.

13. A. Whitney Griswold, *The Far Eastern Policy of the United States* (New York: Harcourt, Brace, 1938), 406–407.

14. Letter, Edwin L. Neville to W. R. Castle, September 24, 1931. Castle Papers, Herbert Hoover Library.

15. Letters, W. Cameron Forbes to W. R. Castle, November 10, November 30, and December 15, 1931. Castle Papers.

16. Letter, Castle to Neville, October 20, 1931. Castle Papers.

17. Cable, Stimson to Hugh Wilson, September 23, 1931. Castle Papers. Clearly neither man had much faith in the League's ability to unscramble the chaos in Manchuria. See Ferrell, *Frank B. Kellogg and Henry L. Stimson,* 224–228.

18. Ellis, *Republican Foreign Policy,* 334–335.

19. Ferrell, *American Diplomacy in the Great Depression,* 19.

20. Castle Diary, October 6, 1931. Hoover Library.

21. The 1910 annexation of Korea had led Japan to seek U.S. recognition of the status quo in return for Japan's acceptance of the existing 5:5:3 Anglo-American-Japanese naval ratio. Secretary of State Charles Evans Hughes had, in the multi-faceted Washington Conference of 1921–1922, sought to eliminate mutual distrust between the United States and Japan by recognizing a new balance of power in Asia which acknowledged the competitive advantages of Japan and the United States while largely ignoring firm pledges to maintain China's territorial integrity.

22. The composition of the Japanese army leadership had begun to change in the democratic 1920s. Young peasant officers, often poorly educated, tended to be recklessly patriotic, suspicious of Western ideas and values, overly "professional." Many spoke of overthrowing the "decadent" Westernized government in Tokyo and establishing a "Showa restoration," a moral regeneration of Japan under a powerful emperor. Many of the younger officers had socialist leanings that alarmed both Japan's civilian leadership and the older officer corps. The socialist tendencies would be purged in 1936, leaving ultrapatriotism in its place. Robert Ferrell, *American Diplomacy: A History,* 3rd ed. (New York: W. W. Norton, 1975), 535. For the most complete account of Japan during the Manchurian incident, see Sadako Ogata, *Defiance in Manchuria* (Berkeley: University of California Press. 1964).

23. For general accounts of U.S.-Japanese relations, see James B. Crowley, "Japan's Military Foreign Policies," in *Japan's Foreign Policy, 1868–1941,* ed. James W. Morley (New York: Columbia University Press, 1974); Ogata, *Defiance in*

Manchuria; William L Neumann, *America Encounters Japan: From Perry to MacArthur* (Baltimore: Johns Hopkins University Press, 1963); Crowley, *Japan's Quest for Autonomy;* Akira Iriye, *Across the Pacific: An Inner History of American–East Asian Relations* (New York: Harcourt, Brace and World, 1967); Akira Iriye, *After Imperialism: The Search for a New Order in the Far East, 1921–1931* (Cambridge, Mass.: Harvard University Press); Christopher Thorne. *The Limits of Foreign Policy: The West, the League, and the Far Eastern Crisis of 1931– 1933* (London: Hamish Hamilton, 1972); Michael Barnhart, *Japan Prepares for Total War* (Ithaca, N.Y.: Cornell University Press, 1987); Justus Doenecke, *When the Wicked Rise* (Lewisburg, Pa.: Bucknell University Press, 1984); Ferrell, *American Diplomacy in the Great Depression.*

24. Thorne, *Limits of Foreign Policy,* 86.

25. N. T. Johnson to Castle, March 25, 1931. Johnson Papers, Box 13, Library of Congress.

26. Castle, speech to American Japanese Society, May 23, 1930. Castle Papers.

27. Castle Diary, September 29 and October 10, 1930. See also R. N. Current, "The Stimson Doctrine and the Hoover Doctrine," *American Historical Review* 59, no. 2 (1954): 513–542.

28. Castle, letter to Stanley Hornbeck, chief of the State Department Division of Far Eastern Affairs. See Hornbeck's "The Case for Japan in Manchuria." Hornbeck Papers, Box 242, Hoover Institution, Stanford, Calif.

29. Stimson Diary, September 23, 24, 25, 1931. Hoover Library.

30. Castle press conference, October 2, 1931, DS7939412022; FRUS, 1931, 111, 108–109, 137–139.

31. Stimson Diary, October 10, 1931, and FRUS, 193, 111, 211–212, 220–221.

32. Stimson Diary, October 13, 15, 1931; Thorne, *Limits of Foreign Policy,* 160.

33. Castle Diary, November 9, 1931.

34. Castle Diary, November 20, 1931.

35. Castle to Stimson, December 4, 1931, DS793.9413101 and FRUS 1931, 111, 431–432.

36. Castle Diary, November 21, 1931.

37. Thorne, *Limits of Foreign Policy,* 194. For a complete

account of China during the Manchurian incident see Parks Coble, *Facing Japan* (Cambridge, Mass.: Harvard University Press, 1991).

38. Letter, Root to Stimson, November 20, 1931, Stimson Papers, Box 303, Herbert Hoover Library. For a later definitive statement of Castle's view of the analogy, see W. R. Castle, Jr., "A Monroe Doctrine for Japan," *The Atlantic,* October 1940, 445–452; W R. Castle, Jr., "Aspects of the Monroe Doctrine," *The Harvard Graduate's Magazine* 40, no. 157 (September 1930): 20–29.

39. Castle Diary, December 4, 1931.

40. Castle Diary, December 7, 1931.

41. Castle Diary, December 31, 1931. See also letter, Eugene Dooman to Castle, December 16, 1931. Castle Papers.

42. Ferrell, *Frank B. Kellogg and Henry L. Stimson,* 235–236.

43. Stimson, Diary, January 6, 1932; FRUS Japan, 1:76. See also Henry L. Stimson, *The Far Eastern Crisis: Recollections and Observations* (New York: Harper and Brothers, 1936), 97–98.

44. Remer, *Foreign Investments in China,* 335. Castle was one of many Republicans who thought that capitalism and democracy at home, and economic interdependence and cultural exchange abroad, had been visualized as the keys to order and stability in the Far East. Akira Iriye, *The Globalizing of America.* Cambridge History of American Foreign Relations, vol. 3 (New York: Cambridge University Press, 1993), 128.

45. *New York Times,* January 5, 1932, 16.

46. *New York Times,* January 7, 1932, 1.

47. Castle Diary, January 7, 1932.

48. Castle Diary, January 8, 1932.

49. Gary B. Ostrower, *Collective Insecurity: The U.S. and the League of Nations During the Early Thirties* (Lewisburg, Pa.: Bucknell University Press, 1979), 112.

50. Ostrower, *Collective Insecurity.* He warned, however, that the Japanese held to political values such as deference to authority and militant patriotism that were different from political values in the United States. This also meant, as he saw it, that Japan would not observe the Washington Conference treaty structure when that structure impeded vital national interests. The United States operated from a different set of "in-

tellectual processes" and assumptions and would therefore feel constrained to honor the details of those treaties.

51. Castle consistently admired Japan's Westernization, civil stability, work ethic, and its courageous rebuilding after the Tokyo fire of 1923. See W. R. Castle, Jr., "Tokyo Today," *National Geographic Magazine*, February 1932, 131–162.

52. Typical among these public exhortations was his speech on January 31 in Baltimore. *New York Times,* February 1, 1932, 4.

53. Castle Diary, February 1, 1932.

54. Castle Diary, February 2, 1932.

55. Castle Diary, February 5–6, 1932.

56. For the full text, see FRUS, Japan, 1931–1941, 1:83–87. The best secondary account of the Borah letter is found in Amin Rappaport, *Henry L. Stimson and Japan, 1931–33* (Chicago: University of Chicago Press, 1963), 1–44. Stimson's memory of the letter is described in Stimson and Bundy, *On Active Service in Peace and War,* 249.

57. Norman A. Graebner, "Hoover, Roosevelt, and the Japanese," in *Pearl Harbor as History: Japanese-American Relations, 1931–1941,* ed. Dorothy Borg and Shumpei Okamoto (New York: Columbia University Press, 1973), 31–32.

58. For a full discussion of these differences, see Current, "The Stimson Doctrine and the Hoover Doctrine."

59. Hoover, *Memoirs,* 3:367–368.

60. Stimson Diary, March 8 and 9, 1932.

61. Stimson Diary, April 3, 1932.

62. *New York Times,* May 5, 1932.

63. Castle Diary, May 2, 1932. Hoover would in future years recall that Castle's independently inspired speech was requested or suggested by him. See Hoover to Castle, February 19, 1942, and Hoover to Charles A. Beard, December 17, 1945. Castle Papers.

64. Castle Diary, May 21, 1932.

65. Stimson Diary, April 3, 16, and May 19, 1932. Hoover had warned Stimson against rebuking the under secretary as he had authorization from Hoover to make the speech. See letter of Stimson to Walter Lippman, May 19, 1932, Newton D. Baker Papers, File 149, Library of Congress; Castle Diary, May 21, 1932.

66. Privately, Castle preferred to see Japan annex Man-

churia, pacify it, and create a viable government there than for the remote area to cause a disastrous war. Moreover, he continued to feel that a strong Japan tied to the United States through economic self-interest would keep the Soviet Union out of Manchuria. Castle Diary, May 24, 1932.

67. Rappaport, *Henry L. Stimson and Japan,* 174; *Thorne, Limits of Foreign Policy,* 275.

68. Castle Diary, July 5, 1932.

69. Castle Diary, September 7, 1932.

70. Castle Diary, August 20, 1932.

71. For the full report, see *Appeal by the Chinese Government: Report of the Commission of Inquiry* (Geneva: League of Nations, 1932).

72. Stimson Diary, December 30, 1932.

73. Dorothy Borg, *The United States and the Far Eastern Crisis of 1933–1938: From the Manchurian Incident through the Initial Stage of the Undeclared Sino-Japanese War* (Cambridge, Mass.: Harvard University Press, 1964), 35; Castle Diary, November 8, 1932.

74. Castle Diary, November 15, 1932.

75. Castle Diary, November 8, 1932.

76. In this, Castle and Stimson agreed fully. As Castle wrote Wilson, "his reason is that he does not want the United States to be put in a position where Japan will blame us for opposing their ambitions, at the same time feeling that the rest of the world might have been friendly." See letter, Castle to Wilson, August 15, 1932. Castle Papers.

77. Castle Diary, November 22, 1932.

78. Ferrell, *American Diplomacy,* 539–540.

79. Castle Diary, January 20, 1933.

80. Crowley, *Japan's Quest,* 185.

81. Castle Diary, January 6, 1933.

82. Castle Diary, February 14, 1933.

83. Castle and Hoover would later point out that Pearl Harbor was attacked in 1941 when FDR unwisely used economic boycotts to coerce Japan. Hoover, *Memoirs,* 2:376.

84. Gerald E. Wheeler, *Prelude to Pearl Harbor: The United States Navy and the Far East, 1921–1931* (Columbia: University of Missouri Press 1963), 192. The London Naval Conference, in which Castle had played a major role, had left the U.S. Navy vulnerable in the Far East, according to many strategic

thinkers. See U.S. Congress, Senate, 71st Congress, Sp. Session, July 18, 1930, *Congressional Record, Vol. 73,* 273.

85. James L. Hollingsworth, "William R. Castle and Japanese-American Relations, 1929–1933" (Ph.D. diss., Texas Christian University, 1971), 208–209.

86. Ellis, *Republican Foreign Policy,* 362. See also Elizabeth Deanne Malpass, "Sir John Simon and British Diplomacy During the Sino-Japanese Crisis, 1931–1933" (Ph.D. diss., Texas Christian University, 1969), 140–141.

87. FRUS, 1932, III, 643, 668–669, and FRUS IV, 55–56.

88. Stimson Diary, April 28, 1931; FRUS, 1932, IV, 232–234.

89. Castle Diary, July 14, 1932.

90. Thorne, *Limits of Foreign Policy,* 301.

91. W. R. Castle, Jr., "United States and the Far East" (unpublished foreign-policy paper, 1937), 329–330. Castle Papers.

7. The Presidential Election of 1936

1. William Allen White, "Republican National Platform," *What It's All About* (New York: Macmillan, 1936), 114.

2. Alfred Landon, letter to William R. Castle, May 29, 1936. Castle Papers, Hoover Library, West Branch, Iowa. Castle liked Landon's "simple honesty." Castle found him less than brilliant but a "clear thinker." Castle Diary, May 27, 1936.

3. W. R. Castle, "Notes on New Deal Foreign Policy" (1936), unpublished manuscript. Castle Papers.

4. Castle, "Notes on New Deal Foreign Policy," 11.

5. W. R. Castle, letter to Alfred Landon, May 30, 1936. Castle Papers.

6. W. R. Castle, letter to Landon, June 9, 1936. Castle Papers.

7. Castle, "Notes on New Deal Foreign Policy," 9–10.

8. Castle, "Notes on New Deal Foreign Policy," 9.

9. Castle, "Notes on New Deal Foreign Policy," 5.

10. Secretly Castle doubted that Landon fully understood the complexities of foreign policy issues and feared that he would not emphasize FDR's weaknesses enough in his speeches. Castle Diary, August 21, 1936.

11. Landon, letter to Castle, June 22, 1936. Castle Papers.

12. Castle, letter to Landon, September 28, 1936. Castle Papers.

13. Transcript of telephone call from William R. Castle to Alfred Landon, October 7, 1936. Castle Papers. See also telegram from Castle to Landon, October 5, 1936.

14. Castle, letter to Landon, October 6, 1936; Castle, letter to Frank Kellogg, October 16, 1936. Castle Papers.

15. Alfred Landon, speech delivered in Indianapolis, Indiana, October 24, 1936. Landon Papers, Kansas State Historical Society, Topeka.

16. Alfred Landon, speech delivered in Charleston, West Virginia, October 30, 1936, Landon Papers.

17. Alfred Landon, letter to Henry Breckinridge, November 9, 1936. Landon Papers.

18. Castle, letter to Landon, November 5, 1936. Castle Papers.

19. Castle, letter to Landon, November 7, 1936. Castle Papers.

20. Landon, letter to Castle, November 25, 1936; Ralph Robey, letter to Alfred Landon, December 13, 1936. Landon Papers.

21. Landon, letters to Castle, December 17, 1936, and January 9, 1937. Landon Papers.

22. Landon, letter to Castle, January 21, 1937. Landon Papers.

23. Castle, letter to Landon, February 4, 1937. Castle Papers.

24. Castle, letter to Landon, February 4, 1937. Castle Papers.

25. Castle, letter to Landon, March 29, 1937. Castle Papers.

26. Landon, letter to Castle, April 16, 1937; Kellogg, letter to Castle, April 9, 1937. Castle Papers.

27. Castle, letter to Landon, June 8, 1937. Castle Papers.

28. Landon, letter to Castle, June 22, 1937. Castle Papers.

29. W. K. Hutchinson, letter to Alfred Landon, July 23, 1937. Landon Papers.

30. Alfred Landon, letter to Harold B. Johnson, August 14 and 20, 1937, Landon Papers.

31. Frank Knox, letter to Annie Knox, September 10, 1937, Knox Papers, Library of Congress, Washington, D.C.

32. Donald R. McCoy, *Landon of Kansas* (Lincoln: University of Nebraska Press, 1966), 346–365.

33. *New York Times,* November 5, 1937.

34. Alfred Landon, letter to John Hamilton, November 23, 1937. Landon Papers.

35. Castle, letter to Landon, November 6, 1937. Castle Papers.

36. Landon, letter to Castle, November 15, 1937. Castle Papers.

37. Alfred Landon, letter to Frank Altschul, December 6, 1937. Landon Papers; *New York Times,* December 11, 1937.

38. Castle, letter to Landon, November 19, 1937; Landon, letter to Castle, November 23, 1937; Castle, letter to Landon, November 26, 1937; Landon, letter to Castle, December 1, 1937. Castle Papers.

39. Alfred Landon, statement to the press, Washington, D.C., December 10, 1937. Landon Papers.

40. Knox, letter to Annie Knox. Knox Papers.

41. Landon, letter to Castle, November 15, 1938. Castle Papers.

8. Opposition to Intervention in Asia, 1939–1941

1. Justus D. Doenecke, "Beyond Polemics: A Historiographical Re-Appraisal of American Entry into World War II," *History Teacher* 12 (1979): 223.

2. For representative traditionalist views of World War II, see Samuel Eliot Morison, *The Rising Sun in the Pacific, 1931– April 1942.* History of United States Naval Operations in World War II, vol. 3 (Boston: Little, Brown, 1948), 111; Walter Millis, *This is Pearl! The United States and Japan—1941* (New York: Morrow, 1947); Selig Adler, *The Isolationist Impulse: Its Twentieth-Century Reaction* (New York: Abelard-Schuman, 1957); Robert H. Ferrell, "Pearl Harbor and the Revisionists," *Historian* 17 (1955): 215–233; Robert E. Sherwood, *Roosevelt and Hopkins: An Intimate History* (New York: Harper, 1948); Herbert Feis, *The Road to Pearl Harbor: The Coming of the War between the United States and Japan* (Princeton, N.J.: Princeton University Press, 1950); and William L. Langer and S. Everett Gleason, *The Challenge to Isolationism, 1937– 1940* (New York: Harper, 1952).

3. For representative revisionist works, see Harry Elmer Barnes, ed., *Perpetual War for Perpetual Peace: A Critical Ex-*

amination of the Foreign Policy of Franklin Delano Roosevelt and its Aftermath (Caldwell, Idaho: Caxton Printers, 1953); Charles A. Beard, *American Foreign Policy in the Making, 1932–1940: A Study in Responsibilities* (New Haven, Conn.: Yale University Press, 1946); Charles A. Beard, *President Roosevelt and the Coming of War, 1941: A Study in Appearances and Realities* (New Haven, Conn.: Yale University Press, 1948); Charles C Tansill, *Back Door to War: The Roosevelt Foreign Policy, 1933–1941* (Chicago: Henry Regnery, 1952).

4. Wayne S. Cole, *America First: The Battle Against Intervention, 1940–41* (Madison: University of Wisconsin Press, 1953); Wayne S. Cole, *Charles A. Lindbergh and the Battle against American Intervention in World War II* (New York: Harcourt Brace Jovanovich, 1974); and Wayne S. Cole, *Roosevelt and the Isolationists, 1932–45* (Lincoln: University of Nebraska Press, 1983). Manfred Jonas, *Isolationism in America, 1935–1941* (Ithaca, N.Y.: Cornell University Press, 1966); Justus D. Doenecke, "Isolationists of the 1930's and 1940's: An Historiographical Essay," in *American Diplomatic History— Issues and Methods,* ed. R. W. Sellen and T. A. Bryson (Carrollton: West Georgia College, 1974), 5–39.

5. Michele F. Stenehjem, *An American First: John T. Flynn and the America First Committee* (New Rochelle, N.Y.: Arlington House, 1976); Ronald Radosh, *Prophets on the Right: Profiles of Conservative Critics of American Globalism* (New York: Simon and Schuster, 1975); James T. Patterson, *Mr. Republican: A Biography of Robert A. Taft* (Boston: Houghton Mifflin, 1972); Joan H. Wilson in *The Hoover Presidency: A Reappraisal,* ed. Martin L. Fausold and George T. Mazuzan (Albany: SUNY Press, 1974).

6. Jonas, *Isolationism in America,* for example, virtually ignores Castle, yet he appeared in numerous public forums throughout the period 1938–1941. Cole's latest book, *Roosevelt and the Isolationists,* also covers Castle's positions inadequately.

7. Manuscripts, speeches, and articles file, October 8, 1939. Castle Papers. See also Castle, untitled article in *Layman's Magazine* (July 1940), 5.

8. See particularly Castle, address to the American Institute of Bankers, Washington D.C., December 5, 1939. Castle Papers.

9. Especially, of course, George Washington's Farewell Address; quoted in J. D. Richardson, ed., *Messages and Papers of the Presidents* (Washington, 1896), 1: 221, 222.

10. Castle, speech on Mutual Broadcasting System, September 13, 1939. Castle Papers.

11. Castle, letter to editor, *U.S. News,* September 7, 1939, 10.

12. W. R. Castle, Jr., "End to Neutrality Act," *New York Times,* October 9, 1939, 9.

13. Castle to Mrs. E. Soher Welch, November 22, 1939. Castle Papers.

14. Speech at Delaware Bankers Association, Rehoboth Beach, September 8, 1939. Castle Papers.

15. Castle, speech at "Tuesday Forum," February 28, 1940. Castle Papers.

16. Castle, "U.S. Japanese Relations," speech delivered at the Jewish Community Center Institute on International Affairs, February 20, 1940. Castle Papers.

17. W. R. Castle, Jr., "The Far East," January 9, 1940, unpublished manuscript. Castle Papers.

18. W. R. Castle, Jr., "A Monroe Doctrine for Japan," *The Atlantic Monthly,* October 1940, 445–452.

19. W. R. Castle, Jr., "Japan and the Monroe Doctrine," *Saturday Evening Post,* July 20, 1940, 38; see also Arthur Krock's commentary in *New York Times,* July 26, 1940, 16.

20. Castle to Hugh R. Wilson, December 20, 1939. Hugh Wilson Papers, Herbert Hoover Library.

21. Castle, address to the 54th annual commencement of Howe School, June 8, 1940. Castle Papers.

22. W. R. Castle, Jr., "Neutrality in the Chinese-Japanese War, *Annals of the American Academy of Political and Social Science* (July 1940): 119–120.

23. Castle, speech to Yale Club, February 15, 1940. Castle Papers.

24. W. R. Castle, Jr., "The Far Eastern Situation," speech delivered in Baltimore, February 20, 1940. Castle Papers.

25. W. R. Castle, Jr., "How to Avoid War with Japan," talk delivered on NBC broadcast "Town Meeting of the Air," December 14, 1939. Castle Papers.

26. W. R. Castle, Jr., untitled, undated, unpublished manuscript, Box 33, Castle Papers.

27. W. R. Castle, Jr., speech to St. Andrews Brotherhood, Baltimore, February 22, 1940. Castle Papers.

28. *Washington Post,* December 12, 1940, 19.

29. W. R. Castle, Jr., "Purposes of the America First Committee," unpublished manuscript, January 15, 1941, 32. Castle Papers.

30. W. R. Castle, Jr., unpublished, untitled manuscript, 1940, articles and speeches file, Box 33, Castle Papers.

31. W. R. Castle, speech at Republican Party Rally at St. Albans, Vermont, October 31, 1940. Castle Papers.

32. *U.S. News,* October 11, 1940, 24–25.

33. W. R. Castle, Jr., address to The Hungary Club, Pittsburgh, December 2, 1940. Castle Papers.

34. W. R. Castle, Jr., "The Mistakes of Roosevelt with Japan," *The Nation,* October 25, 1940, 7. See also Griswold, *The Far Eastern Policy of the United States,* 472–473.

35. W. R. Castle, Jr., "America First," address delivered in Cincinnati, December 4, 1940. Castle Papers.

36. Hoover to Castle, March 1, 1941. Herbert Hoover Papers, Herbert Hoover Library.

37. W. R. Castle, Jr., address to Rotary Club, Washington, D.C., February 19, 1941. Castle Papers.

38. Cole, *Charles A. Lindbergh and the Battle against American Intervention,* 157–158. Of the various groups thought to be most favorable to intervention and smears to discredit the AFC—Anglophiles, Jews, Roosevelt's administration, bankers, munition capitalists, and moral idealists—Castle most suspected the Roosevelt administration.

39. Charles A. Lindbergh, *The Wartime Journals of Charles A. Lindbergh* (New York: Harcourt Brace Jovanovich, 1970), 245. Castle agreed with Lindbergh that Jews had an unhealthy influence over the media but argued that they had good reason to strongly desire intervention. He disagreed with Lindbergh's frank statement about Jewish influence over American foreign policy in the Des Moines speech of September 11, 1941, because his "statement . . . clouds the issue and pins on us, however unfairly, the antisemitic label." See Castle to Stuart, September 15 and 21, 1941. Castle Papers.

40. *New York Tribune,* November 3, 1940, 9.

41. *New York Post,* February 3, 1941, 1. In fact Castle

joined only after he was convinced that it lacked a pro-German taint. see Castle's letter to Morris Stanley, February 25, 1942, quoted in Stanley, "The America First Committee" (M.A. thesis, Emory University, 1942), 9–10.

42. Representative examples are found in William Hocking, *New York Times,* January 26, 1940, 16, and Walter Lippmann, *Washington Post,* February 6, 1941, 9. Both articles accuse Castle of defeatism and unjustified tolerance of Japanese aggression.

43. Castle to Gen. Robert E. Wood, February 4, 1944, and Wood to Castle, February 9, 1944. Robert E. Wood Papers, Herbert Hoover Library.

44. W. R. Castle, Jr., letter to the editor, *New York Herald Tribune,* December 7, 1941, II, 9.

45. Castle to Hoover, December 9, 1941. Castle Papers.

46. Castle to Hoover, December 8, 1941. Hoover Papers.

47. Hoover to Castle, December 8, 1941. Hoover Papers.

48. Castle to Wood, November 15, 1943. Wood Papers. Wood agreed with Castle's desire not to see the AFC reborn. See Wood to Castle, December 3, 1943. Wood Papers.

49. W. R. Castle, Jr., "What Happened at Pearl Harbor: A Retrospective Glance," address delivered to Hardware Manufacturers Statistical Association, New York City, May 21, 1942. Castle Papers. Castle noted that the mistakes at Pearl Harbor included the foolish grouping of planes at Hickam Field and the failure of the F.B.I. to correctly interpret and transmit intercepted messages. He also noted that his brother Alfred, in Honolulu, had anticipated the attack that weekend and had refused to leave the city knowing that public relief agencies would need his help. See also John C. O'Laughlin to Hoover, December 29, 1941. Hoover Papers.

50. W. R. Castle, Jr., speech at Choate School, October 26, 1942. He repeated this plea for calm and critical thinking in his address to the Washington Chapter of the American Church Union at St. Paul's Church, February 7, 1943. Castle Papers.

51. Representative traditional views of Japan's culpability and America's role as patient defender of the status quo in Asia can be found in Sumner Welles, *The Time for Decision* (New York: Harper, 1944); Ferrell, *American Diplomacy in the Great Depression;* David Bergamini, *Japan's Imperial Conspiracy* (New York: Morrow, 1971); Stimson and Bundy, *On Active*

Service in Peace and War; Saburo Ienaga, *The Pacific War: World War II and the Japanese, 1931–1945* (New York: Pantheon Books, 1978).

52. Most current scholarship, for example, is in basic agreement that Roosevelt's administration, far from forcing Japan's hand, lacked clearly established policy priorities and therefore was cautious, passive, and even given to appeasement. Moreover, the Japanese, like many Americans, shared crude, condescending, and often racist images of Westerners. Additionally, as Akira Iriye claims, Japan's attack on Pearl Harbor was part of a larger Asian revolt against Occidental cultural, material, and political domination that ultimately resulted in anticolonialism and the decline of Western power in Asia after 1945. See Iriye, *After Imperialism: The Search for a New Order in the Far East, 1921–1931* and *Across the Pacific: An Inner History of American-East Asian Relations*; Borg, *The United States and the Far Eastern Crisis of 1933–1938*; Neumann, *America Encounters Japan*; and Akira Iriye, "The Failure of Military Expansionism," in *Dilemmas of Growth in Prewar Japan,* ed. James W. Morley (Princeton, N.J.: Princeton University Press, 1971), 107–138.

53. See George F. Kennan, *American Diplomacy, 1900–1950* (Chicago: University of Chicago Press, 1951); Rappaport, *Henry L. Stimson and Japan;* and Richard N. Current, *Secretary Stimson: A Study in Statecraft* (New Brunswick, N.J.: Rutgers University Press, 1954).

54. Ithaca, N.Y.: Cornell University Press, 1958.

55. Crowley, *Japan's Quest for Autonomy;* Waldo H. Heinrichs, *American Ambassador: Joseph C. Grew and the Development of the United States Diplomatic Tradition* (Boston: Little, Brown, 1966); Iriye, *After Imperialism.* New Left historians also have argued that Japan was following the traditional policies of Western powers in its desire to create a political environment favorable to its economic security and prosperity. Representative New Left works include Noam Chomsky, *American Power and the New Mandarins* (New York: Pantheon Books, 1969); William A. Williams, *The Tragedy of American Diplomacy,* rev. ed. (New York: Dell, 1962); Robert F. Smith, "American Foreign Relations, 1920–1942," in *Towards a New Past: Dissenting Essays in American History,* ed. Barton J. Bernstein (New York: Pantheon Books, 1968), 232–262.

56. Christopher Thorne, *Allies of a Kind: The United States, Britain, and the War against Japan, 1941–1945* (New York: Oxford University Press, 1978), and Thorne, *The Limits of Foreign Policy.*

9. Opposition to World War II Foreign Policy

1. Hoover, letter to Castle, December 8, 1941, Post-presidential files, Herbert Hoover Papers, Herbert Hoover Library.

2. Castle Diary, December 12, 1941, Harvard University.

3. Castle Diary, December 12, 1941.

4. Castle learned to his disgust that the former hero, Charles A. Lindbergh, had been denied an opportunity to serve in the U.S. Army Air Forces due to his opposition to the Lend-Lease Act and other support for the Allies prior to Pearl Harbor. Although Castle had disagreed with Lindbergh's speeches, he felt the flyer had been a patriotic opponent to policy and should be allowed to serve. Castle Diary, January 9, 1942.

5. Castle Diary, February 11, 1942.

6. Castle Diary, February 25, 1942.

7. Hoover, letter to Mrs. Ogden Reid, March 10, 1942, Post-Presidential Papers, Hoover Papers.

8. Richard Norton Smith, *An Uncommon Man: The Triumph of Herbert Hoover* (New York: Simon and Schuster, 1984), 315–316.

9. Castle to Gibson, March 16, 1942. Castle Papers, Herbert Hoover Library.

10. Castle, "A Monroe Doctrine for Japan," 445–452.

11. Castle to Gibson, March 16, 1942. Castle Papers.

12. Hoover, letter to Helen Reid, March 10, 1942. Post-Presidential Papers, Hoover Papers.

13. When he read that the reactionary paper edited by Father Charles E. Coughlin would be censored, he agreed with Roosevelt that it would be no real loss to the nation. However,

> On the other hand, when the Government begins to suppress publications which do not happen to agree with its point of view we are getting awfully close to what may easily become complete suppression of free speech, complete suppression of the criticism, some of which must be useful in the war effort. It is a very complicated matter and I certainly should not like to lay down any de-

tailed regulations. Of one thing, however, I am certain, and that is that we are better off when people are allowed to speak their thoughts freely; even seditious thoughts are perhaps less dangerous when expressed than when bottled up, although in war time the control must be infinitely greater than in peace time. (Castle, Diary, April 15, 1942)

14. Castle Diary, May 3, 1942.

15. Speech reported in Herbert Hoover, *Addresses upon the American Road, 1941–1945* (New York, 1945), 160–171.

16. Indeed, the success of the speech seemed to be confirmed on May 30 when Under Secretary of State Sumner Welles gave a speech that incorporated some of Hoover's ideas. Hoover to O'Laughlin, June 5, 1942, Post-Presidential Papers, Hoover Papers.

17. Gary Dean Best, *Herbert Hoover: The Post-Presidential Years, 1933–1964* (Palo Alto, Calif.: Hoover Institution Press, 1983), 210–211.

18. Castle Diary, May 22, 1942.

19. Hoover to O'Laughlin, April 10, 1942. Castle Papers.

20. Hoover to O'Laughlin, August 3, 1942. See also Castle Diary, July 10, 1942.

21. Castle Diary, September 8, 1942.

22. Hoover to Arch Shaw, September 12, 1942. Castle Papers.

23. Castle Diary, September 20, 1942.

24. Castle Diary, February 7, 1943.

25. Castle to Hoover, March 25, 1943. Post-Presidential Papers, Hoover Papers.

26. Castle Diary, May 17, 1943.

27. Castle Diary, May 18, 1943.

28. Castle Diary, May 18, 1943. Castle's charges regarding FDR's undue naivete were later echoed by William Henry Chamberlin, *America's Second Crusade* (Chicago: Henry Regnery, 1950); Barnes, *Perpetual War for Perpetual Peace*; William C. Bullitt, "How We Won the War and Lost the Peace," *Life* 25 (August 30, 1948): 82–97; Chester Wilmot, *The Struggle for Europe* (New York: Harper, 1952); and Hanson W. Baldwin, *Great Mistakes of the War* (New York: Harper, 1949). This school of thought represented the earliest wave of historiography about World War II diplomacy. In the 1980s, this line of

argument was revived by Robert A. Nisbet, *Roosevelt and Stalin: The Failed Courtship* (Washington: Regnery Gateway, 1988), and Frederick W. Marks, *Wind Over Sand: The Diplomacy of Franklin Roosevelt* (Athens: University of Georgia Press, 1988).

29. Castle Diary, May 23, 1943.

30. W. R. Castle, "The Hoover Frame of Mind," *Atlantic Monthly,* August 1943, 27–28.

31. Editor, *Atlantic Monthly,* letter to W. R. Castle, June 10, 1943. Castle Papers.

32. For a summary of these developments, see Stuart Ewen, *Captains of Consciousness: Advertising and the Social Roots of the Consumer Culture* (New York: McGraw-Hill, 1976).

33. O'Laughlin, letter to Hoover, November 8, 1943. O'Laughlin Papers, Herbert Hoover Library.

34. Hoover, letter to Roy Howard, November 2, 1943. Post-Presidential Papers, Hoover Papers.

35. Castle Diary, December 3, 1943.

36. Hoover to O'Laughlin, December 13, 1943. O'Laughlin Papers.

37. At one point, Castle was able to obtain radio coverage on WOL in Washington, D.C., of a speech on food made by Hoover in Kansas City. Castle Diary, October 12, 1943.

38. Hoover, letter to Herbert Lehman, June 23, 1943. Post-Presidential Papers, Hoover Papers.

39. Hoover, letter to Herbert Lehman, June 23, 1943.

40. Castle Diary, December 13, 1943.

41. Castle Diary, January 28, 1944.

42. Castle's sense that the credulity of the Roosevelt administration was part of a larger legacy of U.S. naivete in foreign policy was repeated after the war by George F. Kennan's *American Diplomacy, 1900–1950;* see also Herbert Feis, *Churchill, Roosevelt, Stalin: The War They Waged and the Peace They Sought* (Princeton, N.J.: Princeton University Press, 1957); Gaddis Smith, *American Diplomacy During the Second World War, 1941–1945* (New York: Wiley, 1965); Samuel P. Huntington, *The Soldier and the State: The Theory and Politics of Civil-Military Relations* (Cambridge, Mass.: Harvard University Press, 1957); and William H. McNeill, *America, Britain and Russia: Their Cooperation and Conflict, 1941–1946* (New York: Oxford University Press, 1953). For a summary of an opposing view which saw FDR as more realistic than Castle and

Hoover claimed, see John Snell, *Illusion and Necessity: The Diplomacy of Global War, 1939–1945* (Boston: Houghton Mifflin, 1963) and Raymond G. O'Connor, *Diplomacy for Victory: FDR and Unconditional Surrender* (New York: Norton, 1971).

43. Walter Sloan Poole, "Quest for a Republican Foreign Policy, 1941–1951" (Ph.D. diss., University of Pennsylvania, 1968), 51–60.

44. Hoover to David Lawrence, November 1, 1943. Post-Presidential Papers, Hoover Papers.

45. Castle Diary, February 6, 1944.

46. Castle to Landon, January 31, 1944. Landon Papers, Kansas State Historical Society. Castle found further evidence of FDR's lack of "realism" in dealing with Stalin in his refusal to use lend-lease aid to Russia as a bargaining chip for restraining Stalin's territorial ambitions. Castle Diary, February 28, 1944. For a similar position, see Edward M. Bennett, *Franklin Roosevelt and the Search for Victory: American-Soviet Relations, 1939–1945* (Wilmington, Del.: SR Books, 1990), and Vojtech Mastny, *Russia's The Road to the Cold War: Diplomacy, Warfare, and the Politics of Communism, 1941–1945* (New York: Columbia University Press, 1979).

47. Castle Diary, June 24, 1944.

48. *New York Times,* June 28, 1943.

49. *New York Times,* June 28, 1943.

50. Best, *Herbert Hoover.*

51. Castle to Hoover, November 15, 1944. Castle Papers.

52. Castle to Hoover, December 22, 1944. Castle Papers.

53. Hoover to Castle, November 17, 1944. Post-Presidential Papers, Hoover Papers.

54. W. R. Castle, "Remarks on the Dumbarton Oaks Proposals," *World Affairs* 107 (December 1944): 243–246.

55. Castle Diary, January 29, 1945.

56. Castle Diary, January 29, 1945.

57. Castle Diary, February 9, 1945.

58. Castle Diary, February 13, 1945.

59. For recent similar conclusions about FDR, see Nisbet, *Roosevelt and Stalin;* Keith Eubank, *Summit at Tehran* (New York: William Morrow, 1985); Russell D. Buhite, *Decisions at Yalta: An Appraisal of Summit Diplomacy* (Wilmington, Del.: Scholarly Resources, 1986); Keith Sainsbury, *The Turning Point: Roosevelt, Stalin, Churchill and Chiang Kai-shek,*

1943 (New York: Oxford University Press, 1985). Historians who disagree and believe that FDR got the best deal he could under difficult circumstances include Theodore Draper, "Neo-Conservative History," *New York Review of Books* 16 (January 1986); Melvyn Leffler, "Adherents to Agreements: Yalta and the Experiences of the Early Cold War," *International Security* 11 (summer 1986): 88–123; Warren Kimball, *The Juggler: Franklin Roosevelt as Wartime Statesman* (Princeton, N.J.: Princeton University Press, 1991); Gary R. Hess, *The United States at War, 1941–1945* (Arlington Heights, Ill.: H. Davidson, 1986); and Frank Freidel, *Franklin D. Roosevelt: A Rendezvous With Destiny* (Boston: Little, Brown, 1990).

60. Public statements, 1945, Hoover Papers.

61. Castle to Hoover, February 16, 1945. Castle Papers.

62. Hoover to Castle, February 18, 1945. Castle Papers.

63. Hoover to Landon, February 18, 1945. Post-Presidential Papers, Hoover Papers.

64. Castle to Hoover, February 26, 1945. Castle Papers.

65. Castle Diary, February 21, 1945.

66. Best, *Herbert Hoover*, 262.

67. Castle Diary, April 13, 1945.

68. Castle to Hoover, May 2, 1945. Castle Papers.

69. Memorandum of discussion with Kennedy, May 15, 1945, and memorandum of discussion with Stimson, May 15, 1945. Post-Presidential Papers, Hoover Papers.

70. Castle Diary, May 28, 1945.

71. Castle to Hoover, June 2, 1945. Castle Papers. Castle had spoken eloquently of the spiritual dangers of indiscriminate hate in his Independence Day address at the Church of St. Stephan and the Incarnation, July 4, 1943.

72. Castle Diary, July 23, 1945. For recent accounts of conflicting British-American interests in the Far East, see William Roger Louis, *Imperialism at Bay: The United States and the Decolonization of the British Empire, 1941–1945* (New York: Oxford University Press, 1978); Robert Beitzell, *The Uneasy Alliance: America, Britain and Russia, 1941–1943* (New York: Knopf, 1973); Thorne, *Allies of a Kind*; and Terry H. Anderson, *The United States, Great Britain and the Cold War, 1944–1947* (Columbia: University of Missouri Press, 1981).

73. Castle Diary, July 27–28, 1945.

74. W. R. Castle, speech to the Hardware Manufacturer's Association, New York City, April 18, 1946. Castle Papers.

The New Left attack on Roosevelt and Truman had, ironically, faulted the two for subordinating good relations with the Soviets to an economic agenda of dominating Europe and the Far East. See Williams, *The Tragedy of American Diplomacy;* Lloyd C. Gardner, *Economic Aspects of New Deal Diplomacy* (Madison: University of Wisconsin Press, 1964); Gabriel Kolko, *The Politics of War: The World and United States Foreign Policy, 1943–1945* (New York: Random House, 1968).

75. Public Statements, 1945. Hoover Papers.

76. Castle, speech to the Hardware Manufacturer's Association.

77. Castle Diary, August 8, 1945.

78. For an excellent account of the role racial stereotypes played in wartime policy on both sides, see John Dower, *War Without Mercy* (New York: Pantheon Books, 1986); Clayton R. Koppes and Gregory D. Black, *Hollywood Goes to War: How Politics, Profits, and Propaganda Shaped World War II Movies* (New York: Free Press, 1987); Akira Iriye, *Power and Culture: The Japanese-American War, 1941–1945* (Cambridge, Mass.: Harvard University Press, 1981); and Christopher Thorne, *The Issue of War: States, Societies, and the Far Eastern Conflict of 1941–1945* (New York: Oxford University Press, 1985).

79. Castle Diary, August 15, 1945. Also, for accounts sympathetic to Castle's, see Martin Sherwin, *A World Destroyed: The Atomic Bomb and the Grand Alliance* (New York: Knopf, 1975), and Barton J. Bernstein, "The Perils and Politics of Surrender: Ending the War With Japan and Avoiding the Third Atomic Bomb," *Pacific Historical Review* 46, no. 1 (1977): 1–27.

80. See Alfred L. Castle, "William R. Castle and the Post-War Transformation of Japan," *Wisconsin Magazine of History* (winter 1990–1991): 125–137.

10. Diplomatic Realism and the Postwar Transformation of Japan

1. Harold M. Vinacke, *Far Eastern Politics in the Postwar Period* (New York: Appleton-Century-Crofts, 1956), 423–424.

2. E. J. Lewe Van Advard, *Japan: From Surrender to Peace* (The Hague: M. Nijhoff, 1953), 96–101.

3. Melvyn P. Leffler, "The American Conception of National

Security and the Beginnings of the Cold War, 1945–48," *American Historical Review* 89, no. 2 (1984): 379. See also LaFeber, *The American Age,* 469–470.

4. Edwin O. Reischauer, *The United States and Japan,* 3rd ed. (Cambridge, Mass.: Harvard University Press, 1965). See also Robert E. Ward, "Reflections on the Allied Occupation and Planned Political Change in Japan," in *Political Development in Modern Japan,* ed. Robert E. Ward (Princeton, N.J.: Princeton University Press, 1968), 477–535.

5. Joyce Kolko and Gabriel Kolko, *The Limits of Power: The World and United States Foreign Policy, 1945–1954* (New York: Harper and Row, 1972), 510, 525. See also John W. Dower, "Occupied Japan as History and Occupation History as Politics," *Journal of Asian Studies* 34 (1975): 485–504; Walter LaFeber, *America, Russia and the Cold War, 1945–1990,* 6th ed. (New York: McGraw-Hill, 1991).

6. See Howard B. Schonberger, "The Japan Lobby in American Diplomacy, 1947–1952," *Pacific Historical Review* 46, no. 3 (1977): 327–359, and John G. Roberts, "The 'Japan Crowd' and the Zaibatsu Restoration," *The Japan Interpreter* 12, no. 3/4 (1979): 384–415.

7. Schonberger, "The Japan Lobby," 328–329.

8. For a discussion of the social, educational, and political homogeneity of the State Department to 1950, see Martin Weil, *A Pretty Good Club: The Founding Fathers of the U. S. Foreign Service* (New York: Norton, 1978).

9. *Newsweek* 29 (January 27, 1947): 40.

10. *Newsweek* 29 (June 23, 1947): 36–42.

11. Castle Diary, February 8, 1947.

12. Castle Diary, September 12, 1947. For a recent discussion of Japanese demilitarization, see Meirion Harries and Susie Harries, *Sheathing the Sword: The Demilitarization of Postwar Japan* (London: Hamish Hamilton, 1987).

13. Schonberger, "The Japan Lobby," 332. For an opposing view of a New Dealer, see Theodore Cohen, *Remaking Japan: The American Occupation as New Deal* (New York: Free Press, 1987)

14. Castle Diary, January 9, 1948.

15. James Lee Kauffman, "Report on Conditions in Japan as of September 6, 1947," enclosure in James L. Kauffman to Robert L. Eichelberger, May 13, 1949. Eichelberger Papers, Duke University.

16. George F. Kennan, *Memoirs, 1925–1950* (Boston: Little, Brown, 1967), 395–410.

17. *Newsweek* 30 (December 1, 1947): 37, and 31 (April 19, 1948): 42.

18. Castle Diary, January 14, 1948.

19. *New York Times,* July 27, 1948.

20. Kiba Hirosuke, *Nomura Kichisaburo* (Osaka, 1961), x.

21. Castle Diary, June 29, 1948.

22. "American Policy Toward Japan: Statement for Private Circulation Prepared in Conjunction with Members of the American Council on Japan by Harry Kern," n.d., in Harry F. Kern to William V. Pratt, April 8, 1949. Pratt Papers, Naval War College Archives, Newport, Rhode Island.

23. *New York Times,* January 9, 1950.

24. Castle Diary, October 31, 1952.

25. Castle Diary, March 16, 1950.

26. Kern correspondence with Dodge, in the Joseph Dodge Papers, Detroit Public Library.

27. John G. Roberts, *Mitsui: Three Centuries of Japanese Business* (New York: Weatherhill, 1973), 403, 443.

28. Michael Schaller, *Douglas MacArthur: The Far Eastern General* (New York: Oxford University Press, 1989), 154.

29. Castle Diary, August 16, 1948.

30. Miriam Farley, *Aspects of Japan's Labor Problems* (New York: John Day, 1950), 189–207.

31. Castle Diary, December 8, 1948. Castle's diary entries reveal that he and Kennan continued to meet privately to 1950 in an effort to compare notes on the progress of the "reverse course" strategy.

32. Castle Diary, March 16, 1950.

33. "The Position of Japan in the Framework of American Policy Toward the Far East," n.d., in Harry F. Kern to William V. Pratt, March 22, 1950. Pratt Papers.

34. Schonberger, "The Japan Lobby," 352–353.

35. Frederick S. Dunn, *Peacemaking and the Settlement with Japan* (Princeton, N.J.: Princeton University Press, 1963), 98.

36. Dulles was further impressed when the Emperor Hirohito sent a message through Matsudaira to Kern and Pakenham in which he sanctioned Dulles' receiving his information from highly placed reliable sources. The message read in part: "It has always been His Majesty's hope that Americans in authority visiting Japan for inspection and survey proposed

should be allowed to discuss matters openly and frankly with prominent Japanese on their own comparative level. He is most gratified that a precedent in this regard has been set under the initiative of Mr. Dulles. So far as [the Emperor] knows, this is a unique case." For the full text, see "Pakenham Notes and Emperor's Message" in Harry F. Kern to William V. Pratt, September 8, 1950. Pratt Papers.

37. Castle Diary, August 17, 1951.

38. Harry F. Kern to John F. Dulles, January 15, 1951. Dulles Papers, Princeton University.

39. Harry F. Kern to Robert L. Eichelberger, March 24, 1949. Eichelberger Papers.

40. LaFeber, *The American Age*, 491–493. See also Howard B. Schonberger, *Aftermath of War: Americans and the Remaking of Japan, 1945–1952* (Kent, Ohio: Kent State University Press, 1989), 246–278.

41. Roberts, "The 'Japan Crowd' and the Zaibatsu Restoration," 409.

42. Castle Diary, January 3, 1952.

43. Castle Diary, June 7, 1956.

44. Castle Diary, October 30, 1956. Pakenham had asserted that the Japanese leadership still regarded Castle as their "only American Ambassador." Castle Diary, January 11, 1956.

45. Schonberger, *Aftermath of War*, 284–285.

46. Schonberger, *Aftermath of War*, 144–145.

11. An Aged Realist Examines Cold War Assumptions

1. Castle Diary, February 9, 1947.

2. Gar Alperovitz, *The Decision to Use the Atomic Bomb and the Architecture of an American Myth* (New York: Alfred A. Knopf, 1995), 315.

3. Henry L. Stimson, "The Decision to Use the Atomic Bomb," *Harper's* 194 (February 1947): 97–107.

4. Castle Diary, January 26, 1947, and February 9, 1947.

5. George F. Kennan, *American Diplomacy*, expanded ed. (Chicago: University of Chicago Press, 1984), 178–179.

6. Mark Falcoff, "The Company Man," *The National Interest* 46 (winter 1996–1997): 82.

Bibliography

Adler, Selig. *The Isolationist Impulse: Its Twentieth-Century Reaction.* New York: Abelard-Schuman, 1957.

Alperovitz, Gar. *The Decision to Use the Atomic Bomb and the Architecture of an American Myth.* New York: Alfred A. Knopf, 1995.

American Legislatures and Legislative Methods. New York: Century, 1907.

Anderson, Terry H. *The United States, Great Britain and the Cold War, 1944–1947.* Columbia: University of Missouri Press, 1981.

Baldwin, Hanson W. *Great Mistakes of the War.* New York: Harper, 1949.

Barnes, Harry Elmer, ed. *Perpetual War for Perpetual Peace: A Critical Examination of the Foreign Policy of Franklin Delano Roosevelt and Its Aftermath.* Caldwell, Idaho: Caxton Printers, 1953.

Barnhart, Michael. *Japan Prepares for Total War.* Ithaca, N.Y.: Cornell University Press, 1987.

Beard, Charles A. *American Foreign Policy in the Making, 1932–1940: A Study in Responsibilities.* New Haven, Conn.: Yale University Press, 1946.

————. *President Roosevelt and the Coming of War, 1941: A Study in Appearances and Realities.* New Haven, Conn.: Yale University Press, 1948.

Beitzell, Robert. *The Uneasy Alliance: America, Britain and Russia, 1941–1943.* New York: Knopf, 1973.

Bennett, Edward M. *Franklin Roosevelt and the Search for Victory: American-Soviet Relations, 1939–1945.* Wilmington, Del.: SR Books, 1990.

Bennett, Edward W. *Germany and the Diplomacy of the Financial Crisis, 1931.* Cambridge, Mass.: Harvard University Press, 1962.

Bergamini, David. *Japan's Imperial Conspiracy.* New York: Morrow, 1971.

Bernstein, Barton J. "The Perils and Politics of Surrender: Ending the War With Japan and Avoiding the Third Atomic Bomb." *Pacific Historical Review* 46, no. 1 (1977): 1–27.

Best, Gary Dean. *Herbert Hoover: The Post-Presidential Years, 1933–1964.* Palo Alto, Calif.: Hoover Institution Press, 1983.

Blakewell, Charles M. *The Story of the American Red Cross in Italy.* New York: Macmillan, 1920.

Borg, Dorothy. *The United States and the Far Eastern Crisis of 1933–1938: From the Manchurian Incident through the Initial Stage of the Undeclared Sino-Japanese War.* Cambridge, Mass.: Harvard University Press, 1964.

Braeman, John. "The New Left and American Foreign Policy During the Age of Normalcy: A Re-Examination." *Business History Review* 57, no. 1 (1993). 73–104.

Buckley, Thomas H. *The United States and the Washington Conference, 1921–1922.* Knoxville: University of Tennessee Press, 1970.

Buhite, Russell D. *Decisions at Yalta: An Appraisal of Summit Diplomacy.* Wilmington, Del.: Scholarly Resources, 1986.

Bullitt, William C. "How We Won the War and Lost the Peace," *Life* 25 (August 30, 1948): 82–97.

Burke, Bernard V. "American Diplomats and Hitler's Rise to Power, 1930–1933: The Mission of Ambassador Sackett." Ph.D. dissertation, University of Washington, 1966.

Castle, Alfred L. "Ambassador Castle's Role in the Negotiations of the London Naval Conference." *Naval History* (summer, 1989): 16–21.

———. *A Century of Philanthropy: A History of the Samuel N. and Mary Castle Foundation.* Honolulu: University of Hawai'i Press, 1992.

———. "Christian Realist Values and W. R. Castle's Opposition to Intervention, 1939–1941." *Christian Scholar's Review* (March 1991): 384–401.

———. "William R. Castle and Opposition to U.S. Involvement in an Asian War, 1939–1941." *Pacific Historical Review* 54 (August, 1985): 337–351.

———. "William R. Castle and the Post-War Transformation of Japan." *Wisconsin Magazine of History* (Winter 1990–1991): 125–137.

Castle, William R. "Mary Tenney Castle." *The Friend* (April 11, 1907).

———. *Reminiscences of William Richards Castle.* Honolulu: privately printed, 1960.

Castle, William R., Jr. "Aspects of the Monroe Doctrine." *The Harvard Graduates Magazines* 40, no. 157, 20–29.

———. "The Austrian Collapse." *The Weekly Review* 4 (January 26, 1921): 73–75.

———. Autobiography. In *Twenty-fifth Anniversary Report, Harvard College—Class of 1900,* 133. Harvard University Alumni Association.

———. "Autobiographical Sketch." In *Fiftieth Anniversary Report, Harvard College—Class of 1900,* 119–120. Harvard Archives–Pusey Library.

———. "Barrett Wendell." In *Essays in Memory of Barrett Wendell.* Cambridge, Mass.: Harvard University Press, 1926.

———. "Barrett Wendell." *Scribners* (July, 1921): 60–63.

———. "End to Neutrality Act." *New York Times,* October 9, 1939, 9.

———. "Evaluating the League of Nations." *The Rotarian* (September 1934): 54.

———. "Germany As She Is Today." *New York Evening Post,* November 26, 1920.

———. "Harvard Men in the Foreign Service." *Harvard Graduate's Magazine* (September 1929): 23.

———. "The Hoover Frame of Mind." *Atlantic Monthly,* August 1943, 27–28.

———. "The Hungarian Tangle." *The Review* 1 (November 1, 1919): 535–537.

———. "Japan and the Monroe Doctrine." *The Saturday Evening Post,* July 20, 1940.

———. "The Leopard's Spots." *The Russian Review* 1 (August 19, 1919): 295–297.

———. *Life of Samuel Northrup Castle.* Honolulu: Hawaiian Historical Society, 1960.

———. "The Mistakes of Roosevelt with Japan." *The Nation,* October 25, 1940.

———. "A Monroe Doctrine for Japan." *The Atlantic Monthly* (October 1940): 445–452.

———. "Moscow's Campaign of Poison." *The Review* 2 (January 24, 1920) 77–80.

———. "Neutrality in the Chinese-Japanese War." *Annals of the American Academy of Political and Social Science* (July 1940) 119–120.

———. "Newman and Coleridge." *The Sewanee Review* (1909): 143.

———. "Our Diplomatic Service." *The Weekly Review* 3 (December 15, 1929): 579–580.

———. "Our Foreign Relations." *The Massachusetts Elephant* (June 1928): 3.

———. "The Outlook in Germany." *The Review* 2 (April 10, 1920): 356–358.

———. "Recent American Policy in the Far East." *The Annals of the American Academy of Political and Social Science* 168 (July 1933): 51–53.

———. "Remarks on the Dumbarton Oaks Proposals." *World Affairs* 107 (December 1944): 243–246.

———. "Russia: Conclusions of a Statesman." *Annals of the American Academy of Political and Social Science* 174 (July 1934).

———. "Tokyo Today." *The National Geographic Magazine* (February 1932): 131–162.

———. *Wake Up, America: A Plea for the Recognition of Our Individual and National Responsibilities.* New York, Dodd, Mead, 1916.

Chamberlain, William Henry. *America's Second Crusade.* Chicago: Henry Regnery, 1950.

Chesterton, Gilbert. *Orthodoxy: The Romance of Faith.* New York: Dodd and Mead, 1908.

Chomsky, Noam. *American Power and the New Mandarins.* New York: Pantheon Books, 1969.

Coble, Parks. *Facing Japan*. Cambridge, Mass.: Harvard University Press, 1991.

Cohen, Theodore. *Remaking Japan: The American Occupation as New Deal*. New York: Free Press, 1987.

Cohen, Warren I. *Empire Without Tears: American Foreign Relations, 1921–1933*. Philadelphia: Temple University Press, 1987.

Cole, Wayne S. *America First: The Battle Against Intervention, 1940–1941*. Madison: University of Wisconsin Press, 1953.

———. *Charles A. Lindbergh and the Battle against American Intervention in World War II*. New York: Harcourt Brace Jovanovich, 1974.

———. *Roosevelt and the Isolationists, 1932–45*. Lincoln: University of Nebraska Press, 1983.

Coolidge, Archibald. *The United States as World Power*. New York: Macmillan, 1910.

Costigliola, Frank. "The U.S. and the Reconstruction of Germany in the 1920s." *Business History Review* 50 (winter 1976).

Crowley, James B. "Japan's Military Foreign Policies." In *Japan's Foreign Policy, 1868–1941,* edited by James W. Morley. New York: Columbia University Press, 1974.

———. *Japan's Quest for Autonomy: National Security and Foreign Policy, 1930–1938*. Princeton, N.J.: Princeton University Press. 1966.

Current, Richard N. *Secretary Stimson: A Study in Statecraft*. New Brunswick, N.J.: Rutgers University Press, 1954.

———. "The Stimson Doctrine and the Hoover Doctrine." *American Historical Review* 59, no. 2 (1954): 513–542.

Davis, Joseph S. *The World Between the Wars, 1919–1939: An Economist's View*. Baltimore: Johns Hopkins University Press, 1975.

Dawes, Charles G. *Journal as Ambassador to Great Britain*. New York: Macmillan, 1939.

Diggins, John P. *Mussolini and Fascism: The View from America*. Princeton, N.J.: Princeton University Press, 1972.

Doenecke, Justus D. "Beyond Polemics: A Historiographical Re-Appraisal of American Entry into World War II." *History Teacher* 12 (1979).

———. "Isolationists of the 1930's and 1940's: An Historiographical Essay." In *American Diplomatic History—Issues* and Methods, 5–39, edited by R. W. Sellen and T. A. Bryson. Carrollton: West Georgia College, 1974.

———. *When the Wicked Rise: American Opinion-makers and the Manchurian Crisis of 1931–1933*. Lewisburg, Pa.: Bucknell University Press, 1984.

Dower, John W. "Occupied Japan as History and Occupation History as Politics." *Journal of Asian Studies* 34 (1975): 485–504.

———. *War Without Mercy*. New York: Pantheon Books, 1986.

Draper, Theodore. "Neo-Conservative History." *New York Review of Books* 16 (January 1986).

Dulles, Foster R. *China and America: The Story of Their Relations Since 1784*. Princeton, N.J.: Princeton University Press, 1946.

Dunn, Frederick S. *Peace-making and the Settlement with Japan*. Princeton, N.J.: Princeton University Press, 1963.

Edge, Walter E. *A Jerseyman's Journal: Fifty Years of American Business and Politics*. Princeton, N.J.: Princeton University Press, 1948.

Einstein, Lewis. *American Foreign Policy by a Diplomatist*. New York: Houghton Mifflin, 1909.

———. *A Prophecy of the War*. New York: Columbia University Press, 1917.

Ellis, L. Ethan. *Republican Foreign Policy, 1921–1933*. New Brunswick, N.J.: Rutgers University Press, 1968.

Eubank, Keith. *Summit at Tehran*. New York: William Morrow, 1985.

Ewen, Stuart. *Captains of Consciousness: Advertising and the Social Roots of the Consumer Culture*. New York: McGraw-Hill, 1976.

Fairbank, John K. *The Great Chinese Revolution, 1800–1985*. New York: Harper and Row, 1986.

Falcoff, Mark. "The Company Man." *The National Interest* 46 (winter 1996–1997).

Fallow, Walter, Jr. *President Hoover and Secretary of State Stimson: A Study in International Relations*. Durham, N.C.: Duke University Press, 1957.

Farley, Miriam. *Aspects of Japan's Labor Problems*. New York: John Day, 1950.

Fausold, Martin L., and George T. Mazuzan. *The Hoover Presidency: A Reappraisal*. Albany: SUNY Press, 1974.

Feis, Herbert. *Churchill, Roosevelt, Stalin: The War They Waged and the Peace They Sought.* Princeton, N.J.: Princeton University Press, 1957.

———. *The Diplomacy of the Dollar: First Era, 1919–1932.* Baltimore: Johns Hopkins Press, 1951.

———. *The Road to Pearl Harbor: The Coming of the War between the United States and Japan.* Princeton, N.J.: Princeton University Press, 1950.

Ferrell, Robert H. *American Diplomacy: A History,* 3rd ed. New York: W. W. Norton, 1975.

———. *American Diplomacy in the Great Depression.* New Haven: Yale University Press, 1957.

———. *Frank B. Kellogg and Henry L. Stimson.* The American Secretaries of State and Their Diplomacy, vol. 15. New York: Cooper Square Publishing Co., 1963.

———. *Peace in Their Time.* New Haven: Yale University Press, 1952.

———. "Pearl Harbor and the Revisionists." *Historian* 17 (1955): 215–233.

Freidel, Frank. *Franklin D. Roosevelt: A Rendezvous with Destiny.* Boston: Little, Brown, 1990.

Gardner, Lloyd C. *Economic Aspects of New Deal Diplomacy.* Madison: University of Wisconsin Press, 1964.

Glad, Betty. "Charles Evans Hughes, Rationalism, and Foreign Affairs." In *Traditional Values: American Diplomacy, 1865–1945,* edited by Norman Graebner, 1982.

Graebner, Norman A. "Hoover, Roosevelt, and the Japanese." In *Pearl Harbor as History: Japanese-American Relations, 1931–1941,* 25–52, edited by Dorothy Borg and Shumpei Okamoto. New York: Columbia University Press, 1973.

Grew, Joseph C. *Turbulent Era: A Diplomatic Record of Forty Years, 1904–1945,* 2 vols. Boston: Houghton Mifflin, 1952.

Griswold, A. Whitney. *The Far Eastern Policy of the United States.* New York: Harcourt, Brace, 1938.

Harries, Meirion, and Susie Harries. *Sheathing the Sword: The Demilitarisation of Postwar Japan.* London: Hamish Hamilton, 1987.

Hawley, Ellis. "The Discovery and Study of a 'Corporate Liberalism.'" *Business History Review* 52 (fall 1978).

———. *The Great War and the Search for a Modern Order:*

A *History of the American People and Their Institutions, 1917–1933.* New York: St. Martin's Press, 1979.

Heinrichs, Waldo H. *American Ambassador: Joseph C. Grew and the Development of the United States Diplomatic Tradition.* Boston: Little, Brown, 1966.

Hess, Gary R. *The United States at War, 1941–1945.* Arlington Heights., Ill.: H. Davidson, 1986.

Hogan, Michael J. "Corporatism: A Positive Appraisal." *Diplomatic History* 10, no. 4 (1996): 363–372.

———. *Informal Entente: The Private Structure of Cooperation in Anglo-American Economic Diplomacy, 1918–1928.* Columbia: University of Missouri Press, 1977.

———. "Partisan Politics in the Cold War." In *The End of the Cold War: Its Meaning and Implications,* edited by Michael J. Hogan. New York: Cambridge University Press, 1992.

Hollingsworth, James L. "William R. Castle and Japanese-American Relations 1929–1933." Ph.D. dissertation, Texas Christian University, 1971.

Hoover, Herbert C. *Addresses upon the American Road, 1941–1945.* New York, 1945.

———. *Memoirs,* 3 vols. New York: Macmillan, 1951–1952.

———. *The State Papers and Other Public Writings of Herbert Hoover,* edited by William S. Myers, 2 vols. Garden City, N.Y.: Doubleday, Doran, 1934.

Hornbeck, Stanley K. "William Richards Castle: In Memoriam." Speech delivered at a meeting of The Literary Society of Washington, D.C., Oct. 26, 1963.

Huntington, Samuel P. *The Soldier and the State: The Theory and Politics of Civil-Military Relations.* Cambridge, Mass.: Harvard University Press, 1957.

Huyerford, Edward. *With the Doughboys in France; A Few Chapters of an American Effort.* New York: Macmillan, 1920.

Ienaga, Saburo. *The Pacific War: World War II and the Japanese, 1931–1945.* New York: Pantheon Books, 1978.

Iriye, Akira. *Across the Pacific: An Inner History of American–East Asian Relations.* New York: Harcourt, Brace and World, 1967.

———. *After Imperialism: The Search for a New Order in the Far East, 1921–1931.* Cambridge, Mass.: Harvard University Press, 1965.

———. "The Failure of Military Expansionism." In *Dilemmas of Growth in Prewar Japan,* edited by James W. Morley, 107–138. Princeton, N.J.: Princeton University Press, 1971.

———. *Power and Culture: The Japanese-American War, 1941–1945.* Cambridge, Mass.: Harvard University Press, 1981.

———. *The Globalizing of America. Cambridge History of American Foreign Relations,* vol. 3. New York: Cambridge University Press, 1993.

Jonas, Manfred. *Isolationism in America, 1935–1941.* Ithaca, N.Y.: Cornell University Press, 1966.

———. *The United States and Germany: A Diplomatic History.* Ithaca, N.Y.: Cornell University Press, 1984.

Joslin, Theodore G. *Hoover off the Record.* New York: Doubleday and Doran, 1934.

Kennan, George F. *American Diplomacy, 1900–1950.* Chicago: University of Chicago Press, 1951.

———. *Around the Cragged Hill: A Personal and Political Philosophy.* New York: W. W. Norton, 1993.

———. *Memoirs, 1925–1950.* Boston: Little, Brown, 1967.

———. "The National Interest of the United States." *Illinois Law Review* 45 (January-February 1951): 736–738.

Kiba Kosuke. *Nomura Kichisaburo.* Osaka, 1961.

Kimball, Warren F. *The Juggler: Franklin Roosevelt as Wartime Statesman.* Princeton, N.J. Princeton University Press, 1991.

Kindleberger, Charles P. *The World in Depression.* Berkeley: University of California Press, 1980.

Kolko, Gabriel. *The Politics of War: The World and United States Foreign Policy, 1943–1945.* New York: Random House, 1968.

Kolko, Joyce, and Gabriel Kolko. *The Limits of Power: The World and United States Foreign Policy, 1945–1954.* New York: Harper and Row, 1972.

Koppes, Clayton R., and Gregory D. Black. *Hollywood Goes to War: How Politics, Profits, and Propaganda Shaped World War II Movies.* New York: Free Press, 1987.

LaFeber, Walter. *America, Russia and the Cold War, 1945–1990,* 6th ed. New York: McGraw-Hill, 1991.

———. *The American Age.* New York: W. W. Norton, 1989.

Langer, William L., and S. Everett Gleason. *The Challenge to Isolationism, 1937–1940.* New York: Harper, 1952.

Leffler, Melvyn P. "Adherents to Agreements: Yalta and the Experiences of the Early Cold War." *International Security* 11 (summer 1986): 88–123.

———. "The American Conception of National Security and the Beginnings of the Cold War, 1945–48." *American Historical Review* 89, no. 2 (1984): 346–381.

———. *The Elusive Quest: America's Pursuit of European Stability and French Security, 1919–1933.* Chapel Hill: University of North Carolina Press, 1979.

Lewe van Aduard, E. J. *Japan: From Surrender to Peace.* The Hague: M. Nijhoff, 1953.

Lindbergh, Charles A. *The Wartime Journals of Charles A. Lindbergh.* New York: Harcourt Brace Jovanovich, 1970.

Lodge, Henry Cabot. "Our New Envoy to Japan." *New York Herald Tribune,* January 19, 1930.

Louis, William Roger. *Imperialism at Bay: The United States and the Decolonization of the British Empire, 1941–1945.* New York: Oxford University Press, 1978.

Malpass, Elizabeth Deanne. "Sir John Simon and British Diplomacy During the Sino-Japanese Crisis, 1931–1933." Ph.D. dissertation, Texas Christian University, 1969.

Marks, Frederick W. *Wind Over Sand: The Diplomacy of Franklin Roosevelt.* Athens: University of Georgia Press, 1988.

Mastny, Vojtech. *Russia's Road to the Cold War: Diplomacy, Warfare, and the Politics of Communism, 1941–1945.* New York: Columbia University Press, 1979.

McCormick, Thomas J. "Draft or Mastery: A Corporatist Synthesis for American Diplomatic History." *Reviews in American History* 10 (December 1982).

McCoy, Donald R. *Landon of Kansas.* Lincoln: University of Nebraska Press, 1966.

McNeill, William H. *America, Britain and Russia: Their Cooperation and Conflict, 1941–1946.* New York: Oxford University Press, 1953.

Millis, Walter. *This is Pearl! The United States and Japan—1941.* New York: Morrow, 1947.

Morison, Samuel Eliot. *The Rising Sun in the Pacific, 1931–April 1942.* History of United States Naval Operations in World War II, vol. 3. Boston: Little, Brown, 1948.

Myers, William S., and Walter H. Newton. *The Hoover Ad-*

ministration: A Documented Narrative. New York: Charles Scribner and Sons, 1936.

Nellist, George. *Women of Hawaii.* Honolulu: Paradise of the Pacific Press, 1929.

Neu, Charles E. *The Troubled Encounter: The United States and Japan.* New York: Wiley, 1975.

Neumann, William L. *America Encounters Japan: From Perry to MacArthur.* Baltimore: Johns Hopkins Press, 1963.

Nisbet, Robert A. *Roosevelt and Stalin: The Failed Courtship.* Washington: Regnery Gateway, 1988.

O'Connor, Raymond G. *Diplomacy for Victory: FDR and Unconditional Surrender.* New York: Norton, 1971.

————. *Perilous Equilibrium: The United States and the London Disarmament Conference of 1930.* Lawrence: University of Kansas Press 1962.

Ogata, Sadako. *Defiance in Manchuria: The Making of Japanese Foreign Policy, 1931–1932.* Berkeley: University of California Press, 1964.

Ostrower, Gary B. *Collective Insecurity: The U.S. and the League of Nations During the Early Thirties.* Lewisburg, Pa.: Bucknell University Press, 1979.

Parrini, Carl P. *Heir to Empire: United States Economic Diplomacy, 1916–1923.* Pittsburgh: University of Pittsburgh Press, 1969.

Patterson, James T. *Mr. Republican: A Biography of Robert A. Taft.* Boston: Houghton Mifflin, 1972.

Pearson, Drew, and Robert Allen, *Washington Merry Go Round.* New York: Horace Liveright, 1931.

Perkins, Dexter. "The Department of State and American Public Opinion" In *The Diplomats 1919–1939,* edited by Gordon A. Craig and Felix Gilbert. Princeton, N.J.: Princeton University Press, 1953.

Poole, Walter Sloan. "Quest for a Republican Foreign Policy, 1941–1951." Ph.D. diss., University of Pennsylvania, 1968.

Radosh, Ronald. *Prophets on the Right: Profiles of Conservative Critics of American Globalism.* New York: Simon and Schuster, 1975.

Rappaport, Amin. *Henry L. Stimson and Japan, 1931–33.* Chicago: University of Chicago Press, 1963.

Reinsch, Paul S. *Secret Diplomacy: How Can It Be Eliminated?* New York: Harcourt Brace, 1922.

Reinsch, Paul S. *World Politics at the End of the 19th Century.* New York: Macmillan, 1922.

Reischauer, Edwin O. *The United Stales and Japan,* 3rd ed. Cambridge, Mass.: Harvard University Press, 1965.

Remer, C. F. *Foreign Investments in China.* New York: Macmillan, 1933.

Richardson, James D., ed. *Messages and Papers of the Presidents,* vol. 1. Washington: Bureau of National Literature and Art, 1896.

Rickman, Barney J., III. "Ideology and Influence: William R. Castle, Jr. and the Manchurian Crisis, 1931–33." Paper presented at the Conference of the Society for Historians of American Foreign Relations, University of Maryland, August 1–4, 1990.

Roberts, John G. "The 'Japan Crowd' and the Zaibatsu Restoration." *The Japan Interpreter* 12, no. 3/4 (1979): 384–415.

———. *Mitsui: Three Centuries of Japanese Business.* New York: Weatherhill, 1973.

Sainsbury, Keith. *The Turning Point: Roosevelt, Stalin, Churchill and Chiang Kai-shek, 1943.* New York: Oxford University Press, 1985.

Schaller, Michael. *Douglas MacArthur: The Far Eastern General.* New York: Oxford University Press, 1989.

Schlesinger, Arthur M., Jr. *The Crisis of the Old Order, 1919–1933.* Volume 1 of *Age of Roosevelt.* Boston: Houghton Mifflin, 1957.

Schmitz, David F. *The United States and Fascist Italy, 1922–1940.* Chapel Hill: University of North Carolina Press, 1988.

Schonberger, Howard B. *Aftermath of War: Americans and the Remaking of Japan, 1945–1952.* Kent, Ohio: Kent State University Press, 1989.

———. "The Japan Lobby in American Diplomacy, 1947–1952." *Pacific Historical Review* 46, no. 3 (1977): 327–359.

Schroeder, Paul. *The Axis Alliance and Japanese-American Relations.* Ithaca, N.Y.: Cornell University Press, 1958.

Schulzinger, Robert D. "The Making of the Diplomatic Mind: The Training. Outlook. and Style of United States Foreign Service Officers, 1906–1928." Ph.D. dissertation, Yale University, 1971.

Sherwin, Martin. *A World Destroyed: The Atomic Bomb and the Grand Alliance.* New York: Knopf, 1975.

Sherwood, Robert E. *Roosevelt and Hopkins: An Intimate History.* New York: Harper, 1948.

Smith, Gaddis. *American Diplomacy During the Second World War, 1941–1945.* New York: Wiley, 1965.

Smith, Richard Norton. *An Uncommon Man: The Triumph of Herbert Hoover.* New York: Simon and Schuster, 1984.

Smith, Robert F. "American Foreign Relations, 1920–1942." In *Towards a New Past. Dissenting Essays in American History,* edited by Barton J. Bernstein, 232–262. New York: Pantheon Books, 1968.

———. "Republican Policy at the Pax Americana 1921–1932." In *From Colony to Empire: Essays in the History of American Foreign Relations,* edited by William A. Williams, 253–292. New York: Wiley Press, 1972.

Snell, John L. *Illusion and Necessity: The Diplomacy of Global War, 1939–1945.* Boston: Houghton Mifflin, 1963.

Stanley, Morris. "The America First Committee." M.A. thesis, Emory University, 1942.

Stenehjem, Michele F. *An American First: John T. Flynn and the America First Committee.* New Rochelle, N.Y.: Arlington House, 1976.

Stimson, Henry L. "The Decision to Use the Atomic Bomb." *Harper's* 194 (February 1947): 97–107.

———. *The Far Eastern Crisis: Recollections and Observations.* New York: Harper and Brothers, 1936.

Stimson, Henry L., and McGeorge Bundy. *On Active Service in Peace and War.* New York, Harper: 1948.

Sullivan, Michael J. "Franco-American Relations in the Financial Crisis of 1931." M.A. thesis, Drake University, 1975.

Takeuchi, Tatsuji. *War and Diplomacy in the Japanese Empire.* Chicago: University of Chicago Press, 1935.

Tansill, Charles C. *Back Door to War: The Roosevelt Foreign Policy, 1933–1945.* Chicago: Henry Regnery, 1952.

Thorne, Christopher. *Allies of a Kind: The United States, Britain and the War Against Japan, 1941–1945.* New York: Oxford University Press, 1978.

———. *The Issue of War: States, Societies, and the Far Eastern Conflict of 1941–1945.* New York: Oxford University Press, 1985.

————. *The Limits of Foreign Policy: The West, the League, and the Far Eastern Crisis of 1931–1933.* London: Hamish Hamilton, 1972.

U. S. Department of State. *Foreign Relations of the United States, 1931.*

Van Schaick, John, Jr. *The Little Corner Never Conquered: The Story of the American Red Cross' Work in Belgium.* New York: Macmillan, 1922.

Vinacke, Harold M. *Far Eastern Politics in the Postwar Period.* New York: Appleton-Century-Crofts, 1956.

Wagner, Sandra E. "Mission and Motivation: The Theology of the Early American Mission in Hawaii." *The Hawaiian Journal of History* 19 (1985): 62–70.

Wakatsuki, Baron. "The Aims of Japan." *Foreign Affairs* 13 (1935).

Ward, Robert E. "Reflections on the Allied Occupation and Planned Political Change in Japan." In *Political Development in Modern Japan,* edited by Robert E. Ward. Princeton, N.J.: Princeton University Press, 1968.

Warner, Geoffrey. *Pierre Laval and the Eclipse of France.* New York: Macmillan, 1968.

Weil, Martin. *A Pretty Good Club: The Founding Fathers of the U. S. Foreign Service.* New York: Norton, 1978.

Welles, Sumner. *The Time for Decision.* New York: Harper, 1944.

Wheeler, Gerald E. *Prelude to Pearl Harbor: The United States Navy and the Far East, 1921–1931.* Columbia: University of Missouri Press 1963.

White, William Allen. "Republican National Platform." *What It's All About.* New York: Macmillan, 1936.

Wiebe, Robert H. *The Search for Order, 1877–1920.* New York: Hill and Wang, 1968.

Williams, William A. *American Russian Relations, 1781–1947.* New York: Rinehart, 1952.

————. *The Tragedy of American Diplomacy,* rev. ed. New York: Dell, 1962.

Wilmot, Chester. *The Struggle for Europe.* New York: Harper, 1952.

Wilson, Joan Hoff. *American Business and Foreign Policy 1920–1933.* Lexington: University of Kentucky Press, 1971.

————. *Herbert Hoover: Forgotten Progressive.* Boston: Little Brown, 1975.

Index

Abbott, Frank, 15
Acheson, Dean, 157
Adams, Charles, 81
America First Committee, 106, 107, 112–113, 115, 116, 119, 219n38
American Council on Japan, 145, 146, 148, 149, 150–151, 155. *See also* Japan Lobby
Araki, Sadao, 82
armaments, 39–49, 162
Ashida, Hitoshi, 149
Atlee, Clement, 141
atomic bomb, 141–142, 159–160, 161
Austria, 50

Baker, Newton D., 14–15, 16
Ballantine, Joseph W., 146, 147, 148, 152
Ball, Joseph H., 135

Bank of International Settlement, 57, 58, 64
Barnes, Harry Elmer, 106
Baruch, Bernard, 120
Beard, Charles A., 106, 107
Beaven, J. Ashman, 89
Bischoff, Fritz W., 30
Bliss, Robert Woods, 38
Borah, William E., 45, 58, 80, 98
Bowles, Chester, 112
boycotts, 75–76, 88–89
Brewster, Andrew W., 38
Briand, Aristide, 32–34
Bricker, John, 133
Brooks, Curley, 121
Brownell, Herbert, 134
Brüning, Heinrich, 51, 59, 60, 61, 64
Burke, Arleigh, 150
Butler, Hugh, 121

Butterworth, W. Walton, 150
Byrnes, James F., 142

Carr, Wilbur J., 26
Castle & Cooke, Inc., 1
Castle, Alfred L., 19, 89, 116,
　220n49
Castle, Alfred L., Jr., 19
Castle, Angeline Tenney, 3
Castle, Beatrice, 19
Castle, Donald, 19
Castle, Gwen, 19
Castle, Margaret Farlow, x, xi
Castle, Mary Tenney, 1, 2, 3–9
Castle, Rosamond. *See* Winslow,
　Rosamond Castle
Castle, Samuel Northrup, 1, 3–5
Castle, William Richards, Jr., 2,
　20, 21, 32, 85, 119, 139, 168;
　as ambassador to Japan, 36,
　37–49; and America First
　Committee, 107, 113; and
　American Red Cross, 13–19;
　broadcasts to Japan, 127,
　167–194; on relations with
　China, 71, 73–74, 90–91,
　110–111, 169–171, 212n60;
　on communism, 25, 159; on
　corporatism, 22–23; response
　to criticism, 115, 130; edu-
　cation of, x; foreign policy
　views of, 55–57; and Foreign
　Service School, 27–29; and
　Hoover, 35–36, 55, 66, 87–
　88, 204n25; influence on U.S.
　Japan policy, 156–157; atti-
　tudes toward Japan, xii–xiii,
　35, 168–169; on relations
　with Japan, 37, 40–41, 42–
　43, 45, 56, 72, 84–86, 111–
　112, 115–116, 169–172,

211n50; and Landon, 93–97,
　98, 99, 100–101, 104, 105,
　214n10; and Manchurian
　Incident, 77–79; as noninter-
　ventionist, 107–118; novels
　of, xiii; on peace terms for
　Japan, 140–141, 142; pho-
　tographs of, 13, 14, 19, 27,
　55, 81, 87, 89; on postwar
　treatment of Japan, 122, 147;
　realist values of, 1–2, 9–11,
　27–28, 68–70, 91; and Re-
　publican Party politics, 35–
　36, 100–105; on Roosevelt,
　93–95, 97–98, 107, 114,
　115–116, 121–122, 126; on
　Soviet Union, 25, 56, 124,
　129, 132–133, 137, 141,
　161, 208n5; and Stimson, 47,
　54–55, 83, 87–88, 159–160,
　204n25, 205n39; and war-
　debt moratorium, 30–31, 52,
　58–65, 62, 205n43; on war
　strategy, 126–127, 129
Castle, William Richards, Sr., x,
　1, 7, 19, 81
censorship, 125, 222n13
Chamberlain, Culver B., 77
Chang Hsueh-liang, 75, 187
Chiang Kai-shek, 70, 71, 112,
　122, 129, 137, 155
China, 70, 86, 90–91, 110–111
Churchill, Winston, 131, 136,
　141
Ciechanowski, Jan, 138
Clark, J. Reuben, 98, 99
Claudel, Paul, 34–35, 53, 63, 86
Coffin, William, 30
Cold War, 145, 159, 160–161,
　163
Coolidge, Archibald Cary, 67

Coolidge, Calvin, 35, 53
Coontz, Robert E., 38
Corsi, Edward, 98–99
Cotton, Joseph P., 43, 44
Coughlin, Charles E., 222n13
Cuba, 94
Curtis, John, 146

Dan, Takuma, 182
Dawes, Charles G., 72
Dawes Plan (1924), 56
Debuchi, Katsuji, 77, 79
Dewey, Thomas E., 133, 134, 137
diplomatic realism, 67–70
Disarmament, 96, 97, 162
Ditter, Bill, 121
Dodge, Joseph M., 151, 152
Dooman, Eugene H., 129, 146, 147, 148, 153, 160
Douglas, Lew, 102
Draper, William H., 147, 149, 151
Dulles, Allen W., 154, 199n12
Dulles, John Foster, 150, 153, 154, 155, 156, 157, 229n36

Ebert, Friedrich, 24
Edge, Walter, 54, 58, 59
Eichelberger, Robert L., 152
Eisenhower, Dwight D., 158
Ethiopia, 95, 97

Fish, Hamilton, 100
Flandin, Etienne, 54, 59, 63
Flynn, John T., 107, 112, 113, 115
food relief, 131–132
Forbes, Cameron, 72, 75
Foreign Service, 26–27

Forrestal, James V., 147
France, 31, 53–54, 57, 62, 63, 64, 114
Fukuda, Takeo, 151

Geneva Naval Conference, 35, 62
German-American Claims Commission, 29
Germany, 23–25, 28, 29, 30, 31, 50, 51, 57–66, 174, 185–186, 193
Gibson, Hugh, 122–123, 125, 146
Great Britain, 45, 62, 90, 130, 141
Greece, 114
Green, Joseph C., 129
Green, Theodore F., 130
Green Vase, The, xiii
Grew, Joseph C., 26, 30, 32, 109, 148, 152, 176–177; and Castle, 110, 114, 147, 159; and Japan Lobby, 146, 149

Hamaguchi, Yuko, 37, 41, 42, 45, 47, 48, 49
Hamilton, John, 100, 101, 102, 104
Hard, Billy, 101
Harding, Warren G., 29
Harriman, W. Averell, 147, 157
Harrison, Leland, 199n12
Hart, Thomas C., 146, 153
Harvard University, x, xi
Hawaii, x, xi–xii
Hawaii, Past & Present, xi, xiii
Hays, Will H., 30
Henderson, Arthur, 58, 62
Herrick, Myron T., 35
Hindenburg, Paul von, 53, 60

Hoover, Herbert C., 25, 80, 107, 116, 123, 130, 131, 132, 135; relations with Castle, 35–36, 37, 55, 87–88, 159, 204n25; international agreements, 138–139; and Japan, 81–84; relations with Landon, 103–105; moratorium on war debt, 50–66; photographs of, 23, 33, 51, 55, 87; postwar planning, 122–123, 125, 126, 128, 130, 133, 134, 136; and Republican Party politics, 35–36, 55, 103–105, 134; relations with Stimson, 83, 87–88, 204n25, 212n65; on war strategy, 126–127, 128

Hopkins, Samuel, 3

Hornbeck, Stanley K., 75, 78, 80, 84, 110

Houghton, Alanson, 30, 199n12

Hughes, Charles Evans, 23, 29, 31, 32, 39, 125, 209n21

Hulbertson, Paul, 199n12

Hull, Cordell, 86, 97, 120, 131, 132–133, 134–135, 141

Hullen, Bert, 131

Hungary, 25

Indo-China, 114

Inouye, Kaoru, 182

Inter-American Conference (1936), 94

interventionists, 115

Italy, 78, 95

Japan, 110–112, 117, 120, 209n21; militarists in, 169, 170, 171–172, 177, 181, 186, 190, 192, 209n22; and naval-armaments ratio, 39–49; occupation policy, 144–157; peace treaty, 147–148, 153–155; treatment of prisoners of war, 174–176. *See also* London Naval Conference; Manchurian Incident

Japanese Americans, 179–180

Japan Lobby, 145–146, 147–148. *See also* American Council on Japan

Johnson, Hiram, 43–44

Johnson, Hugh S., 112, 113

Johnson, Nelson T., 74

Johnston, Percy, 149

Joy, Turner, 150

J. P. Morgan and Company, 51–52

Kaihara, Osamu, 154

Katayama, Count, 79

Kato, Kanji, 38, 47, 48

Kauffman, James L., 146, 147, 151

Kauffman report, 148

Kellogg-Briand Pact (1928), 32–35, 73, 74, 76

Kellogg, Frank B., 31, 32–35

Kennan, George F., 117, 147, 148, 151–152, 157, 162, 163, 229n31

Kennedy, Joseph P., 140

Kern, Harry F., 146, 147, 148, 151, 152, 153, 154, 155, 157

Kingsbury, Jeddiah, 3

Knowland, William F., 150, 155

Knox, Frank, 103, 105

Korea, 140, 209n21

Korean War, 154

Kreditanstalt, 50

Krock, Arthur, 127

Kun, Béla, 25
Kurusu, Saburo, 121

LaGuardia, Fiorello, 104
Lamont, Thomas, 51–52
Landon, Alfred M., 92–105, 121, 125, 126, 128, 131
Lansing-Ishii Agreement (1917), 73
Latin America, 94, 123
Latourette, Kenneth S., 146
Lattimore, Owen, 122
Laval, Pierre, 54, 57, 59, 63
Lay, Tracy, 199n12
League of Nations, 91, 96, 97, 133; and Manchurian Incident, 72, 74–76, 84, 86, 90
Lindbergh, Charles A., 107, 112, 115, 219n39, 222n4
Lindsay, Ronald, 58, 70
Lodge, Henry Cabot, Jr., 37–38, 207n75
London Naval Conference, 37–49, 69, 97
Lytton Commission, 84

MacArthur, Douglas, 144, 146–147, 148–149, 152
Machado, Gerardo, 94
MacMurray, John V. A., 75, 117
Makino Nobuaki, 47, 79, 85
Malcolm, Ian, 14
Manchurian Incident (1931), 71–91, 169–170, 186–189
Mao Tse-tung, 70, 129, 137
Marshall, George C., 159
Martin, Joseph, 125
Martino, Giacomo de, 78
Matsudaira, Tsuneo, 46
Matsudaira, Yasumasa, 153, 154
Matsuoka, Yosuke, 172

Mellon, Andrew W., 52, 53, 58, 59, 62–63
Meyer, Clarence C., 146
Mills, Ogden, 51, 52, 53, 60, 62, 98
Moffat, Jay P., 26, 146
Molotov, V. M., 132
Morga, Stokely, 199n12
Morley, Felix, 121
Moscow Conference, 131, 132–133
Murro, Dana, 199n12

Neutrality, 94–96, 108
Neville, Edwin L., 71, 146
New Guinea, 180–181
Newsweek, 147, 148
Nine Power Treaty, 76, 78, 80, 90
Nomura, Kichisaburo, 45, 121, 150
Noninterventionists, 106–107, 119. *See also* America First Committee
Nye, Gerald, 115

Office of War Information, 127, 167
Okada, Kanekazu, 89

Pakenham, Compton, 146, 147, 151, 154, 230n44
Panama, 94
Pan-American Conference (1933), 94
Pearson, Drew, 203n25
Philippines, 112, 116
Phillips, Bill, 26
Pillar of Sand, The, xiii
Pinto, Nicholas H., 99
Poincaré, Raymond, 31

Polk, Frank L., 19, 21
Potsdam Conference, 141
Pratt, William V., 85, 146, 147
Problems of a Lasting Peace,
    122–123, 126, 128, 130

Race, 171–172
Raymond, Antonin, 146
Red Cross, American, xiii, 13–
    20, 129, 197n6
Red Cross, International, 174,
    175
Reed, David A., 32, 42, 46, 48,
    204n25
Reed-Matsudaira Compromise,
    46–48
regional blocs, 123–124
reparations, 31, 56
Republican National Committee,
    92–93, 100, 101–102, 103–
    104, 134
Republican Party, 92–93, 98,
    121–122, 127, 133–134
Rickenbacker, Edward, 113
Robey, Ralph, 100
Rogers Act, 26
Rogers, John Jacob, 26
Roosevelt, Franklin D., 86, 93–
    95, 97, 107, 111, 112, 114,
    117, 120, 131–132
Root, Elihu, 75
Root-Takahira Agreement (1908),
    73
Royall, Kenneth C., 147

Sackett, Frederick, 50, 53, 58,
    59–61, 62, 64
Saionji, Kimmochi, 79, 191
Saito, Makoto, 82, 84–85, 182,
    191
Sarada, Renzo, 153, 154

Scheideman, Philip, 24
Schmitt, Bernadotte E., 199n12
Seiyukai, 42, 49
Sherwood, Robert E., 127, 167
Shidehara, Kijuro, 38, 43, 46, 48,
    71, 74
Short, Dewey, 130
Simon, John, 90
Simpich, Frederick, 131
Smith, Howard Alexander, 150,
    155
Smith, John W. B., 146
Smoot-Hawley Tariff, 73
Solomon Islands, 172–173,
    183–184
South Manchurian Railroad, 43,
    71, 73, 188
Soviet Union, 25, 86, 112. *See
    also* Stalin, Joseph
Spangler, Harrison, 128
Stalin, Joseph, 126, 127, 129,
    131, 132–133, 136, 137,
    141. *See also* Soviet Union
Stettinius, Edward R., Jr., 135,
    139
Stimson Doctrine, 78, 81, 82
Stimson, Henry L., 38, 40, 41,
    81, 90, 117, 206n47; and
    atomic bomb, 159–160;
    relations with Castle, 44, 48,
    159–160, 202n10, 204n25,
    205n39; relations with
    Hoover, 204n25, 212n65;
    and Japan, 40, 41–42,
    44, 45–46, 140, 202n30,
    213n76; and Manchurian
    Incident, 76–78; and war-
    debt moratorium, 52, 53, 65,
    203n24, 204n26
Stowell, Ellery C., 199n12
Stuart, R. Douglas, Jr., 112

Sullivan, Larry, 131
Sun Yat-sen, 70
Suzuki, Tadakatsu, 149
Swanson, Claude, 45

Taft, Robert A., 107, 122, 125, 132
Tanaka, Kunishige, 38
Tenney, Angeline, 3
Tenney, Levy, 3
Tenney, Mary Kingsbury, 3
Teusler, Rudolph B., 176
Thoran, Louise, 197n6
Togo, Shigenori, 181–182, 183
Treaty of Berlin, 29
Truman, Harry S., 139, 141, 142, 145, 152, 157, 159–160, 161
Tucker, Henry St. George, 146

Uchida, Yasuya, 82
Underwood, Oscar W., 29
United Nations, 123, 133, 135–136
United Nations Relief and Rehabilitation Agency (UNRRA), 131, 132, 139–140

Vandenberg, Arthur H., 121
Villard, Oswald Garrison, 107
Vorys, John, 125, 128, 132

Wadsworth, Eliot, 13, 14
Wakatsuki, Reijiro, 44, 46, 76

Wake Up, America, xiii, 12
Wallace, Henry A., 135
War Department, 15, 16, 130
Warner, Langdon, 146
Washington Naval Conference, 39–40, 41, 56, 80, 97, 209n21
Watanabe, Takeshi, 151, 154
Welles, Sumner, 223n16
Wendell, Barrett, 1
West, Rebecca, 130
Whitehouse, Sheldon, 34
White, William Allen, 98
Willkie, Wendell L., 122, 124, 129, 131, 133
Wilson, Hugh, 37, 40, 110, 146
Wilson, Woodrow, 122, 174
Winslow, Alan F., 27
Winslow, Alan F., Jr., 81
Winslow, Rosamond Castle, xi, 13, 80, 81
Wood, Charles W., 146
Wood, Robert E., 112, 139, 220n48

Yalta agreement, 137–139
Yoshida, Shigeru, 149, 151, 153, 155, 156
Young Plan (1929), 51, 53, 56, 58, 64